ROBERT S. McGEE
WM. DREW MOUNTCASTLE

CONQUERING
EATING DISORDERS

A CHRIST-CENTERED 12-STEP PROCESS

Learning Activities by Jim and Annette Florence

D1560561

LifeWay Press
Nashville, Tennessee

ACKNOWLEDGEMENTS

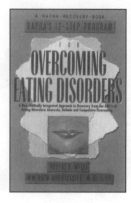

Overcoming Eating Disorders: A Christ-Centered 12-Step Process was originally co-published by Word, Inc. and Rapha Resources, Inc. and is available in its original version in Christian bookstores. We want to thank Rapha Hospital Treatment Centers for making this book available to the LifeWay Press for its use.

Rapha is a manager of inpatient psychiatric care and substance-abuse treatment from a distinctively Christian perspective in hospitals located nationwide. For information about Rapha you may contact Rapha at 1-800-383-HOPE or write to Rapha, 12700 Featherwood, Houston, Texas 77034.

Conquering Eating Disorders: A Christ-Centered 12-Step Process
Copyright © 1993 by Rapha Publishing

LifeWay Press books are published by The Sunday School Board; 127 Ninth Avenue, North; Nashville, Tennessee 37234

For help for facilitators and leaders in carrying out LIFE® Support Group Series ministries in your church, call 1-615-251-5613.

Item 7204-73   ISBN 0-8054-9977-6   Dewey Decimal Number 616.85
Subject Heading: Eating Disorders

Sources for definitions in *Conquering Eating Disorders: A Christ-centered 12-Step Process*:
By permission. From Merriam-*Webster's Collegiate Dictionary, Tenth Edition* ©1993 by Merriam-Webster Inc., publisher of the Merriam-Webster® dictionaries; *Vine's Expository Dictionary of Old and New Testament Words* (Fleming H. Revell Company, 1981).

Printed in the United States of America

Table of Contents

THE AUTHORS

Robert S. McGee is a professional counselor and lecturer who has helped thousands of people experience the love and acceptance of Jesus Christ. He also is the founder of Rapha, a manager of inpatient psychiatric care and substance-abuse treatment from a distinctively Christian perspective in hospitals located nationwide.

Wm. Drew Mountcastle, M.A., LPC-CSAC, is clinical coordinator for the Rapha program at Samaritan Behavior Health Center in Scottsdale, Arizona. He has authored and appeared in an instructional video on eating disorders called *Food Chains*.

Jim Florence is a health education specialist with Meharry Medical College in Nashville, Tennessee. Annette Florence is a personal health consultant.

LIFE® Support Group Series Editorial Team
Kay Moore, Design Editor
Dale McCleskey, Editor
Debbie Colclough, Manuscript Assistant

Johnny Jones, LIFE® Support Group Series Project Coordinator

Graphics by Lori Putnam
Cover Design by Edward Crawford

The Journey Begins

GOD CHANGED MY LIFE!

Today Pam experiences a freedom she once believed never would occur. She credits this freedom to Jesus Christ and to the 12-Step recovery program. She feels freed because she no longer is controlled by compulsive overeating.

Throughout her teenage years and her adult life, Pam struggled with her weight and with something more. When she was depressed, under stress, or feeling any strong emotion, Pam medicated her feelings with food. When she began to eat, she could not stop. She felt shame about her inability to control her compulsive eating, and the shame led her to eat all the more.

In a time of particular stress and out-of-control eating Pam turned to a 12-Step group. There she found people with stories just like her own. They told of the same feelings of defeat and shame, but they also told of something more. They said that by applying the teachings of the 12 Steps they were overcoming their compulsions. Jesus Christ was doing for them what they were unable to do for themselves. They assured Pam that if she would honestly work the program, God would change her life.

Today Pam feels that she has a new life. God gave her life back through His Son Jesus—working through the 12-Step program. She remains abstinent from her compulsive overeating patterns one day at a time through the program, but she says avoiding these patterns is only a small part of her recovery. She says, "The important part is that working the program has taught me how to live. It has helped me to get to know and love God. God changed my life through the 12 Steps!"

What are eating disorders, and what causes them? In *Conquering Eating Disorders: A Christ-Centered 12-Step Process* you will learn more about the three primary forms of eating disorders—anorexia, bulimia, and compulsive overeating. No single cause for eating disorders exists. No single, simple answer exists for why one person develops an eating disorder and another does not.

If you suffer from an eating disorder, the important issue is recovery—how to overcome the compulsion. You can overcome through the power of God. A Christ-centered 12-Step program, coupled with appropriate medical and other professional care will help you to achieve a healthy and Christ-honoring life-style. In this process, you will discover the resources you need to experience these positive changes.

The complexity of eating disorders demonstrates a fact for you to reinforce in your mind. You do not have an eating disorder because you are weak or because you are bad. Many of the most determined people in the world—people with enormous amounts of willpower—have eating disorders. People who deeply love God and desire to live for Him have eating disorders. Shame makes us feel that we are evil, wrong, or defective in a unique way—that we are worse than others. You do not have an eating disorder because you are bad or evil.

You are a person of infinite worth because God created you and because He loves you. You are not bad because you have an addictive behavior. What you are is human.

In a 12-Step meeting you may hear someone say, "I am a grateful recovering _____ (alcoholic, addict, compulsive overeater, etc.)." At first you may be confused by that statement, or you may misunderstand. You may think the person is saying, "I am grateful because I am recovering and am no longer a _____." In time, however, you may understand that some of these individuals are saying, "I am grateful that I have this problem, because the problem has led me to this relationship with God."

You will conquer your problem as you work the Christ-centered 12 Steps. The 12 Steps show us a means for effective living. Many of us are familiar with a booklet called *The Four Spiritual Laws.* The booklet is an effective means by which we can share Jesus Christ with people. Through those concepts many of us have come to understand the facts so we can have a relationship with Christ. *The Four Spiritual Laws* booklet, by Bill Bright, presents basic theology. It organizes the information in the Bible in a practical way, so we can apply it to our lives. The 12 Steps give us an organized plan to live life effectively. *The Four Spiritual Laws* is designed to help save our souls, while the 12 Steps are designed to save our lives.

Twelve-Step programs began with the establishment in the 1930s of the first program, Alcoholics Anonymous. Alcoholics Anonymous was adapted from a Christian revival organization known as the Oxford Group. The Twelve Steps were written in the laboratory of human experience as people sought God's solution for alcoholism, but they do not help only alcoholics. They are for everyone. They are practical.

Those of us who have come to know Jesus through *The Four Spiritual Laws* have a special respect for the little booklet. Those of us who have experienced deliverance from life-crushing problems through the 12 Steps have a similar respect for the 12-Step program—or simply *the program,* as many people call it. We respect the program because the Steps have led us to know and love the Holy God who gave us the Steps. As a reference you'll find the Twelve Steps of Alcoholics Anonymous on page 223 and our adaptation of them—the Christ-Centered 12 Steps—on page 224.

The purpose of this book is to help you begin and work the 12-Step process in your life. You will find *Conquering Eating Disorders: A Christ-Centered 12-Step Process* is true to the proven 12-Step recovery tradition. Without apology we identify Jesus Christ as our Higher Power.

On the inside back cover you'll find a course map showing steps out of eating disorders. This drawing represents a further explanation of how the Christ-Centered 12 Steps work. On the unit page of each Step, you'll find a cutaway drawing of some steps that will highlight and give a brief synopsis of the Step.

If you are new to the 12-Step process you will encounter some unfamiliar terms in this book. They are expressions frequently used in 12-Step groups. Below we have given you an overview of some of these terms.

Definitions

• **Recovery**—The entire process of healing from the painful effects of dysfunctional behavior is called recovery. In a larger sense everything in Christian ministry is recovery. You may think of it this way: God created us with a glorious purpose. Sin warped and twisted that purpose. Theologians call this the "fall" of humanity. We also might call it the loss—loss of our innocence, purpose, dignity, and of our relationships to God and to others. Recovery is the process of restoring what sin has taken away.

Recovery is for everyone. For some of us it is specialized. For example, for the alcoholic, recovery is restoration of sobriety. For the codependent, recovery includes restoration of healthy boundaries and separateness. For the person with an eating disorder, recovery includes abstinence from eating-disordered behavior, but recovery goes beyond abstinence.

By their sheer determination some people refrain from addictive behavior. They become hard and brittle from the strain. The goal of recovery is to live a life of joyful obedience—to maintain abstinence because we want to, not because we have to.

• **The Program**—When we speak of "the program" we mean the entire process of restoration that comes through working the 12 Steps. The program includes attending meetings, the sponsoring model of personal accountability and discipleship, and doing the written and verbal work to apply the Steps to a person's life. The program essentially applies the classical disciplines of the Christian faith to practical life situations.

• **Sponsor**—The 12-Step program uses the ancient biblical practice of apprenticeship for spiritual growth. Each person is encouraged to enlist a sponsor—an older brother or sister in the program. This is someone who has progressed in the recovery process. The sponsor does not take care of, rescue, or fix the person he or she sponsors. The sponsor makes assignments and guides the newcomer to work the Steps.

• **Working the Steps** (or **"Step-work"**)—The goal of the program is to glorify God as we develop healthy, Christ-honoring behavior. God makes these changes in our lives as we work this discipleship program called the 12 Steps. Working the Steps is the entire process of learning and growing. The key parts of working the Steps include the relationship with a sponsor, attendance and sharing at meetings, and completing certain written work. *Conquering Eating Disorders* is a workbook to help you work the Steps.

Distinctives

Conquering Eating Disorders: A Christ-Centered 12-Step Program is distinct in at least three ways. It is Christ-centered. It is based on the biblical 12-Step process for life change. It is written in an interactive style we call "writing for life change."

The information in this workbook is Christ-centered. We recognize that the life-threatening problem of eating disorders is, in part, the result of damaged relationships. The ultimate solution includes relationships. We need healthy relationships with God and with each other. Only in Jesus Christ do we find the forgiveness and grace to achieve those healing relationships. As you study

Conquering Eating Disorders: A Christ-Centered 12-Step Process and as you participate in a 12-Step support group, you will have opportunities to establish and deepen your relationship with God and with others.

The purpose of this book is to help you begin and work the 12-Step process in your life. The writers have many years' experience in recovery and with the 12 Steps. You will find *Conquering Eating Disorders: A Christ-Centered 12-Step Process* is true to the proven 12-Step recovery tradition. Without apology we identify Jesus Christ as our Higher Power.

Conquering Eating Disorders: A Christ-Centered 12-Step Process is not merely designed for you to understand concepts. The purpose of this material is life change.

How this course fits in

Conquering Eating Disorders is part of the LIFE® Support Group Series. The LIFE® Support Group Series is an educational system of discovery-group and support-group resources for providing Christian ministry and emotional support to individuals in the areas of social, emotional, and physical need. These resources deal with such life issues as chemical dependency, codependency, recovery from sexual abuse, eating disorders, divorce recovery, and how to grieve the losses of life. Persons using LIFE® Support Group Series courses will be led through recovery to discipleship and ministry by using these courses.

Conquering Eating Disorders is an integrated course of study. To achieve the full benefit of the educational design, complete your written work in the book, share it with your sponsor, and participate in the group sessions. This is not a course which you will study and then forget. It represents an opportunity to understand and change basic areas which have generated pain in your life.

Study Tips. This book is written as a tutorial text. Study it as if Robert S. McGee or Drew Mountcastle is sitting at your side helping you learn. When the book asks you a question or gives you an assignment, you will benefit most by writing your response. Each assignment is indented and appears in **boldface type**. When you are to respond in writing, a pencil appears beside the assignment. For example, an assignment will look like this:

✎ **Read Psalm 139:13. Write what the verse tells about God's care for you.**

Of course, in an actual activity, a line would appear below each assignment or in the margin beside the assignment. You would write your response as indicated. Then, when you are asked to respond in a non-written fashion—for example, by thinking about or praying about a matter—a ⇨ appears beside the assignment. This type of assignment will look like this:

⇨ **Pause now to pray and thank God for accepting you unconditionally.**

In most cases your "personal tutor" will give you some feedback about your response—for example, you may see a suggestion about what you might have written. This process is designed to help you learn the material and apply the concepts more effectively. Do not deny yourself valuable learning by skipping the learning activities.

Set a definite time and select a quiet place where you can study with little interruption. Keep a Bible handy for times in which the material asks you to look up Scripture. Memorizing Scripture is an important part of your work. Set aside a portion of your study period for memory work. Make notes of problems, questions, or concerns that arise as you study. You will discuss many of these with your sponsor or during your 12-Step meetings. Write these matters in the margins of this textbook so you can find them easily.

Your 12-Step support group will add a needed dimension to your learning. If you have started a study of *Conquering Eating Disorders* and you are not involved in a group, try to enlist some friends or associates who will work through this material with you. Approach your church leaders about beginning such a group. *Conquering Eating Disorders: A Christ-Centered 12-Step Process Facilitator's Guide* provides guidance in how to begin a Christ-centered 12-Step group. (Send orders or inquiries to Customer Service Center; 127 Ninth Avenue, North; Nashville, TN 37234; call 1-800-458-2772; or visit your Baptist Book Store or Lifeway Christian Store. Ask for item # 7205-73.)

A key decision

Conquering Eating Disorders: A Christ-Centered 12-Step Process is written with the assumption that you already have received Jesus Christ as your Savior and Lord and that you have Him guiding you in the healing process. If you have not yet made the important decision to receive Christ, you will find guidance for how to do so in Step 3. You will benefit far more from *Conquering Eating Disorders: A Christ-Centered 12-Step Process* if you have Jesus working in your life and guiding you in the process.

MAJOR ISSUE ALERT

Conquering Eating Disorders: A Christ-Centered 12-Step Process is not intended to be a substitute for professional counseling. Because of the physical and psychological effects of the condition, a high percentage of people with eating disorders need to begin their recovery with hospitalization and in-patient care.

As you begin the process of recovery from an eating disorder—or even if you are uncertain if you have an eating disorder—we encourage you to take these actions.
- See a medical doctor with experience in treating patients with eating disorders.
- Talk to a qualified professional Christian counselor—one with experience in treating patients with eating disorders—for an evaluation.
- Seek out a support group for individuals with eating disorders.

If you require treatment to begin recovery, you will find a treatment center to be a source of great help. In the setting of an eating-disorders treatment center, you will have the support of a trained and skilled team specializing in helping people with your condition. Just as importantly, you will have the support of others in your same situation.

Seeking and receiving professional help, outpatient or inpatient, is neither unchristian nor a sign of failure. Proverbs 15:22 says, "Plans fail for lack of counsel, but with many advisors they succeed" (NIV). Deciding to get help is a sign of courage. God bless you as you begin your recovery journey.

Admitting My Powerlessness

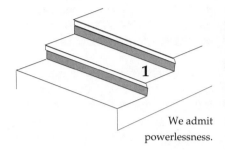

We admit
powerlessness.

OVERCOME BY PAIN AND SHAME

Barbara was a high achiever who had struggled with her body weight and image since high school. She maintained what she considered the "ideal weight" by limiting her food intake and exercising compulsively. During college, these habits intensified. Because she had been depriving her body, she had become preoccupied with food. When under pressure she lost control and resorted to binge-eating. Riddled with guilt and shame from her out-of-control behavior, she then made herself vomit to get rid of the food she had consumed during the binge. This happened time after time, until all she could think about was food and her next binge.

After graduating from college Barbara landed a job as a sales representative for a national pharmaceutical company. Within 15 months she climbed to the top. The pressure and lack of structure associated with her job caused Barbara more problems with her eating-disordered behavior and then with her job. She began to run late for her appointments. Then she began missing important calls from clients because her time was increasingly absorbed by the binge/purge cycle of her disorder. Over time, she was unable to attend to her clients' needs. Her sales volume fell, gradually at first and then sharply over the course of five months until finally, she was unable to produce. The company let her go. (Read more about Barbara on pages 29-30.)

Step 1   *We admit that by ourselves we are powerless over our eating behavior—that our lives have become unmanageable.*

Memory verse   *Blessed are the poor in spirit, for theirs is the kingdom of heaven.*
                                                                        –Matthew 5:3

Overview for Step 1   **Lesson 1: Defining the Problem**
            Goal: You will identify the three primary eating disorders and describe some of the reasons they occur.
        Lesson 2: Describing the Results
            Goal: You will describe your eating-disordered behaviors and begin to describe the consequences of the behaviors.
        Lesson 3: Declaring Our Powerlessness
            Goal: You will admit that you are powerless to conquer your eating disorder.
        Lesson 4: Discovering the Solution
            Goal: You will learn the steps to the Christ-centered approach to conquering eating disorders.
        Lesson 5: Deciding to Begin
            Goal: You will begin the process of healing and victory God provides over eating disorders.

LESSON 1

Defining the Problem

We admit that by ourselves we are powerless over our eating behavior—that our lives have become unmanageable.

> *Be not far from me, for trouble is near; for there is none to help.*
> —Psalm 22:11

Key Concept:
An eating disorder is a compulsive behavior that controls my life.

This unit began with part of Barbara's story. You'll hear more about her later. In this lesson you'll also meet Annie, Cathy, and Doug. You will follow their stories as you go through this workbook. You will see them discover and experience the same power that can help you conquer your eating disorder. As you read their stories, look for things you have in common with these individuals.

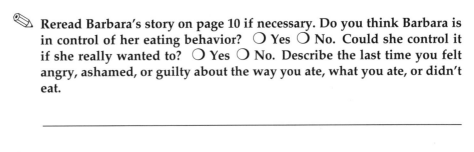 **Reread Barbara's story on page 10 if necessary. Do you think Barbara is in control of her eating behavior?** ○ Yes ○ No. **Could she control it if she really wanted to?** ○ Yes ○ No. **Describe the last time you felt angry, ashamed, or guilty about the way you ate, what you ate, or didn't eat.**

_____

_____

Barbara has a progressive eating disorder that she cannot control. As time passes she may become more out of control. In the next story Cathy has a different, but equally out-of-control, eating disorder.

Cathy's story

Cathy is a secretary for a well-known law firm. She makes a good salary and seems to have a bright future. She performs her work to perfection. On her last job evaluation her boss wrote, "Cathy is the best secretary we've ever had." She also is married to her handsome high school sweetheart who last month earned "Salesman of the Year." With two beautiful daughters, a new puppy, and a nice home, it seems Cathy's life couldn't be better. Down deep inside Cathy is miserable and frustrated about being overweight. She could still hear her physician say at her last checkup: "You should lose 50 to 60 pounds." Over and over again Cathy tried to lose weight. Each new diet brought temporary weight loss followed by regaining it all and then some. She lost count of the number of times she tried and of the number of times she thought, "This time it will work; this time I'll keep it off." That was a lifetime ago, it seemed. She since had adjusted to the giggles of the neighborhood children as they saw her and to the unappreciated humor from her husband—about her figure "going south for the winter." The expected mask of jolliness was difficult to maintain. She found it more and more difficult to laugh at herself along with the others.

**Cathy is
out of control . . .**

_____

_____

_____

_____

_____

Do you think Cathy feels out of control? ○ Yes ○ No. **In the margin box describe in what ways you believe her behavior is out of control.**

Doug's story

Doug is a Sunday School director for a growing church. He loves God and takes his church work seriously. Someday he would like to go to seminary and serve full time in the ministry. Doug always has been overweight. Terms like *blob, fatso,* and *the beached whale,* have followed him all his life. Now his eating seems to be out of control. It threatens his health and his marriage.

After Doug had a nose bleed and after dizziness caused him to miss a day of work, Doug recently visited his doctor . His doctor told him he had high blood pressure. Doug says his less-than-understanding wife causes his blood pressure woes. "She nags me about my eating . . . she nags about the grocery bill . . . she nags about everything." He says, "She really let me have it the other day when I sat on and broke one of her mother's old kitchen chairs. The pressure at work, at home, and at church just seem to drive me to eat. I sometimes find myself looking into an empty carton of ice cream or bag of cookies I just finished. I don't even remember opening the package."

✎ **What is/are Doug's problem(s)? (Check all that apply.)**

○ He is trying to do too many things at once.
○ His eating is out of control.
○ He has high blood pressure.
○ He has a "nagging" wife.
○ He isn't satisfied in his present job.

addiction–n. the quality or state of being devoted or surrendered to something habitually or obsessively

Addiction counselors say that **addictions** such as chemical dependency and eating disorders are *chronic, primary, progressive,* and *terminal* illnesses. Addictions are *chronic;* they are always present. They are *progressive;* they keep growing and becoming more destructive. They are *terminal;* unless something stops the process, these addictions result in death. And they are *primary.* That means the addiction must be halted before treatment for any other disease will be effective. All of the answers to the learning activity represent things happening in Doug's life. Only one is his primary problem—his food addiction. His eating is out of control.

What Are Eating Disorders?

compulsive–adj. having power to compel (drive or urge forcefully)

Barbara, Cathy, and Doug have eating disorders—**compulsive** abnormal eating behaviors that control their lives. They have addictions as strong as that of a drug addict. In their cases, the drug of choice is not crack, cocaine, or heroin. The drug is food.

Not every abnormal eating pattern is an eating disorder. The strange food cravings women may have during pregnancy are not eating disorders. Overeating and gaining weight, or skipping meals to lose weight—though not healthy—are not in themselves eating disorders. Not being able to stick to a diet is not an eating disorder, either.

✎ **Which of the following *are* eating disorders?**

○ Yes ○ No Frequent snacking between meals
○ Yes ○ No Crash dieting for an athletic event
○ Yes ○ No Fasting as a spiritual discipline
○ Yes ○ No Eating dill pickles and ice cream during pregnancy
○ Yes ○ No Trying several fad diets with little success

None of these eating patterns is an eating disorder—though activities like dieting or eating unhealthy foods may lead to an eating disorder in some cases. Most of these examples are temporary activities that are not compulsive in nature. True eating disorders occur in three main types.

The ABC's of Eating Disorders

Anorexia Nervosa. The name literally means "nervous lack of appetite," which is not an accurate description since appetite and thoughts of food aren't lost. Anorexia is an addiction to dieting or self-starvation. It usually is accompanied by a compulsive drive for perfection and control.

Bulimia Nervosa. The word literally means "hungry as an ox." A pattern of powerful, and often secret, binge eating—quickly eating large amounts of high-calorie, sugary, fatty foods, or high-fiber watery vegetables, like salads. The eating binge usually is followed by purging—removing the food eaten during the binge—by using laxatives, diuretics, self-induced vomiting, compulsive exercise, or starvation. The goal is to "get rid of everything quick." Most bulimics are not anorexic, and only a small number of anorexics practice bulimic-like behaviors. Anorexia and bulimia are distinct eating disorders.

Compulsive Overeating. Overeating that resembles the binges in bulimia (which may or may not be done secretly) or "grazing" (constant eating) over a few hours. This usually is done to escape or deaden unwelcome emotions like anger, inadequacy, embarrassment, fear, loneliness, or boredom. Since compulsive overeaters don't purge, the extra calories eaten in frequent binges quickly add up to gains in body fat and weight.

✎ **Match each of the following activities with the phrase that describes it best:**

_____ 1. bingeing	a. eating proper amounts of food regularly
_____ 2. purging	b. eating lots of food quickly
_____ 3. overeating	c. eating too little
_____ 4. starving	d. eating too much
	e. quickly removing food from the body

✎ **Describe any of the above activities you have practiced.**

_____

_____

The answers to the above statements were 1: b; 2: e; 3: d; 4: c.

Why Do Eating Disorders Occur?

Events may trigger eating-disordered behaviors.

Many professionals believe that certain life events, such as illness or death of a loved one, divorce, or sexual abuse may trigger eating-disordered behaviors. These behaviors often are supported by the comments of others (positive or negative) and by deep-seated personal and relationship needs. Some researchers also believe that physical or hereditary factors play a part in eating disorders. In the same way that some persons are genetically more likely to become alcoholic than others, some persons may be more susceptible than others to becoming eating disordered.

✎ **Read Annie's story and underline any clues you can find which may have triggered her eating disorder or supported it once it began.**

Annie's story

Annie is a college freshman. She attends a well-known university. Her father picked the school for her. "Only the best for my little girl," he said when the selection was made. Annie's parents now are divorced, and she lives on campus. She tries to keep in touch with both parents but lives with her mom during the summers. She still remembers the day she came home to find that her father had moved out to live with another woman. The memory still causes pain.

Annie is also good at something else—dieting.

Annie enjoys college and has made a few new friends. She performs well in her studies but found she can excel in physical education. Not that she's on a school team or plays sports, but she loves to exercise . . . jogging, hiking, and aerobics class are her favorites. She's also good at something else—dieting. When Annie arrived at college, she decided to lose a few pounds. Losing weight didn't seem to take much effort at all. In fact, the pounds seemed to melt off. She received lots of compliments from her classmates and, when she went home for spring break, she received nothing but praise from her family. Even her grandmother, who always told her she ate too much, commented on her nice, new figure. With all that positive support, Annie decided to lose even more weight. The compliments have stopped now. Annie barely tips the scale at 90 pounds. She eats only what she must to keep from feeling too weak or lightheaded.

As you underlined clues in this exercise, did you underline the divorce of Annie's parents and her father's over-control? Did you also note the positive reinforcement she received for her initial weight loss? Might Annie's feeling of accomplishment—that she is *good at* exercise—play a part?

✎ **Think back on your own experience. Write down any life events that may have triggered or supported your own compulsive eating behavior.**

____

____

➔ **Take a few moments right now to pray. Ask God to help you as you begin to look honestly at your past and at your present eating behavior.**

Key Concept for Lesson 1

An eating disorder is a compulsive behavior that controls my life.

✎ **Pray and ask God how this concept can apply in your life. Now review this lesson. What has God shown you that you can use?**

____

____

Describing the Results

Key Concept:
I must honestly admit the harmful results of my eating disorder.

The purpose of the recovery process is not to blame but to get help.

How do you rate?

We admit that by ourselves we are powerless over our eating behavior—that our lives have become unmanageable.

O LORD, do not rebuke me in Thine anger, nor chasten me in Thy wrath. Be gracious to me, O LORD, for I am pining away; heal me, O LORD, for my bones are dismayed.

–Psalm 6:1-2

You are reading this because you either suspect or know that you have an eating disorder or because someone who cares about you wants you to get help. Whatever the reason, examine your life for signs of any compulsive eating behaviors. A complex set of factors combine to cause eating disorders. The purpose of the recovery process is not to blame but to get help. Consult with a physician to explain any symptoms and rule out any physical factors which may be contributing to your behavior.

 In the following list you will find eating behaviors which are typical of one or more of the following conditions: anorexia nervosa, bulimia nervosa, or compulsive overeating. Begin by answering the questions as honestly and as accurately as possible. Check each question that describes your situation (past or present).

  ☑ 1. Do thoughts about food occupy much of your time? *Pr*
  ☑ 2. Are you preoccupied with a desire to be thinner?
  ○ 3. Do you starve to make up for eating binges?
  ○ 4. Are you overweight, despite concern by others for you to lose weight?
  ○ 5. Do you binge and then vomit afterward?
  ○ 6. Do you exercise excessively to burn off calories?
  ○ 7. Do you overeat by bingeing or by "grazing" continuously?
  ○ 8. Do you eat the same thing every day and feel annoyed when you eat something else?
  ○ 9. Do you binge and then take enemas or laxatives to get rid of the food you have eaten?
  ○ 10. Do you hide stashes of food for future eating or bingeing?
  ○ 11. Do you avoid foods with sugar in them and feel uncomfortable after eating sweets?
  ○ 12. Is food your friend?
  ○ 13. Would you rather eat alone? Do you feel uncomfortable when you must eat with others?
  ○ 14. Do you have specific ways you eat when you are emotionally upset, sad, angry, afraid, anxious, or ashamed?
  ○ 15. Do you become depressed or feel guilty after an eating binge?
  ☑ 16. Do you "feel" fat even when people tell you otherwise?
  ○ 17. Are you ever afraid that you won't be able to stop eating?
  ○ 18. Have you tried to diet repeatedly only to sabotage your weight loss?
  ○ 19. Do you binge on high-calorie, sugary, "forbidden" foods?

○ 20. Are you proud of your ability to control the food you eat and your weight?
☑ 21. Do you have weight changes of more than 10 pounds after binges and fasts?
☑ 22. Do you feel your eating behavior is abnormal? Do you try to hide it from others?
○ 23. Does feeling ashamed of your body weight result in more bingeing?
○ 24. Do you make a lot of insulting jokes about your body weight or your eating?
☑ 25. Do you feel guilty after eating anything not allowed on your diet?
○ 26. Do you follow unusual rituals while eating, such as counting bites or not allowing the fork or food to touch your lips?

If you checked five or more of the questions numbered 1, 2, 6, 8, 11, 13, 14, 16, 17, 20, 22, 25, 26, you have eating behaviors typical of anorexia nervosa.

If you checked five or more of the questions numbered 1, 3, 5, 6, 9, 10, 13, 14, 15, 17, 19, 21, 22, 26, you have eating behaviors common in bulimia nervosa.

If you checked five or more of the questions numbered 1, 4, 7, 10, 12, 13, 14, 15, 17, 18, 19, 22, 23, and 24, you may be dealing with compulsive overeating.

Does this self-test confirm your suspicions or what you already know? Does it provide the first strong evidence that you may have an eating disorder? If so, complete the following statement and repeat it aloud:

> "I have an addictive eating disorder.
>
> I believe it to be _____."

Congratulations if you have admitted to yourself that you have a problem! You have just taken a giant step toward recovery. Many people cannot see their own problem. They are in **denial**. They rationalize their behavior or blame someone else. Others know they have a problem but won't face it. They continue their behaviors in spite of painful consequences. They may not admit the problem because they fear what others will think, they think they can stop whenever they want, or they don't know where to turn for help.

denial–n. refusal to admit the truth or reality. (Webster's) Addicts develop a denial which blinds them to the truth about their condition.

Some people first break through denial by responding to an exercise like the one you just completed. Some seek help after seeing the harm that their compulsive actions can cause—to themselves and others. Strained relationships, problems on the job, or damaged physical health get their attention. Addictive eating disorders are behaviors that cause serious physical problems, even death.

Important Information

> The self-test you took shows patterns and helps to pinpoint suspicions. It is not a diagnostic tool. *Only your physician is qualified to make a diagnosis and/or label your eating disorder, if one exists.* This is an exercise in self discovery designed to help you realize the seriousness of any compulsive eating habits. If you think you have identified an eating disorder in yourself for the first time, using this self-test, please see your physician for further evaluation.

The following pages contain important facts about the effects of eating disorders on our bodies. For general information you may want to read the results of all three eating disorders. Read and respond to the one you checked most on the self-test.

The Harmful Effects of Anorexia Nervosa

Many of the health problems caused by anorexia nervosa occur because of lowered hormone production.

Feeling cold. The body has a marvelous life-preserving instinct built in by God, our Creator. When the food or calorie intake is reduced, the body slows its internal level of activity—the metabolic rate. Fewer calories are used to maintain life. One of the effects of the lowered metabolic rate is a decreased production of body heat. This makes it more difficult to tolerate cold temperatures. In the process of starving their bodies, many anorexics simply can't stand the cold.

Digestive problems. The digestive tract works less efficiently: digestion is slowed; stomach bloating, gas, constipation, and pain often occur.

osteoporosis–n. a condition that is characterized by decrease in bone mass with decreased density and enlargement of bone spaces producing porosity and fragility; results from a disturbance of nutrition and mineral metabolism (Webster's)

Weak bones. Weakening of the bones—**osteoporosis**—is caused by insufficient calcium and a lowering of the female hormone—estrogen—which is responsible for bone cell growth and replacement.

Heart problems. As the entire body is affected by anorexic starvation, the heart rate slows and the heart muscles weaken. This leads to a drop in blood pressure and delivery of oxygen throughout the body. The heart may beat irregularly. These changes can cause death.

Destruction of muscle. Due to lowered calorie intake the body will use lean tissue, or muscle, for food. This leads to a wasting away of the body, its protein, and a further lowering of the metabolic rate.

Effects on the brain. The brain also requires food. Starvation results in depression and mood swings. If blood sugar levels fall too low, you will experience blackouts.

Hair and skin. Hair and skin become dry. A fine hair called *lanugo* may replace normal body hair.

Reproductive system problems. A common symptom of anorexia is decreased ovulation and loss of the menstrual period in women. In men, lowered testicular function and impotence may occur.

 List any of the above symptoms you have experienced or are experiencing now.

_____

_____

The addiction hides behind the addictive logic called denial.

Addictions always share a common trait. The addiction behaves like a living thing—it hides behind the addictive logic called denial. If you have

Your addiction is telling you the symptom really isn't important.

experienced any of the symptoms of anorexia, your addiction is telling you that the symptom really isn't important. Go back to the list you just described, and multiply the importance of your answers by 100. Your eating disorder is important—it is a matter of life and death!

The Harmful Effects of Bulimia Nervosa

Take a look at bulimia nervosa—the behavior of binge eating and then purging. It sounds like a simple act: overeat, then get rid of it. However, serious medical complications result, especially if you practice this behavior often. The more frequently you vomit, or use laxatives or diuretics, the greater the risk for developing serious health problems. These risks include:

Upset body chemistry. Frequent vomiting causes low blood potassium. This is one of the more common and more serious problems related to bulimia. This is especially true if laxatives and/or diuretics are also used to lose weight. These practices also cause the body to lose potassium. The resulting low blood levels can cause fainting and irregular heartbeat. They can put you at risk for sudden cardiac arrest and death.

Sudden cardiac arrest

Heartburn and raw, bleeding sore throat. Stomach acid causes heartburn. The acid irritates the lining of the esophagus leading into the stomach. Vomiting and putting fingers or other objects down the throat to induce vomiting irritates the delicate tissues.

Lung problems. During vomiting you run the risk of accidentally breathing the vomit into your lungs. This can cause pneumonia or suffocate you.

Stomach tearing. The physical act of vomiting can cause stretching of the stomach and even rupture the stomach or esophagus. This results in a very serious medical emergency or death.

Dental problems. Since most of the foods eaten during a binge are high in sugar, tooth decay may occur as the sugar and bacteria combine to damage the surface of the teeth. This can cause cavities. Tooth decay also may be caused by the action of the stomach acid present in vomit. This eats away at the teeth.

✎ **From the following list check those medical problems that can arise from bulimia.**

- ○ dental cavities
- ○ heart attack
- ○ irregular heart beats
- ○ suffocation
- ○ pneumonia
- ○ heartburn
- ○ rupture of the stomach
- ○ death

All of these medical problems are linked to bulimia. All are progressive. Some of them show up early in the process as tension headaches and heartburn. Others remain hidden until they erupt in a crisis.

✎ **What medical problems have you experienced from bulimia?**

_____

_____

The Harmful Effects of Compulsive Overeating

Compulsive overeating carries with it all the health risks linked to obesity, and then some.

High blood pressure. Being overweight increases the risk of hypertension. High blood pressure increases the risk of health problems such as stroke.

Greatly increased risk

Coronary artery disease: Obesity can raise cholesterol and other blood chemistry levels. Along with increased blood pressure these changes greatly increase risk of heart disease.

Hyperglycemia and diabetes. In addition to heart disease and stroke, compulsive overeating increases blood sugar levels—hyperglycemia—which increases the risk for diabetes.

osteoarthritis–n. arthritis marked by degeneration of the cartilage and bone of joints (Webster's)

Orthopedic problems. Obesity causes or aggravates a variety of skeletal problems including low back pain, **osteoarthritis**, and problems with feet and ankles.

Other problems. Overeating contributes to several skin disorders and to nerve problems of many kinds. When people binge, they usually eat foods high in sugar and fats. Many health problems are linked to eating large amounts of sugar and fats. These health problems include heart disease, strokes, diabetes, cancer, and low blood sugar.

✎ **List your 10 favorite foods.**

1. _____	6. _____
2. _____	7. _____
3. _____	8. _____
4. _____	9. _____
5. _____	10. _____

✎ **Do you feel that these foods are your "friends"?** ○ Yes ○ No
How do you feel when you are eating these foods?

_____

_____

✎ **How do you feel after you have eaten them?**

_____

_____

For Thou didst know my inward parts; Thou didst weave me in my mother's womb. I will give thanks to Thee, for I am fearfully and wonderfully made; Wonderful are Thy works, and my soul knows it very well.
–Psalm 139:13-14

Regardless of how you may see yourself or your body, you are a creation of God. You are an awesome, wonderful, special creation that was no accident. Both you and your body are worthy of care. Read the words of King David in the margin. He wrote with awe about the marvelous work of creation he saw in his own body.

✎ **Write a prayer thanking God for creating you. Ask Him to help you see your body as His marvelous creation.**

_____

_____

_____

The Scripture in Recovery

Accept one another, just as Christ also accepted us to the glory of God.
                    –Romans 15:7

We hope you will feel free and accepted. Some people may have been deeply misunderstood and hurt by church people. Our uses of Scripture are intended to affirm and encourage—not to communicate shame—just as the group's purpose is to communicate love, acceptance, and strength.

Key Concept for Lesson 2
I must honestly admit the harmful results of my eating disorder.

✎ **Pray and ask God how this concept can apply in your life. Now review this lesson. What has God shown you that you can use?**

_____

_____

➜ **Memorize this Step's memory verse:**
Blessed are the poor in spirit, for theirs is the kingdom of heaven.
                    –Matthew 5:3

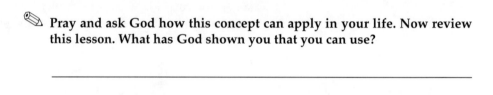

LESSON 3

Key Concept:
Admitting my powerlessness is the first step to victory over my eating disorder.

Declaring Our Powerlessness

We admit that by ourselves we are powerless over our eating behavior—that our lives have become unmanageable.

> _For he will deliver the needy when he cries for help, the afflicted also, and him who has no helper._
>   –Psalm 72:12

You probably have tried—and failed—to change your compulsive relationship to food. Now you have an opportunity to apply the spiritual power of a Christ-centered 12-Step program to the problem. You will find that God does what you cannot and that He works this miracle as you work the 12 Steps.

The 12 Steps begin in a seemingly strange manner. One must admit that he or she is powerless over the addiction. Then the power of God begins to work.

Although the three major eating disorders—anorexia nervosa, bulimia nervosa, and compulsive overeating—have different eating habits or styles, a common underlying problem exists. That problem is powerlessness. In all three behaviors we are powerless over food; it has control over us.

✎ **Answer the following questions as you take a closer look at your dietary habits.**

What best describes your compulsive eating behavior? Circle the phrases that apply:

- bingeing and/or purging
- hoarding food
- avoiding meals
- skipping meals
- excessive exercise
- using laxatives/diuretics
- continuous "grazing"
- self-starvation

When did you first begin these behavior(s) and why? _____

_____

Why do you think you have continued them? _____

_____

Did social pressure cause you to stop or change?

Did social pressure cause you to stop? ⊘ Yes ○ No

How often do you think about eating, calories, or your weight?

- ○ 1-4 times a day
- ○ 5-10 times a day
- ⊘ 11-20 times a day
- ○ more than 20 times a day

If you binge and purge, how frequently do you binge?
_____ times daily, _____ times weekly

how frequently do you purge?
_____ times daily, _____ times weekly

Most everyone at some time will skip meals, exercise, take a laxative/diuretic, or overeat. These behaviors, however, usually are short term, done within safe guidelines under a doctor's order, or accomplished for a special reason. Do you think your answers to the above questions indicate "normal eating habits?" Do you suppose that most other people would give similar answers?

Have you tried to change your food consumption, purging, self-starvation, or other eating behaviors? ○ Yes ○ No

If so, how? _____

_____

Did you change your behavior for a time? ⊘ Yes ○ No

At best, how long? _____

Did you ultimately fail? ⊘ Yes ○ No

Did you fail to give up bingeing or starving yourself even when you had health problems? ⊘ Yes ○ No

Have you ever been frightened because you've passed out or coughed up blood when you purged? ⊘ Yes ○ No

How has your food behavior been embarrassing, inconvenient, or destructive to you and/or to others?

_____

_____

Do you think you've lost self-respect as a result of your secret eating compulsion? ☑ Yes ○ No

If so, how? _____

_____

✎ **In the box appearing in the margin describe your typical eating habits. By responding to the following:**

If you are anorexic, list all you allow yourself to eat in a typical day. What are your "safe" foods? What are your "scare" or "off limits" foods?

If you are bulimic or a compulsive overeater, describe a typical binge. What are your favorite binge foods?

From the answers you gave to these questions, can you see the lack of power you have over food? These questions focus on situations which would cause most people to change. For some it is rigid perfectionism.

Having an unmanageable life is another sign of powerlessness. Unmanageability is the lack of control.

✎ **Answer the following questions to determine if your life is "out of control."**

What is your current physical condition? _____

_____

_____

_____

_____

Can you no longer empty your bowels without using laxatives?
○ Yes ○ No

Do you either require chemical assistance or several attempts to make yourself vomit or are you so "accomplished" that you can make yourself vomit on demand? ○ Yes ○ No

Are you losing your sensory abilities, especially your sense of hearing or sense of touch? ○ Yes ○ No

Did you have any of these problems before you began your compulsive eating behavior(s)? ○ Yes ○ No

Have you experienced any mood swings or weakness because of blood sugar fluctuations? ○ Yes ○ No

Have you experienced blackouts or fainting? ○ Yes ○ No

If you are a woman, have your monthly periods slowed or stopped for no other apparent reason? ○ Yes ○ No

---

My eating habits—

_____

_____

_____

_____

_____

_____

_____

_____

_____

_____

_____

➜ **Congratulations for answering these questions. This process is difficult, but worthwhile. Take a five-minute break before you continue your study.**

Anorexia, Bulimia, and Compulsive Overeating

For whichever eating disorder you are concerned, answer the following questions.

✎ **Give examples of "social unmanageability" on your part as a result of your eating behavior.**

Social unmanageability–n. The term refers to situations in which our eating behavior has interfered with our normal life and relationships. Examples include—
• feeling a need to binge when expecting an important phone call, and feeling resentment toward the caller;
• taking the phone off the hook in order to binge, resulting in an inability to cope with the business which the call involved;
• staying home from a dinner party for fear of having to eat.

_____

_____

_____

Name ways your eating behavior has led you to antisocial behavior (a behavior which challenges your conscience or values, such as lying, shoplifting, etc.)

_____

_____

_____

Name ways your eating behavior has or may have caused you to mismanage or jeopardize your education or job.

_____

_____

_____

Have you been in treatment for eating disorders? ○ Yes ○ No
More than once? ○ Yes ○ No How many times have you been in treatment? _____

From these questions and answers, can you admit that your eating behavior is unmanageable—that it is an addiction?

I've tried to change but nothing works.

Don't despair. You may think, *So now where do I go? I've tried to change but nothing works.* Hope exists for you! You cannot be free from the problem through willpower and self-control. You have a relationship with food in which food controls you. You cannot control the food-related behavior by exercising more willpower and self-effort. You need the power that comes from Jesus Christ.

To receive Christ's power you must start with the first Step. You must admit you have a problem which you cannot control. The problem is controlling you. For the last two lessons you have been answering questions about your habits, thoughts, health, and life situation which all show you have a addiction—a behavior that you cannot control.

Reread your questions and answers at this time to see the whole picture. Note that no person would have all the symptoms listed. Do your answers indicate the direction your addiction is taking you? If so, finish the following statement and repeat it out loud several times. Do not continue until you have completed this action.

> I have an eating disorder, I am (anorexic, bulimic, a compulsive overeater, etc.) _____. I have no control over food. It controls me. I am powerless.

No person would have all of the symptoms.

Was it difficult to say *I have no control over food. I am powerless*? The statement is difficult because it seems to take away your control. By refusing to admit powerlessness you may have maintained the illusion that you were able to control your addiction. Stating the fact "I have no power" seems to be giving up. What you actually are doing is choosing to live in reality.

Live life on life's terms.

One of the slogans in the 12-Step program is "live life on life's terms." The slogan means becoming honest and living with reality rather than living in a dream world. We have realized that we cannot control our addictions. The harder we try to control them the more control they exercise over us. Step 1 frees us from the bondage of attempting the impossible.

Look deep into your mind and heart. How do you feel now that you have admitted you have no power? Do you feel that if someone else doesn't step in and take over, you cannot function? Does the thought of losing control frighten you?

That is the good news. By admitting we are powerless over our lives—specifically over the eating behavior—we open a door for Christ to come in and do for us what we cannot do for ourselves.

"My grace is sufficient for you, for power is perfected in weakness." Most gladly, therefore, I will rather boast about my weaknesses, that the power of Christ may dwell in me.
–2 Corinthians 12:9

✎ **Read 2 Corinthians 12:9 that appears in the margin. Check the following response which more nearly fits the statement "(God's) power is perfected in weakness."**

- ○ 1. God wants me to be weak and helpless.
- ○ 2. God won't change my life unless I let Him.
- ○ 3. I best depend on God's power when I realize my own weakness.
- ○ 4. I must use my willpower to serve God.

The apostle Paul prayed in Ephesians 3:16: *that He would grant you, according to the riches of His glory, to be strengthened with power through His Spirit in the inner man.* Answer 3 seems best to express the meaning of the passage. God's power works when we realize our lack of power.

Key Concept for Lesson 3
Admitting my powerlessness is the first step to victory over my eating disorder.

✎ Pray and ask God how this concept can apply in your life. Now review this lesson. What has God shown you that you can use?

_____

_____

➔ Spend five minutes memorizing this Step's memory verse, Matthew 5:3.

Discovering the Solution

We admit that by ourselves we are powerless over our eating behavior—that our lives have become unmanageable.

> *In my distress I called upon the LORD, and cried to my God for help; He heard my voice out of His temple, and my cry for help before Him came into His ears.*
>
> –Psalm 18:6

Key Concept:
Recovery includes my mental, social, physical, and spiritual healing.

The goal of recovery is progress—not perfection. You probably have thought "If I can just _____, then everything will be OK."

An eating disorder is an extremely complex problem. The ongoing process for effective, lasting change involves all of the parts of your being—mental, social, physical, and spiritual. The same way that Jesus grew and developed in these areas while He was on earth, God will help you develop in each area the strengths you will need in your recovery.

And Jesus increased in wisdom and stature and in favor with God and men.
                    –Luke 2:52

✎ **Read the Scripture in the margin. Draw lines to connect the Bible words with the modern terms for each of the areas in which Jesus developed.**

1. *wisdom*   a. spiritual
2. *stature*   b. social
3. *favor with God*   c. physical
4. *favor with men*   d. mental

Does the realization that Jesus had to grow and develop in all areas of His life help you to deal with your own perfectionism? He was perfect in that He never sinned. He was perfect in that He became exactly what the Father had planned. He was not perfect in the unrealistic sense of compulsive perfectionism. He knew that the way to be happy was not to be found by being the most attractive, most slender, strongest, best athlete, or most popular. The answers were 1. d, 2. c, 3. a, 4. b. In your process of recovery, here are some ways you will develop in the above four areas.

Mental (also called *psychological* or *cognitive*). As you gain a better understanding of your background, feelings, thoughts, and the truths found in God's Word, you will be able to apply specific biblical truths to your deepest needs, hurts, and desires. God will renew your mind, reform your will, and heal your emotions as you learn to trust and obey Him.

Be anxious for nothing, but in everything by prayer and supplication with thanksgiving let your requests be made known to God. And the peace of God, which surpasses all comprehension, shall guard your hearts and your minds in Christ Jesus.

–Philippians 4:6-7

✎ **Read Philippians 4:6-7 printed in the margin. How do you feel about the promise that God will renew your mind and heal your emotions? Check all the responses you feel.**

○ hopeful   ○ afraid   ○ doubtful   ○ angry

○ other _____

We all would like a "magic pill" kind of solution for our problems—a quick and easy solution. Read again Philippians 4:6-7. What does the writer tell us to do before the peace of God comes in our lives?

_____

_____

Did you note that we are told to stop concentrating on our problems and instead to begin concentrating on our relationship with God? Step 1 leads us to recognize reality so we can begin to move toward a Christ-honoring life of victory.

Social (also called *relational*). Fellowship is vital to your recovery. You need the acceptance and encouragement of others to do important recovery-related tasks like personal reflection and application. To conquer the painful causes and effects of an addiction by yourself is difficult if not impossible. You need the support of others who have gone through (or are going through) this process of healing.

You need support

Unfortunately, just relying on family and friends for the support you need may not be enough. Often those closest to you, though they may mean well, have come to doubt your sincerity about wanting to change. They have heard your repeated promises and seen your efforts to reform come and go. Yet your compulsive behaviors and the pain they cause still remain. Family and friends understandably are doubtful that you mean business this time. But those who have been where you are understand. Let them help you while you help them. Together you can conquer.

Two are better than one because they have a good return for their labor. For if either of them falls, the one will lift up his companion. But woe to the one who falls when there is not another to lift him up. Furthermore, if two lie down together they keep warm, but how can one be warm alone? And if one can overpower him who is alone, two can resist him. A cord of three strands is not quickly torn apart.

–Ecclesiastes 4:9-12

✎ **Read the words of Solomon printed in the margin. In the program you may hear this slogan: "Only you can do it, but you can't do it alone." Describe what you think the slogan and the passage from Ecclesiastes mean.**

_____

_____

_____

_____

Proverbs 27:17 says *Iron sharpens iron, So one man sharpens another.* Did your answer note that we need each other? Addictive persons isolate themselves and either blame themselves or blame others. The Scripture and the slogan both teach that we need each other and that we must become responsible for our own actions. We need other people in our recovery process.

Physical (also called *somatic*). Eating disorders are health-threatening and life-threatening. They produce strains on the body's internal organs, biochemistry, and hormone levels. Your months or years of abusing your body by compulsive eating behaviors have caused some physical problems, some of which you may or may not recognize. You may have experienced one or more of the conditions discussed in lesson 2.

Bless the LORD, O my soul, and forget none of His benefits; Who pardons all your iniquities; Who heals all your diseases.
–Psalm 103:2-3

The good news is that God created your body with a remarkable ability to heal itself when you give it a chance. In time, you can expect complete physical recovery, in most cases. But your actions here are most important. To read or think about the Steps you need to take for recovery . . . or even to decide you should take them is not enough. You must take the actions. God will provide the strength for the journey, but you must work the Steps.

Spiritual (also called *moral*). As in any relationship, the more time you spend with someone, the more you get to know the person, and the more he or she influences you. The same is true with God—the more time you spend with Him in prayer, Bible study, and reflection on His character, the more He will change you.

But we all, with unveiled face beholding as in a mirror the glory of the Lord, are being transformed into the same image from glory to glory, just as from the Lord, the Spirit.
–2 Corinthians 3:18

As you examine God's truths and begin to experience His forgiveness and strengths, you will grow in your understanding of His character and purposes for your life. You also will gain a new attitude about accepting others and sharing yourself with them.

Not a Quick Fix

An eating disorder is no simple problem. You probably waver between despair and the desire for a simple solution.

 Carefully read the Scripture in the margin. The passage is a benediction—a combination blessing and prayer. The passage requests that you be sanctified—made holy, or suitable for God's use. What parts of your being are included in this blessing?

Now may the God of peace Himself sanctify you entirely; and may your spirit and soul and body be preserved complete, without blame at the coming of our Lord Jesus Christ. Faithful is He who calls you, and He also will bring it to pass.
–1 Thessalonians 5:23-24

_____

_____

You noted that God is vitally interested in all the parts that make you a distinct person—your spirit, soul, and body. He is the One who will bring you to blameless completion. The solution to your problem must include your spirit, mind, and body. By following the disciplines in the Steps, you will grow in the spiritual, mental, social, and physical areas of your life.

The Plan

The course map on the inside back cover illustrates the 12-Step model for recovery used in this workbook. Each of the 12 Steps builds on the prior Steps. Work through each as completely as possible, because you will take strengths and successes from one to the next. The Steps are the principles you will use again and again. You will use them first for recovery and then for victorious living.

work out your own salvation with fear and trembling; for it is God who is at work in you both to will and to work for his good pleasure.

–Philippians 2:12-13

Note the apostle Paul's instructions found in the margin. He said we are to work out our salvation, but then Paul also said it is God who is doing the work. In terms of the Steps we might say that it is our job to work the Steps and God's job to change our lives.

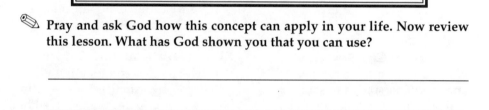 **Rewrite Philippians 2:12-13 in your own words. Focus on how God will work in and with you to free you from your eating disorder.**

_____

_____

_____

One day Jesus found His disciples tired and frustrated from fishing all night and catching nothing. He told them to throw their nets from the other side of the boat. To the disciples' amazement they caught so many fish the net began to break. The disciples had to throw out the nets; Jesus supplied the fish!

You may be tired and frustrated by repeated failures at trying to control your compulsive behavior. You can take hope in the fact that God wants you free, and it is His good pleasure to work in you to bring about that freedom.

> ### Key Concept for Lesson 4
> Recovery includes my mental, social, physical, and spiritual healing.

Pray and ask God how this concept can apply in your life. Now review this lesson. What has God shown you that you can use?

_____

_____

➜ Memorize this Step's memory verse.

LESSON 5

Key Concept:
Recovery means I will go through a grief process.

Deciding to Begin

We admit that by ourselves we are powerless over our eating behavior—that our lives have become unmanageable.

> _Save me, O God, for the waters have threatened my life. I have sunk in deep mire, and there is no foothold; I have come into deep waters, and a flood overflows me. I am weary with my crying; my throat is parched; my eyes fail while I wait for my God._
>
> –Psalm 69:1-3

Recovering from eating disorders is never simple or easy. It may be the most difficult task in your life. But it's much better than not recovering.

People experience deep feelings of loss as they give up addictive habits.

Prepare yourself for an odd fact of recovery. In spite of the negative symptoms, effects, and problems of addictive food behavior, and in spite of the many positive benefits that occur in recovery, many people experience deep feelings of personal loss as they give up addictive habits. Although these feelings of personal loss eventually will become less frequent and less severe, they may last from several weeks to several years, depending on the strength of the addiction.

Many pastors and counselors identify five stages experienced by dying patients or persons losing someone or something important to them.[1] Though the idea seems strange, giving up an addiction is like losing a cherished friend. People withdrawing from eating-disordered behaviors pass through similar stages of grief during the recovery process. The five stages are:

Denial ➡ Bargaining ➡ Anger ➡ Grief ➡ Acceptance

Denial

Most people with an eating disorder are unable or unwilling to admit—to others or to themselves—that they have a problem. In spite of obvious signs that the disorder drives their lives, they continue to experience the blindness of denial.

We cling to our denial because staying a victim gives us an excuse for our behavior. If we go through the grieving process, we become more responsible.

 As you read more of Barbara's story, underline the phrases that show her denial at work.

More about Barbara

Barbara rinsed her mouth with water and then wiped her face with a cool cloth. She usually felt better after vomiting, but this time angry memories of recent events flooded her mind. As the tears welled up in her eyes, she stared into the bathroom mirror. "Why don't they leave me alone?" she practically yelled. "It's my life, not theirs. I know what I'm doing."

Barbara's boss had said that her work needed to improve. He told her that it seemed her mind was on matters other than her job. He insisted she visit the employee assistance program counselor. One of Barbara's co-workers said she "looked terrible" and asked if something were wrong. Barbara didn't mean to, but before she could stop herself, she said some rather mean things to her friend—things she immediately regretted.

In what ways has your eating disorder made you say or do things you later regretted?

_____

_____

Barbara blamed her boss for his lack of understanding. She blamed the company because the job was "too demanding." After she was fired she was unable to find work due to the all-consuming demands of her disorder. She

"What problem?"

blamed God, who she said has "had it out for me since the beginning." Many times Barbara's co-workers, friends, and family members confronted her about her "food problem." "Problem? What problem? I've just had a rough go of things," she said.

Did you underline the statement that Barbara blamed her company? Then she blamed God. Finally, she simply said she had no problem.

 Review Barbara's story on page 10 and in the previous paragraphs. Look for the progression of her addiction. Number the stages of progression as her addiction grows. For example, you might put a 1 by the statement that she struggled with her body weight by diet and exercise. Then you would put a 2 by the fact that she became preoccupied with food. See how many stages you can identify.

You may have identified many stages as Barbara's addiction gained more and more control over her life. Isn't it amazing that her denial could be so strong that she still could not see her eating disorder realistically?

 Apply the things you have just learned to your situation. Write a list of the people, institutions, and situations you have blamed as part of your denial.

_____

_____

_____

Bargaining

Bargaining is an attempt to postpone quitting.

Bargaining usually marks the beginning of the dependent person's recognition of his or her addiction. Bargaining is an attempt to postpone quitting. Persons bargain with themselves: "I need to kick this, but I'm just too upset right now. What difference is one more little binge going to make? I promise this will be the last time!" They bargain with others: "Of course I'm still serious about giving this up, and I will—right after this project at work blows over." They bargain with God: "God, help me get rid of all this food I've eaten, then I promise I'll never binge again!"

 Describe at least two instances when you have bargained with God, yourself, or others.

_____

_____

_____

Anger

When you no longer can escape the facts pointing to your addiction, or when you enter treatment, anger is a normal response. You probably will vent your anger toward God, family members, and friends. You may feel that all of them contributed to your addiction or entry into treatment. You also may feel angry about the circumstances of needing to enter recovery and angry at yourself for continuing in this condition and for feeling helpless to overcome it alone.

Depression

The experience of grief during recovery is an unwelcome surprise.

The majority of eating-disordered persons have become experts at avoiding painful emotions. The experience of deep distress or grief during recovery is often an unwelcome surprise.

Most people recognize sadness as a normal response to loss, but many do not realize that feelings of grief are a normal response to the loss of anything we consider important. The eating disorder has been the victim's closest— although most destructive—friend. Losing this friend brings a great feeling of loss.

Rigid control

Compulsive food behavior provides an immediate payoff. It calms the nerves; blocks feelings of pain, failure, or disappointment; and gives a sense of courage or power to control. Because the cycle of addiction turns its victims increasingly inward, compulsive eating or rigid control over food consumption becomes an important part of the victim's life. When this "support" is taken away, it's like losing a good friend. Grieving about such a loss is a normal, healthy aspect of recovery—even though it doesn't feel good. Grieving properly occurs when persons give themselves the freedom to feel the loss whenever it comes to mind.

Acceptance

Over time, those who continue on their journey to recovery accept their addiction and their need for treatment. Gradually, most can maintain a life apart from addictive patterns of behavior with a sense of peace and eventually with joy.

✎ **These stages often overlap in actual experiences. Which one(s) are you in now? You may feel more than one at the same time.**

      ○ Denial   ○ Grief
      ○ Bargaining ○ Acceptance
      ○ Anger

Write a statement describing your feelings now.

_____

_____

_____

_____

Remaining aware of your condition and the possibility that you have needs will help you make clear and honest decisions about your problem.

```
┌─────────────────────────────────────────────────────┐
│                                                       │
│              Key Concept for Lesson 5                 │
│        Recovery means going through a grief process.  │
│                                                       │
└─────────────────────────────────────────────────────┘
```

➡ **Memorize this Step's memory verse.**
Blessed are the poor in spirit, for theirs is the kingdom of heaven.

–Matthew 5:3

Step Review

✎ **Step 1 says:** *We admit that by ourselves we are powerless over our eating behavior—that our lives have become unmanageable.* **What does powerless mean to you?**

_____

_____

_____

_____

Are you powerless over your eating disorder? In what ways?

_____

_____

_____

In what ways has your life become unmanageable?

_____

_____

_____

Describe how you plan to apply Step 1 daily to your life and recovery.

_____

_____

_____

_____

_____

Notes
[1]Adapted from the work of Elizabeth Kubler-Ross in her book *On Death and Dying* (New York: MacMillan Publishing, 1969).

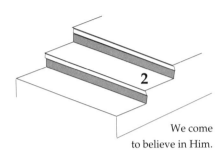

STEP 2

We come
to believe in Him.

Coming to Believe

ANNIE MAKES A NEW START

Annie hit bottom when she passed out at school and had to be taken to the hospital. She spent three months of her junior year in an inpatient eating-disorders treatment program. Although she protested at first, Annie finally admitted she was out of control and needed help.

With the encouragement of her support group, she began to realize that if she were going to stay alive, she needed a power outside of herself. Annie didn't have an easy time admitting her powerlessness. But as she did, she realized that she couldn't even trust her own mind to make the right decisions about eating.

She knew all the answers for successful recovery and at one time thought she would never have to face her "problem" again. She only weighed herself once or twice a day now, instead of 20 to 30 times a day like she did before her hospitalization. Then it happened. She caught the flu and lost five pounds in a week. A flood of excitement rolled through her mind. Before she knew it, she was planning how she could lose even more. Instead of acting on that plan, she realized that her old destructive patterns were trying to sneak back in. She knew she was in a life-or-death struggle and needed God's help.

Step 2   *We come to believe that God, through Jesus Christ, can restore us to sanity.*

Memory verse   *Ah Lord GOD. Nothing is too difficult for Thee.*   –Jeremiah 32:17

Overview for Step 2   **Lesson 1: Baffling Behaviors**
     Goal: You will identify attitudes and actions characteristic of distorted thinking.
Lesson 2: Distorted Views of God
     Goal: You will distinguish between guilt, shame, and blame.
Lesson 3: Burdens of the Past
     Goal: You will analyze past relationships with your parents.
Lesson 4: Bridge to the Present
     Goal: You will describe the impact of your past relationships on your view of God.
Lesson 5: Believing the Truth about God
     Goal: You will take steps to correct elements of your faulty concept of God.
Lesson 6: Believing the Truth about You
     Goal: You will take steps to correct elements of your faulty self-concept.

Baffling Behaviors

We come to believe that God, through Jesus Christ, can restore us to sanity.

> *Again therefore Jesus spoke to them, saying, "I am the light of the world; he who follows Me shall not walk in the darkness, but shall have the light of life."*
>
> –John 8:12

Key Concept:
Eating disorders represent a form of insanity.

insanity–n. As a recovery term insanity describes unsound judgment. The term is not used here in a clinical sense to refer to a mental disorder.

You may find the word *sanity* puzzling or even disturbing in Step 2. When told that the 12 Steps represent the road to their healing, many persons get only as far as this word. They then protest, "I am *not* insane!"

Webster's New World Dictionary defines sanity as "soundness of judgment." How sane are the behaviors your eating disorder has led you to practice? One friend described her actions before recovery. She said of the description, "It's graphic, but nothing is pretty about the binge/purge cycle—nothing pretty about standing over a toilet throwing up!"

 Remember the general questions about eating disorders in Step 1? Think about these attitudes and actions again, but this time decide which ones you feel are sane and which ones are insane. Check the appropriate response.

Sane	Insane	
○	○	For women, missing more than three periods and failing to consult a doctor.
○	○	"Feeling" fat, when others insist that you are not.
○	○	Believing that others are out to control us when they fearfully point out that we look like we just got out of a concentration camp.
○	○	Exercising three to four hours to burn off calories.
○	○	Taking 30 laxatives to get rid of a cookie.
○	○	Hoarding food like a squirrel hoards nuts, even when you resist eating it.
○	○	Eating a cookie and then starving yourself for two days to punish yourself.
○	○	Thinking of a food as a "friend" or an "enemy."
○	○	Being afraid of having others see you eat.
○	○	Spending tremendous amounts of money on "junk food," eating it, then making yourself throw up.
○	○	Continuing to overeat when your doctor says that your body weight is affecting your health.
○	○	Waiting anxiously for everyone else in the house to go to bed so that you can prepare something to eat.
○	○	"Wolfing" down food like a wild animal does.

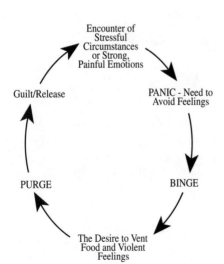

Encounter of Stressful Circumstances or Strong, Painful Emotions

PANIC - Need to Avoid Feelings

BINGE

The Desire to Vent Food and Violent Feelings

PURGE

Guilt/Release

The Binge/Purge Cycle

The cycle of bingeing and purging that characterizes bulimic behavior is an example of an abnormal eating pattern. If you are bulimic, you sometimes cope with stressful events or strong emotions (such as anger, hurt, or fear,) by bingeing. This usually brings on other strong emotions (such as guilt, shame, and more anger), with which you often try to cope by purging. In turn, this produces more strong feelings (such as frustration, hopelessness, and more guilt), which may lead to more bingeing. This creates a vicious cycle you can't seem to break. The chart in the margin on page 34 illustrates the binge/purge cycle.

The "insanity" works two ways. Not only is the behavior harmful, it also fails to solve the problems that cause the strong emotions. The behavior actually makes the emotions worse. "Sanity" means looking for the causes of your intense feelings and then dealing with them. Solving the problem(s) is a sane response. Acting out an eating-disordered ritual is insane.

Dealing with causes

Unless you learn to deal with unwelcome emotions, you are not likely to break free from the insanity of addiction. The addiction is a means of avoiding problems and solutions.

✎ **List occasions when you have acted in such a way that an honest observer, who knows you and your circumstances, might say, "That's insane!" (You may wish to refer to the list of sane and insane activities on page 34, if any apply to you).**

_____

_____

_____

_____

God Can Restore Your Sanity

Psalm 23 contains a beautiful picture of God's sanity-restoring activity. Here God is described as the Shepherd who restores your soul. In the Scripture the soul is the decision-making and emotional nature of human beings—their total being. God is the One who can restore your soul—your sanity.

The LORD is my shepherd, I shall not want. He makes me lie down in green pastures; He leads me beside quiet waters. He restores my soul; He guides me in the paths of righteousness for His name's sake.
–Psalm 23:1-3

✎ **Read Psalm 23:1-3 in the margin at left. Name four things the Shepherd does for you that these three verses describe.**

1. _____

2. _____

3. _____

4. _____

A shepherd makes sure his sheep are fed and watered (provides green pastures and leads them to quiet waters). His gentle presence and caring activity also calms their fears, settles their nerves, and provides peace (restores the soul). Finally, he directs the sheep in the safe path they should follow (guides in the paths of righteousness).

God wants to restore your soul. He does His restoring work primarily through His Word. As you grow in recovery, you will grow in your understanding of God's Word. Ask the Holy Spirit to reveal the deep riches of healing and restoration contained in Scripture. Claim the promises He shows you. Obey the commands He gives you.

The law of the Lord is perfect, restoring the soul.
                                    –Psalm 19:7

➔ **Take a moment right now to pray and thank God for being your Shepherd and for restoring your sanity. Trust Him as He continues His work in you.**

```
┌─────────────────────────────────────────────┐
│                                             │
│          Key Concept for Lesson 1           │
│   Eating disorders represent a form of insanity. │
│                                             │
└─────────────────────────────────────────────┘
```

➔ **Memorize this Step's memory verse.**
Ah Lord GOD. Nothing is too difficult for Thee.   –Jeremiah 32:17

LESSON 2

Key Concept:
A distorted concept of God makes trusting Him difficult.

Distorted Views of God

We come to believe that God, through Jesus Christ, can restore us to sanity.

for the Son of Man did not come to destroy men's lives, but to save them.
                                    –Luke 9:56

If thinking about God makes you feel uncomfortable, that is perfectly understandable. You may see God as a restrictive, controlling parent; as an all-too-powerful and vengeful righter of wrongs; or as some other negative figure of authority. Humans tend to "make God in our own image" or to think of Him in terms of the characteristics you've observed in other authority figures. If you have experienced abuse or neglect from a parent or authority figure, you will expect the same from God.

Cathy's view of God

Seeing God as a loving, kind, and willing source of strength didn't occur easily for Cathy. She saw Him as a restrictive, controlling parent or a punishing avenger—much as she saw her own strict and controlling father. Forced to attend church when she was a child, Cathy quit all religious activities after she eloped with her high-school sweetheart. For a brief time she told people that she no longer believed God existed. That was after her father died of cancer. She blamed herself indirectly for causing her father's death. She thought, *if only I had been a better child . . . .*

Cathy also blamed God for letting her father die. After all, He is God; He can do anything. Why didn't He stop it? And why didn't He help her cope better with the loss . . . and where was He when she needed help with her out-of-control eating? She finally admitted that God did exist. But to acknowledge Him as source of the sanity and control she so desperately needed was too much to ask. And yet, where else could she go?

 Do you share some of Cathy's feelings about God? Explore your feelings on the matter. Respond to the statements on the next page as thoughtfully and honestly as you can.

	Often	Sometimes	Rarely	Never
I feel uncomfortable praying or talking to God.	O	O	O	O
I see God as an angry, controlling parent—just waiting to punish me for doing wrong.	O	O	O	O
I feel guilty or ashamed before God because of my disordered behavior.	O	O	O	O
I want to be in control of my own life without outside interference from God.	O	O	O	O
I blame God for failing me when I needed Him.	O	O	O	O

You may have feared God would condemn and punish you for your failures.

In the past, you may have avoided God because of your personal sense of inadequacy and especially because of your sense of guilt and shame. These feelings may have caused you to shy away from Him. You may have feared that He would condemn and punish you for your failures and shortcomings.

Perhaps you feel guilty about the behaviors you indicated as abnormal. Or, as in the case with many who are bound by eating disorders, perhaps you were abused in some way when you were a child. Believing that you somehow were to blame for the abuse, you feel a sense of shame.

If you answered any of the above questions as "often" or "sometimes," you may need to give extra attention to this lesson. You will explore the nature and operation of guilt and shame.

Guilt, Shame, and Blame

For purpose of this Step, we will distinguish between real guilt and false guilt. We will use the terms *guilt* and *perceived guilt*. *Guilt* is a judicial fact. It is the truth that you have done something that was wrong. *Perceived guilt* is the feeling that you are guilty, even though you may not have done anything wrong.

Perceived Guilt

Sue was mad at Cliff because he had revealed to a friend something which she had told him in confidence. Finally, when she could bear her anger no longer, she confronted Cliff with his wrongdoing—she expressed her anger in an appropriate way. Now Sue has the uneasy feeling of perceived guilt. She is not really guilty of any wrongdoing, but because she confronted Cliff, she perceives guilt on her part. After all, she was reared to believe, "If you can't say anything nice, don't say anything at all."

Appropriate Guilt

Arthur is in trouble. His neighbor has two small children, each of whom seems able to produce the noise and disruption of 10 children. They threw a baseball through one of Arthur's new storm windows. Arthur picked up the ball, and in his anger, threw it at one of the children. The ball hit the child in the head. The children didn't see Arthur, and no one seems to know who hit the child with the baseball. Now Arthur feels guilty, and well he should. He actually is guilty of vengefully hurting his neighbor's child.

Sally and Mark seem like the perfect couple. They communicate well, have many mutual interests, and obviously enjoy each other's company. They are head-over-heels in love with each other, which is unfortunate since each is married—to someone else. They have been sexually intimate with one another a number of times, but they feel no regret for their behavior because they are, as they say, so "in love with each other." They neglect their spouses and their children because they are so "in love with each other." They feel no guilt because they are so "in love with each other." But they really are guilty of adultery, whether or not they feel guilty.

Shame

Shame often results when you fail to measure up, either to your own expectations or to those of another. Like guilt, shame may be real or perceived. Feelings of inadequacy and hopelessness often result, along with feelings of real or perceived guilt about your own or another's wrongdoing.

Barbara's shame

Barbara's father sexually abused her throughout her adolescence. These experiences horrified and shocked her and yet gave her pleasure, as well. On the one hand, she enjoyed being her father's "special girl" and his "little princess." Of course, she could not help physically responding to his touch. On the other hand, she felt disgusted and violated by his behavior. She was frightened by the thought that he might harm her or reject her if she failed to do what he asked. She feared what others might say or do if they knew.

As Barbara grew into adulthood, she longed for intimacy in her relationships with men and attempted to find it in the only way she knew how—through sexual activity. Although she seemed confident and sure, Barbara felt inadequate in almost every respect outside of the bedroom. She felt that she had nothing but her body to offer or contribute to life. The fact that she allowed men to use her later caused her to despise all men. But her primary target of hatred was herself. It was a hatred that showed itself in her self-ridiculing jokes, her tendency toward perfectionism, her self-sacrificing workaholism, and in her eating disorder.

Barbara was not to blame for her father's behavior.

When she was in her late forties, Barbara became a Christian and began working through her sexual-abuse issues. She eventually realized that besides the appropriate guilt she felt for her promiscuity, she also felt deep shame for her behavior with her father. She was strongly convinced that she had led him on—thus, she perceived the beginning of the abuse as her fault. Helping Barbara understand that she was not to blame for her father's abusive behavior marked the beginning of her freedom from falsely-based shame.

When you perceive guilt and feel shame, do (or did) you turn to eating-disordered behaviors to push those feelings away?

○ Yes, much of the time
○ Yes, some of the time
○ Yes, in the past but not now
○ No

If you answered yes to any of the choices, write a brief statement about how guilt or shame affected the following relationships in your life:

your self-esteem _____

_____

_____

with family _____

_____

_____

with friends and acquaintances _____

_____

_____

with God _____

_____

_____

Blame   Still another barrier to close fellowship with God is blame. "Find a scapegoat!" says blame. Looking for a way to escape pain, blame goes for the closest target. The problem is, whether you blame others or yourself, blame cannot change your situation. It cannot reverse your circumstances; it cannot correct anything. It simply is a waste of time and emotional energy. Blame promises power to right a wrong, but it cannot deliver on its promise.

Complete the following exercises to discover what role blame has played in your eating disorders and in sabotaging your relationship with God.

✎ **Place a check below the face which best describes how you feel when you fail at something important.**

✎ **From the list below, check all the ways you typically feel or respond when you fail.**

○ Angry   ○ Inclined to Give Up
○ Sad   ○ Inclined to Try Again
○ Frustrated   ○ Other: _____
○ Inclined to Blame
○ Shameful   _____

How do you *feel* when others fail? _____

_____

How do you *act* toward others when they fail? _____

_____

When you fail, do you blame God? If so, describe how and why. _____

_____

_____

Do you believe God has a condemning attitude toward you? If so, describe how and why.

_____

_____

```
Key Concept for Lesson 2
A distorted concept of God makes trusting Him difficult.
```

→ **Memorize this Step's memory verse.**
   Ah Lord GOD. Nothing is too difficult for Thee.   –Jeremiah 32:17

<table>
<tr><td>

LESSON

3

</td><td>

Burdens of the Past

We come to believe that God, through Jesus Christ, can restore us to sanity.

I would have despaired unless I had believed that I would see the goodness of the LORD in the land of the living.

–Psalm 27:13

</td></tr>
</table>

Key Concept:
My concept of God comes
primarily from my parents.

You may have desired to please God, but after you failed Him again and again, you began to believe that you just weren't able to please Him. You may have decided that you didn't have enough faith—and you may have given up on ever having His approval, His love, or His acceptance. You may have pushed yourself to the limits of your people-pleasing abilities by thinking that "just a little more" would do the trick, but you never have felt accepted and loved by God.

Your Parents and You

Why is it often so hard to stay close to God? If you feel distant from Him, you may do so partly because of a faulty relationship with one or both of your parents.

If your parents were supportive, you probably believe that God is loving and strong.

Your views about God, your self-concept, and your ability to relate to others are shaped by a complex set of factors. Perhaps the most powerful of these factors is your relationship with your parents or those who reared you. If your parents were loving and supportive, you probably believe that God is loving and strong. If, however, your parents were harsh and demanding, you may feel that God is impossible to please. Either way, the foundation of your emotional, social, and spiritual health usually is formed by observing your parents' model. The results can be wonderful or tragic.

To gain a better understanding of this "shaping" process, you can look at some personal characteristics of your parents and how they related to you. The following exercise will help you evaluate your relationships with your mother and your father as you were growing up.

Think back to how your parents related to you when you were young and place an *F* (for Father) and an *M* (for Mother) in the appropriate boxes after each characteristic. If you were reared by someone other than your birth parents, relate the characteristics to your primary caretakers. You will find it most helpful if you complete the checklist for one parent at a time.

To help you get an accurate reflection of your relationships with your parents, turn each characteristic into a question. For example, ask, "How often did (or do) I feel that my father/mother was gentle . . . stern, etc.?" Leave room for up to three letters per box. Below is an example.

Characteristics	Always	Very Often	Some- times	Hardly Ever	Never	Don't Know
Gentle		M	F			
Stern	F			M		
Loving			F	M		
Disapproving		F,M				
Distant			F		M	

 Carefully fill in the chart below. Do this first for one parent then the other.

Characteristics	Always	Very Often	Some- times	Hardly Ever	Never	Don't Know
Gentle						
Stern						
Loving						
Disapproving						
Distant						
Close, intimate						
Kind						
Angry						
Caring						
Demanding						
Harsh						
Trustworthy						
Joyful						
Forgiving						
Good						
Cherished me						
Impatient						
Unreasonable						
Strong						
Protective						
Passive						
Encouraging						
Sensitive						
Unpredictable						

Evaluating Your Relationship with Your Father

✎ **What does this inventory tell you about your relationship with your father?**

_____

_____

What were his strengths? _____

_____

Give two examples of a time when he related to you in a positive way.

1. _____

2. _____

What were his weaknesses? _____

_____

Give two examples of a time when he related to you in a negative way.

1. _____

2. _____

✎ **If you were an outside observer of the type of relationship you have just described, how would you feel toward the father?**

○ Angry   ○ Sad   ○ Sympathetic   ○ Happy
○ No feeling   ○ Afraid   ○ Other _____

✎ **Write a letter to your father. Tell him your feelings this exercise revealed about some of the issues from your past. (Note: Whether or not your father is living, you will benefit from completing this exercise. The benefit is in the reflecting and writing. You do not have to give the letter to your father if he is living. Consult your sponsor or counselor, pray, and wait before you even consider sending the letter.)**

Evaluating Your Relationship with Your Mother

✎ **What does this inventory tell you about your relationship with your mother?**

_____

_____

What were her strengths? _____

_____

Give two examples of times when she related to you in a positive way.

1. _____

2. _____

What were her weaknesses? _____

_____

Give two examples of times when she related to you in a negative way.

1. _____

2. _____

✎ **If you were an outside observer of the type of relationship you have just described, how would you feel toward the mother?**

  ○ Angry   ○ Sad   ○ Sympathetic   ○ Happy
  ○ No feeling ○ Afraid   ○ Other _____

✎ **Write a letter to your mother. Tell her your feelings this exercise revealed about some of the issues from your past. (Note: Whether or not your mother is living, you will benefit from completing this exercise. The benefit is in the reflecting and writing. You do not have to give the letter to your mother if she is living. Consult your sponsor or counselor, pray, and wait before even considering sending the letter.)**

✎ **If you have a strained relationship with a parent, how do you think that relationship might impact your food addiction?**

_____

_____

_____

_____

_____

People respond in a variety of ways to feeling unloved. Several responses can cause or support an eating disorder. Some of us use food as a substitute friend, to keep people at a distance, to numb emotional pain, or to gain control back from an overpowering parent.

┌───┐
│   **Key Concept for Lesson 3**   │
│   My concept of God comes primarily from my parents. │
└───┘

➤ **Memorize this Step's memory verse.**
  Ah Lord GOD. Nothing is too difficult for Thee.   –Jeremiah 32:17

LESSON 4

Key Concept:
My concept of God comes primarily from my parents.

Bridge to the Present

We come to believe that God, through Jesus Christ, can restore us to sanity.

I speak the things which I have seen with My Father; therefore you also do the things which you heard from your father.

–John 8:38

Evaluating Your Relationship with God

In the previous lesson you examined your relationship with your parents. Now look at your relationship with God. By first evaluating your present relationship with Him and then comparing it with your past relationship to your parents, you can begin to see how your relationship with your parents has influenced your view of God. The following inventory will help you determine some of your feelings toward God. Because it is subjective, no right or wrong answers exist. To make sure that the test shows your actual feelings, please follow the instructions carefully.

- Go back to the inventory you completed in the last lesson and take it again. This time evaluate your relationship with God.

- Turn each characteristic into a question. For example: "To what degree do I really feel that God loves me?" or "To what degree do I really feel that God understands me?"

- Place a *G* in the appropriate column to the right of the characteristic for your answer. Your answers may or may not match those for your parents' characteristics. Mark these answers without thinking about the previous ones.

- Answer openly and honestly. Don't give answers from your knowledge of theology or church doctrine but from personal experience, especially as you reflect on your feelings.

Reflect on your feelings

- Don't describe what the relationship *ought* to be, or what you *hope* it will be, but what it *is* right now.

God is pleased with our honesty.

- Some people feel God might be angry if they give a negative answer. Nothing is further from the truth. God is pleased with our honesty. He wants us to know we can trust His love enough to share our deepest feelings with Him. Openness and honesty form the foundation of growth.

✎ **Complete the inventory on page 41.**

✎ **Now look at your responses. What does this inventory tell you about your relationship with God?**

_____

_____

✎ If you were an outside observer of the relationship you have just described, what would you think of the God who was described? Check all that apply. God seems to be—

    ◯ loving   ◯ caring   ◯ understanding
    ◯ harsh   ◯ critical   ◯ other_____
    ◯ angry   ◯ sympathetic   _____

✎ Write a letter to God. Express whatever feelings this exercise has brought to your awareness about Him. Be honest with Him. He can tolerate your anger, grief, doubt, and fear. You may be like the little girl who was angry because her father had refused a request. She wrote him a note that read, "Dear Dad, I hate you. Love, Jodi." Express your feelings—including confusion—as they are.

Your Parents' Influence on Your Relationship with God

You examined your present relationship with God. Now look at how your relationship with your parents has influenced your view of your Heavenly Father.

✎ To make the comparison, do the following:

• Turn back to the chart on page 41. For each characteristic, circle each response where you placed a *G* in the same box with an *F* or an *M*. Below is an example:

Characteristics	Always	Very Often	Some-times	Hardly Ever	Never	Don't Know
Gentle		M	F,G			
Stern	F			M,G		
Loving			F	M		G
Disapproving		F,M				
Distant			F,G		M	

If few or none of your responses were in the exact same boxes, circle the responses which were close to the same.

✎ List the characteristics which are the same (or similar) of your parents and of God.

Of your father and of God: _____

_____

Of your mother and of God: _____

_____

✎ List the characteristics which are quite different (two or more boxes away from each other):

Of your father and of God: _____

_____

Of your mother and of God: _____

_____

What patterns (if any) do you see? _____

_____

_____

_____

✎ Write a summary paragraph about how your relationship with your father has shaped your view of God.

_____

_____

_____

_____

✎ Write a second paragraph telling how your relationship with your mother has shaped your view of God.

_____

_____

_____

_____

┌───┐
│   │
│   **Key Concept for Lesson 4**   │
│   My concept of God comes primarily from my parents. │
│   │
└───┘

➔ Thank you for taking time to evaluate honestly your relationships with your father, mother, and God.

➔ Write in the margin three times this Step's memory verse, Jeremiah 32:17.

LESSON 5

Believing the Truth About God

We come to believe that God, through Jesus Christ, can restore us to sanity.

And Jesus said to him, "If You can! All things are possible to him who believes."

–Mark 9:23

Key Concept:
Correcting my faulty concept of God is an important recovery task.

When we do the work in the past two lessons, many of us discover an amazing fact. We discover that our concept of God—the God we had been trying to serve or trying to avoid—originated more from our own life experiences and dysfunctional families than from reality.

 Check the statement below that most nearly expresses the meaning of the paragraph above.

○ 1. The God in your head may not be similar to the real God.
○ 2. Our concept of God comes primarily from our parents.
○ 3. We need to get to know God rather than just our concept of God.
○ 4. Just as we can have a wrong impression of a person, we may have a wrong impression of God.

Every person's greatest task is to know God. Often a faulty concept of God stands in the way. All the statements reflect ideas from the paragraph, but number 1.

Knowing God from Psalm 139

Some passages in Scripture teach God's nature and character. Psalm 139 is one of the greatest passages for this purpose. Studying this psalm can help you understand how God knows you so completely and loves you so thoroughly. You may want to read the entire psalm from your Bible before you examine it more carefully in the following activities.

God Knows Me Thoroughly

O Lord, Thou hast searched me and known me. Thou dost know when I sit down and when I rise up; Thou dost understand my thought from afar. Thou dost scrutinize my path and my lying down, and art intimately acquainted with all my ways. Even before there is a word on my tongue, behold, O Lord, Thou dost know it all.
–Psalm 139:1-4

 Read verses 1-4 in the margin. Answer the questions below.

God always knows everything about you. You can keep no secrets from Him, yet He loves you unconditionally! How does this make you feel?

○ afraid   ○ excited   ○ condemned
○ hopeful   ○ sad   ○ grateful
○ glad   ○ accepted   ○ _____

In what ways does God's powerful knowledge give you courage and strength?

_____

_____

_____

He Protects Me

✎ **Read verses 5-6. Answer the questions below.**

Thou hast enclosed me behind and before, and laid Thy hand upon me. Such knowledge is too wonderful for me; it is too high, I cannot attain to it.
                                    –Psalm 139:5-6

God's perfect knowledge about you makes Him able to protect you (to hem you in). From what do you need His protection?

_____

_____

Is it difficult for you to understand the Lord's complete knowledge that this passage mentions? Why or why not?

_____

_____

He Always Is Present

✎ **Read verses 7-12. Answer the questions below.**

Where can I go from Thy Spirit? Or where can I hide from Thy presence? If I ascend to heaven, Thou art there; If I make my bed in Sheol, behold, Thou art there. If I take the winds of the dawn, if I dwell in the remotest part of the sea, even there Thy hand will lead me, and Thy right hand will lay hold of me. If I say, "Surely the darkness will overwhelm me, and the light around me will be night," even the darkness is not dark to Thee, and the night is as bright as the day. Darkness and light are alike to Thee.
                                    –Psalm 139:7-12

The most important promise to one who has strayed is that he is not lost! How close is God to you?

_____

_____

How close does He seem to be? _____

_____

How far can you get from Him? _____

_____

Some of us have looked with a distorted view at God's nearness. We have heard, "Where can I go from Thy Spirit?" as if God were pursuing us to do us harm. The entire passage speaks of God's great love and care. His love will follow us—no matter where we go.

He Is a Sovereign Creator

For Thou didst form my inward parts; Thou didst weave me in my mother's womb. I will give thanks to Thee, for I am fearfully and wonderfully made; wonderful are Thy works, and my soul knows it very well. My frame was not hidden from Thee, when I was made in secret, and skillfully wrought in the depths of the earth.

–Psalm 139:13-15

 Read verses 13-15. Answer the questions below.

What is God's opinion of you and of your body? _____

_____

The psalmist said he was a marvelous creation of God. He said all of God's works—including you—are wonderful. God made you, and He did it well.

The psalmist felt awe at the realization that God created his body. Describe what you think it would be like to feel totally accepting of your own body.

_____

_____

How do you normally respond to your appearance? _____

_____

How does your view of your appearance affect your self-image?

_____

_____

Do you think (or worry) about what other people think of your appearance? Why or why not?

_____

_____

How could this psalm help free you from the fear of what others think of you?

_____

_____

God Has a Plan for You

Thine eyes have seen my unformed substance; and in Thy book they were all written, the days that were ordained for me. When as yet there was not one of them.

–Psalm 139:16

 Read verse 16. Answer the questions below.

Describe any comfort you gain from knowing that God has a plan for your life.

_____

_____

Here are some examples of God's plans for you:

- He wants to strengthen you (Isaiah 40:29).
- He wants to provide for your welfare and give you a future and a hope (Jeremiah 29:11).
- He wants to give you things that will be good for you (Matthew 7:7-11).
- He wants you to spend eternity with Him (John 14:1-3).
- He wants you to have a love relationship with Him through His Son, Jesus Christ (John 3:16-18).
- He wants to give you a full and abundant life (John 10:10).

God Is Constant and Consistent

How precious also are Thy thoughts to me, O God! How vast is the sum of them! If I should count them, they would outnumber the sand. When I awake, I am still with Thee.
—Psalm 139:17-18

✎ **Read verses 17-18. The Lord is infinite (never ending), and He is thinking about you all the time! How does that fact comfort and encourage you?**

_____

_____

Your Response

Search me, O God, and know my heart; try me and know my anxious thoughts; and see if there be any hurtful way in me, and lead me in the everlasting way.
—Psalm 139:23-24

✎ **Read verses 23-24. Are you open to God's correction and guidance? Why or why not?**

_____

_____

Openness to God's correction and guidance is the way the psalmist responds to the secure position he has with God. You also can have a secure position with God, through Jesus Christ, who died to pay for your sins and who rose from the dead to give you new life.

Your Sponsor

Being open to God's correction and guidance often involves dealing with input and feedback from persons who have developed some maturity, both in their relationship with God and in a life apart from compulsive-addictive behavior. A mature sponsor can be a tremendous help to your recovery. Preferably this person is someone who also is in recovery from eating disorders and who is working through a 12-Step format like yours. This person has at least one year's time (preferably more) in recovery and can supervise your Step work and be available to you in emergencies. A trusted friend or minister will do, although your best bet is with a sponsor in recovery or a Christian counselor who specializes in eating disorders.

A sponsor should be someone who has maturity and wisdom about recovery issues and who is willing to set up proper boundaries with you. This means having an ability to help without trying to "save" you when what is best for your growth and development is responsibly facing problems, making choices, and living with the consequences. A good sponsor teaches and helps but leaves you free to make your own decisions.

➔ Memorize this Step's memory verse: Jeremiah 32:17.

LESSON 6

Key Concept:
Correcting one's faulty concept of self is an important recovery task.

He (Jesus) said, "It is not those who are healthy who need a physician, but those who are ill. But go and learn what this means, 'I desire compassion, and not sacrifice,' for I did not come to call the righteous, but sinners."

–Matthew 9:12-13

Believing the Truth About You

We come to believe that God, through Jesus Christ, can restore us to sanity.

> *As far as the east is from the west, so far has He removed our transgressions from us.*
> –Psalm 103:12

✎ **Read Matthew 9:12-13. For whom did Jesus show the greatest concern?**

_____

_____

From the statement "I desire compassion and not sacrifice," which of the following pleases God? He is pleased for you to be—

○ 1. a perfect person who never makes mistakes.
○ 2. a righteous person who obeys all the laws.
○ 3. a caring person who has experienced failure.

Jesus' concern always has been for hurting people. He showed concern for two groups of people—those who were ill and those who saw themselves as sinners.

> Do you believe that God, through Jesus Christ, can restore you to "sanity"—a life free from eating disorders? ○ Yes   ○ No

> Describe how you think it would feel really to *believe* that Jesus wants to restore you.

_____

_____

Mark 9:16-28 tells of a father whose demon-possessed son was desperately ill. The father asked Jesus to help his son. Jesus said, "All things are possible to him who believes."

Immediately the boy's father cried out and began saying, "I do believe; help me in my unbelief."
–Mark 9:24

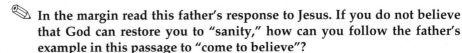 In the margin read this father's response to Jesus. If you do not believe that God can restore you to "sanity," how can you follow the father's example in this passage to "come to believe"?

_____

You can ask God to help you overcome your unbelief just as the boy's father asked. Are you willing to ask God to help you in your unbelief?

If you are willing to have God help you to overcome unbelief, will you write a prayer asking Him to give you faith in Him? If you feel that you are not yet willing, write the prayer honestly expressing your feelings.

_____

_____

_____

_____

Belief Systems

In the last two lessons you have described both your perception of God and what the Bible reveals of His nature and character. Understanding the truth of God's Word is the beginning of our restoration. Jesus repeatedly emphasized the importance of believing Him, because our actions usually are based on what we believe.

Jesus repeatedly emphasized the importance of believing Him.

Search for Significance LIFE Support Edition identifies four false beliefs which distort our perceptions of God and ourselves.[1] All of these lies are based on the primary belief that our self-worth equals our performance plus others' opinions. In other words we suffer from a misconception that what we do and what others think of us determines our significance, or worth.

Each of these four false beliefs results in a specific fear:

False Belief: *I must meet certain standards to feel good about myself. If I fail to meet these standards, I cannot really feel good about myself.* This belief results in the fear of failure.

False Belief: *I must be approved (accepted) by certain people to accept myself. If I do not have the approval of these people, I cannot accept myself.* This belief results in the fear of rejection.

False Belief: *Those who fail are unworthy of love and deserve to be blamed and condemned.* This belief leads to the fear of punishment and the tendency to punish others.

False Belief: *I am what I am. I cannot change. I am hopeless.* This means I am simply a total of all my past performances, both good and bad. I am what I have done. This belief leads to a sense of shame.

Each of these false beliefs has a corresponding truth from God's Word, the Scriptures:[2]

False Beliefs	Painful Emotions	God's Truths
The Performance Trap: *I must meet certain standards to feel good about myself.*	**The fear of failure**	I am completely forgiven by and fully pleasing to God. I no longer have to fear failure (Romans 5:1).
Approval Addict: *I must have the approval of certain others to feel good about myself.*	**The fear of rejection**	I am totally accepted by God. I no longer have to fear rejection (Colossians 1:21-22).
The Blame Game: *Those who fail (including myself) are unworthy of love and deserve to be punished.*	**Guilt**	I am deeply loved by God. I no longer have to fear punishment or punish others (1 John 2:2).
Shame: *I am what I am. I cannot change. I am hopeless.*	**Feelings of shame**	I have been made brand-new, complete in Christ. I no longer need to experience the pain of shame (2 Corinthians 5:17).

Rich and rewarding

Renewing your perception of God, others, and yourself by changing your belief systems will take time, study, and experience. It has taken years to develop patterns of behavior that reflect a false belief system. It will take time to change. Throughout this workbook we will continue to examine these beliefs. The process of learning to apply God's truths to our lives may be painful at times, but it also is rich, rewarding, and exciting!

Summary

Step 2 is a means for examining your overall belief system. Remember that the Steps are helps you will use for the rest of your life. The process of examining your concept of God and growing in your belief will continue as you recover.

You are now ready for Step 3, in which we will deal with another aspect of your believing. Step 3 is the most important aspect of faith. As you increasingly admit reality in Step 1 and grow in the ability to trust God in Step 2, you will become more capable of making life's key decision—the decision to turn your life and will over to Jesus Christ.

Relapse

relapse–n. returning to an addictive behavior (such as an eating disorder) after a period of abstinence

Before moving to Step 3, you need to learn something about **relapse**. Relapse is returning to an addictive behavior (such as an eating disorder) after a period of abstinence. Relapse is possible for anyone in recovery, regardless of how long he or she has abstained from a particular behavior. Be alert to signs pointing toward relapse.

Warning Signals

Relapse is a process rather than an event. A group of behaviors, attitudes, feelings, and thoughts develop first. Then these lead to an action—namely the return to acting out the eating disorder. One may fall into a relapse over a period of hours, days, weeks, or even months. Warning signals to alert you to a possible relapse include:

Signs of relapse
- Feeling uneasy, afraid, and anxious about abstaining from the addictive behavior. This begins to increase as "serenity" decreases.
- Ignoring feelings of fear and anxiety, and refusing to talk about them with others.
- Having a low tolerance for frustration.
- Becoming defiant, so that rebelliousness begins to replace what has been love and acceptance. Anger becomes one's ruling emotion.
- The "ISM" (I-Self-Me) attitude grows. Self-centered behavior begins to rule one's attitudes and feelings.
- Increasing dishonesty, whereby small lies begin to surface as deceptive thinking again takes over.
- Increased isolation and withdrawal characterized by missing group meetings and withdrawing from friends, family, and other support.
- Exhibiting a critical, judgmental attitude—a behavior which often is a process of projection as the person in recovery feels shame and guilt for his or her negative behaviors.
- Lack of confidence about oneself manifested by self-derogatory remarks, overwhelming feelings of failure, a tendency to set up oneself for failure.
- Overconfidence manifested by statements such as, "I'll never do that again," or by simply believing that one is the "exception" to all rules about recovery.

Special Stressors

In addition to these warning signals, be alert to certain times which can make a person more vulnerable to relapse. Some of these include:

- Completing the first week of abstinence from eating-disorder behavior.
- Completing the first 21 days of abstinence, and any anniversaries thereafter, specifically: 90 days, six months, nine months, one year.
- Holidays.
- Personal anniversaries, birthdays, or other special days.
- Experiencing "high" moods of exuberance, perhaps after receiving a raise, getting a job, or becoming engaged or getting married. (Many people fail to realize that "high" moods are as stressful as low moods.)
- Becoming overly hungry, angry, lonely, or tired. Using the acronym, HALT, (Hungry, Angry, Lonely, Tired) can help avoid a potential relapse.
- Playing with food.
- Having trouble eating in front of others.

You often can defeat "triggers" to compulsive behavior by recognizing them and by planning ahead. Step 10 explores a specific strategy we can use to prevent relapse. Feel free to turn to that Step now if you foresee needing help with this issue.

Should you relapse and begin the cycle of your eating disorder again, do not let feelings of failure, guilt, or a sense of "blowing it" dominate your actions so that you "give in" to the behavior in increasing amounts. Talk to your sponsor, counselor, physician, or pastor. Secrecy only perpetuates addictive behavior. Look at a "slip" as a deviation from your plan, and then immediately resume your plan for recovery.

Key Concept for Lesson 6
Correcting my faulty concept of self is an important recovery task.

➔ **Write this Step's memory verse.**

_____

_____

Step Review

✎ **Step 2 says:** *We come to believe that God, through Jesus Christ, can restore us to sanity.* **Write in your own words what Step 2 means.**

_____

_____

_____

_____

Describe how you will daily apply Step 2 to your life and recovery.

_____

_____

_____

_____

_____

Notes
[1]Robert S. McGee, *Search for Significance* LIFE Support Edition (Houston: Rapha Publishing, 1992), 11.
[2]Ibid.

STEP 3

Turning It Over

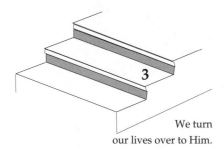

3

We turn
our lives over to Him.

> **BARBARA SURRENDERS**
>
> Barbara's recovery from bulimia took a positive turn a few months ago. She decided to give up her resistance. She decided to surrender to reality. For years Barbara rebelled against people who said she had a problem. She denied the truth. Then after she finally admitted the truth, for three years she fought the bulimia on her own. First she tried to stop on her own. Then she tried group therapy, but the real progress—the kind she feels will last—has just begun. With the help of her group sponsor, Barbara surrendered her life to Jesus Christ.
>
> Barbara's decision just seemed to fit. She needed Christ, and He wanted her just the way she was—but with no intention of leaving her that way. It seemed funny how it made sense now when it didn't before. For years she had accepted the facts about Christ and His love. She just found it difficult to trust Him with her life after all that she had been through. She wanted to trust, but she hadn't been able to trust—not even Him.
>
> Her Christian sponsor told her that believing was only the first step. She said believing was like "knowing that a life preserver thrown to you can keep you from drowning. Without grabbing the life preserver," her sponsor continued, "all the facts, or even belief in the facts, would be useless."
>
> Tired of fighting the raging waters, Barbara gave her life to Christ. She knew that now she would not make her journey of recovery alone. Christ would walk beside her, and that would make all the difference in the world.

Step 3   *We make a decision to turn our lives over to God through Jesus Christ.*

Memory verse   *I urge you therefore, brethren, by the mercies of God, to present your bodies a living and holy sacrifice, acceptable to God, which is your spiritual service of worship.*
                                                                            –Romans 12:1

Overview for Step 3   **Lesson 1: Help from God**
         Goal: You will describe the twofold nature of Step 3.
   Lesson 2: God's Provision in Christ
         Goal: You will explain God's plan to deliver people from the power of sin.
   Lesson 3: Your Position in Christ
         Goal: You will identify the complete forgiveness Christ gives.
   Lesson 4: Working the Step, Part One
         Goal: You will have an opportunity to express personal faith in Christ.
   Lesson 5: Working the Step, Part Two
         Goal: You will describe the ongoing process of applying Step 3 to practical problems.

LESSON 1

Key Concept:
I must make a decision.

Help from God

We make a decision to turn our will and our lives over to God through Jesus Christ.

> *Hence, also, He is able to save forever those who draw near to God through Him, since He always lives to make intercession for them.*
>
> –Hebrews 7:25

Do you see the beauty and simplicity of the Steps beginning to emerge? We have lived in self-deception. We have attempted to control our emotions and our physical appearance. We have attempted to control other people's opinions of us. We have attempted to control everything, and in the process our lives have become more and more chaotic and painful—unmanageable. Now the Steps teach us to—

(Step 1) admit honestly that we are human beings—powerless to control many things, especially our addictions;

(Step 2) begin to believe that God cares and that He can bring order to our lives;

(Step 3) make the only possible sane decision—to let God be God in our lives. We can let Him begin to give us wisdom and strength to deal with our circumstances.

It's Your Choice

God respects you!

God respects you! This may seem an odd concept, but it is true. You can measure respect by the amount of freedom someone gives you to make personal choices and decisions. God made you in His image and gave you the ability to make choices.

God's gift of choices is both a blessing and a danger. Human beings are not capable of absolute freedom. We find the only true freedom in obedience to God. Either we will choose to obey God, with wonderful results, or we will choose to obey some selfish desire, which leads to bondage.

> Do you not know that when you present yourselves to someone as slaves for obedience, you are slaves of the one whom you obey, either of sin resulting in death, or of obedience resulting in righteousness?
>
> –Romans 6:16

 Read Romans 6:16 in the margin and Penny's story below. Identify the desires Penny sought to serve—desires that became her masters and resulted in slavery.

Penny was a minister's wife in a small town. Though Penny was severely anorexic, she was known for her excellent cooking. Penny did not cook for herself; she cooked for others. She cooked from early in the morning until late at night in order to please her family and her many guests. Penny denied food to herself while she provided huge, sumptuous gourmet meals to her family, friends, and total strangers.

Even when Penny finally went to treatment for her eating disorder, she insisted on preparing a full month's food for her family before she left. Only after an extended time in treatment did Penny begin to identify the hidden motives behind her serving.

✎ **What do you suppose Penny was attempting to do by her compulsive service? Check all that apply.**

○ unselfishly serve and meet the needs of others;
○ look good to her friends and neighbors;
○ control others by controlling their perceptions of her;
○ work hard enough to earn the respect and love of others;
○ other _____

Blind to her motives

As Penny began to face her addiction honestly, she realized that control was at the core of her disorder. She sought to control her weight, but mostly she sought to control other people. She wanted to control their opinions—how they saw her. Penny was blind to the motives behind her behavior. She was a slave, but she did not know how or why.

✎ **From the following list check each of the goals that people commonly value—goals that according to Romans 6:16 lead to slavery.**

○ to have the perfect body
○ to be loved and accepted
○ to be in control so I cannot be hurt again
○ to numb emotions and avoid pain
○ others _____

You could have checked every one of the items above. All are things people commonly value. If someone were to observe your behavior, what would they identify as your goals in life?

_____

Are your goals leading you to a growing relationship with God—a relationship of freedom and joy—or are they leading you to guilt, slavery, and pain? Explain your answer.

_____

_____

What do you want your number one goal in life to be?

_____

The Twofold Nature of Step 3

Step 3 works in two distinct ways. One is a once-in-a-lifetime decision. The other is a moment-by-moment decision. A woman in a group compared the Step to marriage. She said, "I was married on a specific day and time, but each day I have to live out that decision. I decide to act married."

✎ **Read the paragraph at the top of the next page. Identify the two different expressions of Step 3 you find there. Underline the descriptions of the once-for-all decision and draw a circle around the descriptions of the decision which we must repeat.**

submission–n. yielding to the authority or control of another

Placing your trust in Christ alone for your salvation is a one-time event through which you forever are saved from your sins and brought into an eternal relationship with God. However, living in **submission** to Him is a daily (sometimes hourly!) choice. Probably few people like the concept of being submissive in a relationship, but God's Word says you will become slaves of that which you obey (Romans 6:16).

Did you underline such phrases as "placing your trust in Christ alone," "salvation," and "brought into a relationship with God"? Did you circle such phrases as "daily submission"?

Savior and Lord

"Working" Step 3 has both meanings. Some people have made the decision to accept Jesus as their Savior, but they aren't making the decision to turn their will over to Him daily. Others seek to surrender to God their daily issues—such as their eating disorder—but they never have received Jesus Christ as their Savior. The way of joy and effective living comes through working Step 3 in both ways—the Bible calls it having Jesus as Savior and Lord.

Why Step 3 Is Necessary

The Old Testament describes in detail the origin of sin and the fall of humanity. Adam and Eve were perfect in body, mind, and spirit, and they were free with one exception to enjoy all that was within their perfect environment. A single tree was forbidden. God gave humanity an opportunity to choose obedience or disobedience. The verse in the margin describes the choice God offered. Adam and Eve followed Satan's suggestion and disobeyed God.

And the LORD God commanded the man, saying, "From any tree of the garden you may eat freely; but from the tree of the knowledge of good and evil you shall not eat, for in the day that you eat from it you shall surely die."
–Genesis 2:16-17

 Go back and read Romans 6:16 in the margin of page 57. As long as Adam and Eve chose to obey God, they lived in the freedom of paradise. What happened when instead they chose to be their own boss and run their own lives?

_____

_____

_____

As a result of their decision they became slaves. The slavery appears in many forms. Humanity lost the glory God had intended for humankind and forfeited fellowship with God—effects all people since have felt. Adam's and Eve's deliberate rebellion also aided Satan's purpose. It gave Satan power and authority on earth. From that moment on, all of history would lead to a single hill outside of Jerusalem, where God appointed a Savior to pay the penalty for humanity's sin and rebellion. The payment would be valid not only for Adam's and Eve's acts of rebellion but for the sins of all people.

```
Key Concept for Lesson 1
I must make a decision.
```

✎ Pray and ask God how this concept can apply in your life. Now please review this lesson. What has God shown you that you can use?

_____

_____

➜ Write this Step's memory verse three times in the margin. Begin to memorize it.

<table>
<tr><td>

LESSON

2

</td><td></td></tr>
</table>

God's Provision in Christ

We make a decision to turn our will and our lives over to God through Jesus Christ.

> *to the praise of the glory of His grace, which He freely bestowed on us in the Beloved.*
>
> –Ephesians 1:6

Key Concept:
I must decide to turn over my will.

Humanity's problem is self-will. Individually and collectively we have chosen to be our own bosses and run our own lives. Step 3 is the decision to reverse that self-will. As a result of Step 1—realizing that I am incapable of being God and of managing my own life—and as a result of Step 2—coming to realize that God loves me and is willing and able to save me from sin and myself, Step 3 is a decision to turn control over to God.

When humankind rebelled, God instituted a plan to save and forgive. By His death on the cross, Christ paid for the sin of all people. On the basis of that payment God now recreates fallen humanity by restoring to their former glory all who accept Christ. God's eternal purpose is to save all who have rebelled against Him—members of the entire human race—if they are willing to return.

God's Eternal Purpose

When Adam sinned, he brought on all people both the burden and the penalty of sin. As a result, people by nature rebel against God, are separated from Him, and deserve His righteous judgment.

Your iniquities have made a separation between you and your God, and your sins have hidden His face from you, so that He does not hear.
–Isaiah 59:2

✎ **Circle the words *you* and *your* each time they appear in the passage in the margin.**

Describe how your self-will has damaged your life in the following areas:

in my relationship with others _____

_____

_____

in my health. _____

_____

in my finances _____

_____

in my relationship with God _____

_____

repentance–n. to change one's mind or purpose (Vine's)

The decision to turn our will over to God is part of what the Bible calls **repentance**. The word means a changed mind. Repentance is not something people do completely on their own. The change is a miracle that God works in a person's life. The decision in Step 3 could be called the door to repentance. The entire 12 Steps represent a path to repentance. The reason to work the Steps is to have a changed mind and as a result, a changed life. Humanity's problem originates from the fact that we all have attempted to take control of our will and lives. The solution begins with the decision to turn that control back to God.

Repentance means we turn from our sin, much like a soldier who makes an about face and marches in the opposite direction from which he was traveling before. It also means to change your mind and thoughts about something.

Or do you think lightly of the riches of His kindness and forbearance and patience, not knowing that the kindness of God leads you to repentance? But because of your stubbornness and unrepentant heart you are storing up wrath for yourself in the day of wrath and revelation of the righteous judgment of God.
    –Romans 2:4-5

✎ **The word *repentance* is used in Romans 2:4-5 almost as if it is a place. The kindness of God leads you to this place. Describe in your own words how the first two Steps could lead you to repentance.**

_____

_____

For a suggested answer to the learning activity, look back to the paraphrase of Steps 1, 2, and 3 on page 57.

God's Provision for Your Sin

Having created you for fellowship with Him, God also created a way by which you can be united with Him. He sent His Son to die in your place, and through Christ's death, to pay the price for your sins. As a result you can have fellowship with God.

For Christ also died for sins once for all, the just (_____) for the unjust (_____), in order that He might bring us to God.
    –1 Peter 3:18

✎ **In the verse on the left "just" means righteous—without sin. In the appropriate blanks in the verse in the margin write the name "Jesus" and your name.**

✎ **According to the verse on the left, what is the result of Christ's dying for you?**

_____

_____

All that the Father gives Me shall come to Me; and the one who comes to Me I will certainly not cast out.

–John 6:37

In the verse Jesus is the just, and we are the unjust. God's open acceptance and forgiveness is the result of Christ's death—to "bring us to God." He has paid for all sin. When we come to Him, He promises He will receive us and as the verse on the left promises, He will not cast us out. In Christ, God loves us just as if we never had sinned.

➡ **Stop for a moment to pray. Thank God for loving you enough to give His only Son to die for your sin. Thank Him for His promise to accept you, to cleanse you, and to forgive you.**

```
┌─────────────────────────────────────────────┐
│          Key Concept for Lesson 2            │
│        I must decide to turn over my will.    │
└─────────────────────────────────────────────┘
```

✎ **Pray and ask God how this concept can apply in your life. Now please review this lesson. What has God shown you that you can use?**

_____

_____

➡ **Take five minutes to memorize this Step's memory verse:**

I urge you therefore, brethren, by the mercies of God, to present your bodies a living and holy sacrifice, acceptable to God, which is your spiritual service of worship.

–Romans 12:1

LESSON 3

Key Concept:
In Christ I am unconditionally forgiven and totally accepted by God.

Your Position in Christ

We make a decision to turn our will and our lives over to God through Jesus Christ.

being justified as a gift by His grace through the redemption which is in Christ Jesus.

–Romans 3:24

Annie cried when she got a B in her English Literature class. Not that she cared for all the stuff she had to read, but it hurt that she no longer had a perfect 4.0 grade point average. She tried hard to be the perfect student. In fact, she tried hard to be perfect at everything . . . even anorexia. Of course, in the early stages she didn't recognize anorexia as a problem. Anorexic behavior was just her way of eating.

Annie also worked hard to be the perfect social activist. She studied different cultures and attempted to use her membership in several campus clubs to help needy people. But for Annie it was more than a way to lend a helping hand; it was a way to gain God's acceptance. To earn God's approval would have been the high point of her life, but she never seemed to manage it. When Annie was a child, she pleased her Sunday School teachers with her quick answers and ability to quote lengthy Bible texts. The feeling of God's acceptance, however, was something she never quite achieved, so she tried even harder. She joined an Eastern meditation club on campus; she went to different churches two and three times a week; she knew all the formulas for prayer and all the rituals for worship . . . and really believed them. Yet something was terribly wrong. She still felt so empty, so alone.

 What was wrong with Annie's search for God? Underline the activities that she did that you also have tried in an attempt to please God or to approach Him. What other things have you done to gain His acceptance and salvation?

_____

_____

Could it be that Annie's search for God was based on her own efforts? Annie somehow got the message that she must be perfect in order to be accepted and loved. She could not understand and accept God's grace—because grace is the opposite of performance-based acceptance. Annie was unable to have what she so desperately wanted—a position of acceptance with God—precisely because what she wanted to earn is a gift that cannot be earned.

Somebody Special

A television commercial contained an intriguing line. The commercial showed a parent and child discussing a gift someone had given them. The parent said to the child: "Somebody must think we're special." We all need to feel that we are special. Sacrificing His only Son's life on your behalf is the proof of God's love for you. The Creator of the universe thinks you are special.

The Bible states the basic message that God considers you special in many ways. 1 John 4:9-10 tells how He loves you and introduces a wonderful concept. Read the verse and watch for the second big, unfamiliar word.

By this the love of God was manifested in us, that God has sent His only begotten Son into the world so that we might live through Him. In this is love, not that we loved God, but that He loved us and sent His Son to be the propitiation for our sins.
—1 John 4:9-10

The first big word—manifested—simply means "showed" or "demonstrated." God demonstrated His love in Jesus. But did you catch the second big word? In the margin is the definition of the word **propitiation**.

Here is some background to help you appreciate the meaning of propitiation. Have you ever watched an old movie in which one character challenged another to a duel? The character may have said something like, "You have offended my honor, and I demand satisfaction!" The idea behind "satisfaction" was that someone must pay for the insult to one's honor or reputation. The biblical idea of propitiation comes from a similar background. Our sin has offended God. He is holy and righteous, and He simply cannot overlook our offense. He would cease to be righteous if He ignored sin. His holiness must be satisfied. Payment must be made. In the Old Testament

The Creator of the universe thinks you are special.

propitiation–n. describes what happened when Christ, through His death, became the means by which God's wrath was satisfied and God's mercy was granted to the sinner who believes on Christ.

system that payment would be called the propitiation. The propitiation had to be a perfect sacrifice which was offered to pay for the person's sin.

✎ **Read again 1 John 4:9-10. This time we printed it in the margin. Describe how the propitiation was made for our sin.**

_____

_____

> By this the love of God was manifested in us, that God has sent His only begotten Son into the world so that we might live through Him. In this is love, not that we loved God, but that He loved us and sent His Son to be the propitiation for our sins.
> —1 John 4:9-10

Did you see it in the verse? God "sent" Jesus to be the propitiation for our sin. Jesus' death on the cross made the payment. He became the satisfaction for all of humanity's sin.

✎ **The passage said God's wrath—His righteous anger—was satisfied. How much of His wrath was satisfied?**

○ 1. Only God's wrath about the sins of other people.
○ 2. Only God's wrath about sins committed in ignorance.
○ 3. Only God's wrath for my sins before I became a Christian.
○ 4. God's wrath about very single sin I've ever committed or ever will commit.

Jesus is the absolutely perfect sacrifice. His payment was complete. He did not satisfy some of God's wrath. He satisfied it all. The answer is number four.

✎ **Read the passage on the left. Jesus' death was for all people. He loves everyone. But the payment does not automatically apply to all people. Describe what you must do for Jesus' payment for sin to be effective in your life.**

_____

> For God so loved the world, that He gave His only begotten Son, that whoever believes in Him should not perish, but have eternal life. For God did not send the Son into the world to judge the world, but that the world should be saved through Him. He who believes in Him is not judged; he who does not believe has been judged already, because he has not believed in the name of the only begotten Son of God.
> —John 3:16-18

God loved the world so much He gave His only Son to die for us, yet only those who believe in Christ can experience God's unconditional love. Believers in Jesus will not perish—experience God's wrath—but will have eternal life instead. They will not be judged for their sins since they have accepted Christ's judgment on the cross on their behalf. Unbelievers will die without eternal life and will be judged for their own sins since they rejected Christ's payment for them.

✎ **Write your name in each of the blanks below.**

For God so loved _____, that He gave His only begotten Son,

that if _____ believes in Him, _____ should not

perish, but have eternal life. For God did not send the Son into the world

to judge _____, but so that _____ should be saved

through Him. If _____ believes in Him _____ is not

judged.

➔ Stop and thank God for sending His only Son, Jesus, to the world specifically for you.

You Are Completely Forgiven by God

Christ's death not only prevented the wrath of God from falling on all of us who believe in Him, but He fully paid our debt of sin so that we are completely forgiven.

When you were dead in your sins . . . God made you alive with Christ. He forgave us all our sins, having canceled the written code, with its regulations, that was against us and that stood opposed to us; he took it away, nailing it to the cross.
–Colossians 2:13-14, NIV

➔ **Read the passage in the margin. The words "the written code" refer to the Old Testament law. The law points out our sin so that we will come to Christ for forgiveness. Pray as you read Colossians 2:13-14 and the paragraph below. Picture Jesus taking your sin and nailing it to His cross. Express to Him your thanks, love, fear, doubt, and any other emotion you feel.**

All the sins you've ever committed, all the lies you've ever told, all the evil thoughts you've ever had, all the missed opportunities for doing good you, all of these and more make up your indebtedness to God. But in one eternally sufficient act through Christ's death, He covered your guilt, buried your sin, and completely forgave you of every wrong you ever committed or ever will commit.

You cannot be too bad or "too far gone" to be deeply loved and totally forgiven by God.

➔ **Ask God to forgive you for the sins in your life that have built barriers between you and Him. Thank Him for His forgiveness and for His love, even though you do not deserve it, and you cannot earn it.**

You Are Totally Accepted by God

Christ's payment for your sins removed the barrier between Him and you; you can be His beloved child and friend. Shortly before Jesus went to die on the cross for our sins, He spoke the words found in the margin.

No longer do I call you slaves; for the slave does not know what his master is doing; but I have called you friends, for all things that I have heard from My Father I have made known to you.
–John 15:15

✎ **Describe how you think it would feel to believe that Jesus considers you His valued and trusted friend.**

_____

_____

_____

_____

> ### Key Concept for Lesson 3
> In Christ I am unconditionally forgiven and totally accepted by God.

Please pray and ask God how this concept can apply in your life. Now please review this lesson. What has God shown you that you can use?

_____

_____

→ Memorize this Step's memory verse, Romans 12:1.

Working the Step, Part One

We make a decision to turn our will and our lives over to God through Jesus Christ.

> *But as many as received Him, to them He gave the right to become children of God, even to those who believe in His name.*
>
> –John 1:12

LESSON

4

Key Concept:
I can begin a new relationship with God.

As you learn to apply the Steps, you will discover these principles apply to many different areas of your life. On page 58 you learned about two ways to apply Step 3. In this lesson you will explore Step 3 and your relationship with God. In the next lesson you will explore Step 3 and your relationship with recovery from an eating disorder.

Trusting in Christ

God desires to have an intimate relationship with you. He has provided you with continual access to Himself through His Son, Jesus Christ.

Are you trusting in your own abilities to earn acceptance with God?

Are you trusting in your own abilities to earn acceptance with God, or are you trusting in the death of Christ to pay for your sins? Are you trusting in what you can accomplish, or are you trusting in the resurrection of Christ to give you new life?

 Take a moment to reflect on this question. On a scale of 0 to 100 percent, how sure are you that you would spend eternity with God if you died today? Circle your response.

Unsure										Sure
0	10	20	30	40	50	60	70	80	90	100

An answer of less than 100 percent may indicate that you are trusting, at least in part, in yourself. You may be thinking, *Isn't it arrogant to say that I am 100 percent sure?* Indeed, it would be arrogant if you were trusting in yourself—your abilities, your actions, and good deeds—to earn your salvation. However, if you no longer trust in your own efforts but in the all-sufficient payment of Christ, then 100-percent certainty is a response of humility and thankfulness, not arrogance.

If you were to die today and stand before God, and He were to ask you, "Why should I let you into heaven?" What would you tell Him?

➜ Reflect on the question to the left. Would you mention your abilities, church attendance, kindness to others, Christian service, abstinence from a particular sin, or some other good deed?

Paul wrote to Titus:

But when the kindness of God our Savior and His love for mankind appeared, He saved us, not on the basis of deeds which we have done in righteousness, but according to His mercy.

–Titus 3:4-5

And to the Ephesians he wrote:

For by grace you have been saved through faith; and that not of yourselves, it is the gift of God; not as a result of works, that no one should boast.

–Ephesians 2:8-9

✎ **From these two passages, which of the things listed below are necessary in order to be saved? (Check all that apply.)**

- ○ God's grace
- ○ good deeds
- ○ a positive attitude
- ○ attempts to reform

- ○ self-punishment
- ○ help from others
- ○ willpower
- ○ faith in God

Only the first and last items in the list—God's grace and faith in God—are essential to salvation. The others actually may block the way because of a false sense of pride in your own efforts.

Give up your own efforts to achieve righteousness. Instead, trust Christ's death and resurrection alone to pay for your sin and separation from God.

In Acts 16:31, Luke wrote, "Believe in the Lord Jesus, and you shall be saved."

Coming to Christ

If you have not done so already, you can receive Jesus Christ right now by invitation. The Scripture says:

But as many received Him, to them He gave the right to become children of God, even to those who believe in His name.

–John 1:12

If you are not 100 percent sure that you would spend eternity with God if you died today, and if you are willing to trust Christ and accept His payment for your sins, tell God in prayer right now. You may use this sample prayer to express your faith.

Lord Jesus, I need You. I want You to be my Savior and my Lord. I accept Your death on the cross as payment for my sins, and I now entrust my life to Your care. Thank You for forgiving me and for giving me a new life. Please help me grow in my understanding of Your love and power so that my life will bring glory and honor to You. Amen.

_____ (signature) _____ (date)

If you have placed your trust in Jesus Christ before you read this, consider reaffirming your faith and commitment to serve Him. You may do so by using this prayer:

Lord Jesus, I need You and thank You that I am Yours. I confess that I have sinned against You, and I ask You to "create in me a clean heart, and renew a steadfast spirit within me" (Psalm 51:10). I renew my commitment to serve You. Thank You for loving me and forgiving me. Please give me Your strength and wisdom to continue growing in You so that my life can bring glory and honor to You. Amen.

_____ (signature) _____ (date)

Not instant deliverance

Trusting in Christ does not guarantee that you will be delivered instantly from eating-disordered behavior or from any other problem in life. It means that you are forgiven; that you are restored to a relationship with Him that will last throughout eternity; and that you will receive His unconditional love and acceptance, as well as His strength, power, and wisdom, as you continue to grow in recovery.

> **Key Concept for Lesson 4**
> I can begin a new relationship with God.

➜ **Say aloud five times this Step's memory verse, Romans 12:1.**

LESSON 5

Working the Step, Part Two

Key Concept:
A new relationship with God can help me overcome my addiction.

We make a decision to turn our will and our lives over to God through Jesus Christ.

> *He who has found his life shall lose it, and he who has lost his life for My sake shall find it.*
> –Matthew 10:39

In the last lesson you had an opportunity to express your decision to turn your will and life over to God or to renew your previous decision. That decision applies Step 3 to your relationship with God. The Bible compares that decision to a spiritual birth. Just as physical birth is a once-in-a-lifetime experience, spiritual birth is permanent. When you are born into the Father's family, you never will be rejected again. You never will be able to commit a sin for which Jesus has not paid. Your relationship with God is absolutely secure in Jesus.

The wonderful truth in the last paragraph does not mean that your problems all are solved. Now you are ready to begin applying Step 3 in the second way. God wants to help you grow and learn to trust Him in all areas of your life.

As you therefore have received Christ Jesus the Lord, so walk in Him.

–Colossians 2:6

✎ **Colossians 2:6 is a wonderful verse that describes the two ways we work Step 3. Read the verse in the margin carefully. Answer the following questions.**

Describe how you received Christ. _____

_____

Therefore, how are you to continue in your life? _____

_____

_____

Someone paraphrased Colossians 2:6 this way, "The way you get in is the way you go on." Did you note that you received Christ entirely by faith and not by any act of your own? You may have used the words of the Step. Those words said that you made a decision to turn your will and life over to Jesus Christ. Therefore, the only workable solution to living problems is to make the same decision in practical matters every day.

Making the responsible choice to trust God moment by moment, day by day, begins your new life of healing, growth, and renewal. When troubles arise, your response can be the same—to turn your life over to God through Jesus Christ. When circumstances threaten to overwhelm you and your eating disorders call to you—turn your life over to God through Jesus Christ. When you need to make an important personal decision—turn your life over to God through Jesus Christ. When you are tempted to worry about others or yourself, when anxiety and fear threaten to overtake you, when you experience trouble and hardship—your decision can be the same. Turn your life over to God through Jesus Christ.

And we know that God causes all things to work together for good to those who love God, to those who are called according to His purpose.

–Romans 8:28

remember that you were at that time separate from Christ, excluded from the commonwealth of Israel, and strangers to the covenants of promise, having no hope and without God in the world.

–Ephesians 2:12

Christ in you, the hope of glory.

–Colossians 1:27

Blessed be the God and Father of our Lord Jesus Christ, who according to His great mercy has caused us to be born again to a living hope through the resurrection of Jesus Christ from the dead.

–1 Peter 1:3

The Promise of Hope

The Bible word *hope* means the confidence or certainty that comes from God. He is completely dependable so we can have hope—confidence—that what He says He will do.

✎ **Four verses about our hope in Christ are printed in the margin. Match the passages to the following statements. Write the reference of the Scripture next to the statement which best reflects the passage.**

_____ 1. Before I received Christ, I had no hope.

_____ 2. My hope is assured by Jesus' victory over death.

_____ 3. God will use all the events in my life to bring about His glory and my good.

_____ 4. My hope comes from the fact that Jesus Christ lives in me.

_____ 5. My hope comes not from my performance but from God's mercy.

The verses reveal that we have hope because of Christ. His love, forgiveness, and power gives hope for a new life. We can be confident in knowing that absolutely nothing happens to the believer that God doesn't use to his or her betterment. The answers were: 1. Ephesians 2:12; 2. 1 Peter 1:3; 3. Romans 8:28; 4. Colossians 1:27; 5. 1 Peter 1:3.

This hope—confidence in God's power—is key to conquering your eating disorder. Complete the following statement and memorize it.

> By the authority and power of the Son of God, I have hope that I
>
> will conquer _____

The Promise of Faithfulness

God is faithful in times of temptation.

God's faithfulness is His very nature. Christ always is faithful to do what He has promised. Read the following Scripture. Then respond to the statements that follow.

No temptation has overtaken you but such as is common to man; and God is faithful, who will not allow you to be tempted beyond what you are able, but with the temptation will provide the way of escape also, that you may be able to endure it.
                                                                      –1 Corinthians 10:13

✎ **Mark the following statements as *T* (True) or *F* (False).**

_____ God is not strong enough to keep me from falling.
_____ I have uncommonly powerful temptations.
_____ Many of my temptations are beyond my ability to resist.
_____ Being tempted is as bad as sinning.

All but one of the above statements are false. Your temptations may be beyond your ability to resist, but they are not beyond God's power to work in your life. Look for God's faithfulness as you trust Him to help you when you are tempted to eat compulsively, restrict, skip meals, binge, purge, or exercise compulsively.

Let us hold fast the confession of our hope without wavering, for He who promised is faithful.
–Hebrews 10:23

✎ **Read Hebrews 10:23 appearing in the margin. In light of the earlier statement about your hope of conquering your eating disorder, paraphrase and personalize the verse.**

_____

_____

_____

Several years ago, a young woman who had bulimia nervosa shared the following Scripture. Out of her understanding about her eating disorder and out of her experiences during her recovery, she had come to an appreciation of the saving, healing grace of Jehovah Rapha, "The Lord who heals."

The hungry soul He has filled with what is good. He brought them out of darkness and the shadow of death, and broke their bands apart. For He has shattered gates of bronze, And cut bars of iron asunder. Their souls abhorred all kinds of food; and they drew near to the gates of death. Then they cried out to the LORD in their trouble. He sent His word and healed them, and delivered them from their destructions.

–Psalm 107:9b,14,16,18-20

God will be faithful to see us through.

These verses taught her that no matter how her bulimia had distorted her life, God still heard her prayer and would give her the wisdom and strength to make change. He would be faithful to see her through.

✎ **In what ways is your experience with Christ similar to her experience?**

_____

_____

_____

_____

In what ways is it different?

_____

_____

_____

_____

Continued courage

Steps 1, 2, and 3 serve as preparation for the work you will do in recovery. To move beyond this point will require continued courage.

In the Old Testament Joshua was Moses' successor. As he prepared to assume leadership and bring the nation of Israel into the promised land, he undoubtedly felt anxious at the enormous task before him. God promised Joshua, "Just as I have been with Moses, I will be with you; I will not fail you or forsake you" (Joshua 1:5).

Jesus made the same promise. He said, "I am with you always, even to end of the age" (Matthew 28:20).

God told Joshua three times, "Be strong and courageous" (Joshua 1:6-7,9). In Step 4 you will learn exactly what courageous means and how to be "strong and courageous." As you prepare to take the Step, you may find helpful the words of an old hymn.

> "Fear not, I am with thee; O be not dismayed,
> For I am thy God and will still give thee aid;
> I'll strengthen thee, help thee, and cause thee to stand,
> Upheld by My righteous, omnipotent hand.

"When thro' fiery trials thy pathway shall lie,
My grace, all-sufficient, shall be thy supply;
The flame shall not hurt thee; I only design
Thy dross to consume, and thy gold to refine.

"The soul that on Jesus hath leaned for repose,
I will not, I will not desert to his foes;
That soul, tho' all hell should endeavor to shake,
I'll never, no never, no never forsake."[1]

Key Concept for Lesson 5

A new relationship with God can help me overcome my addiction.

Step Review

➔ **Write this Step's memory verse.**

_____

_____

✎ **Step 3 says:** *We make a decision to turn our lives over to God through Jesus Christ.* **Write in your own words what Step 3 means.**

_____

_____

_____

_____

Have you made that decision? Describe how you will daily apply Step 3 to your life and recovery.

_____

_____

_____

_____

_____

Notes
[1]John Rippon's *Selection of Hymns*, 1787, "How Firm a Foundation," *The Baptist Hymnal* (Nashville: Convention Press, 1991).

Taking My Inventory

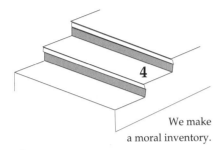

We make
a moral inventory.

BROKEN BY THE PRESSURE

Before Annie went into the hospital for treatment, she experienced what she called a "major burnout." She was deeply depressed. Tired of juggling so many different time-consuming activities and feeling pressured by trying to be perfect at everything, her body systems and her mind couldn't handle the physical and emotional stress. As she looked back on the experience, she observed something she failed to see at the time. She had become quite a master at lies and half-truths—sometimes simple, sometimes elaborate—but all designed to hide the truth of her condition.

Ironically, she was so successful, she even deceived herself into thinking that the problem wasn't with her but was with others who challenged her. When she was in public, she wore large, baggy clothing to hide her thinness, but she thought it would be very normal and desirable to be even thinner. She pretended to eat all the food her parents left for her when she went home for weekends. She secretly fed it to her all-too-willing Irish setter. "It wasn't really lying," she justified. "They just gave me too much food."

Annie continued to lose weight. At one point she weighed 82 pounds. Her father became concerned. He demanded that she see a doctor. Tests showed that Annie's anorexia was affecting her bodily functions and that her kidneys were failing. The doctor immediately admitted her to the hospital.

Even when she was an inpatient and talked about her failings and behaviors, Annie had trouble distinguishing the truth from a lie. (Read more about Annie on page 78).

Step 4   *We make a searching, courageous moral inventory of ourselves.*

Memory verse   *Let us examine and probe our ways, and let us return to the Lord.*
                                                        –Lamentations 3:40

Overview for Step 4   **Lesson 1: Why Take a Moral Inventory?**
        Goal: You will describe what a moral inventory is and what a moral inventory is not.
Lesson 2: Dishonesty and Resentment
        Goal: You will write an inventory of dishonesty and resentment.
Lesson 3: Self-Pity and False Pride
        Goal: You will write an inventory of self-pity and false pride.
Lesson 4: Criticism and Destructive Anger
        Goal: You will write an inventory of criticism and destructive anger.
Lesson 5: Fear and Impatience
        Goal: You will write an inventory of fear and impatience.

LESSON 1

Why Take a Moral Inventory?

We make a searching, courageous moral inventory of ourselves.

He is on the path of life who heeds instruction, but he who forsakes reproof goes astray.

–Proverbs 10:17

Key Concept:
A moral inventory is an honest look at the good and the bad in my life.

As you work the first three Steps you become willing to—
- admit reality—that you have no power over your eating disorder;
- believe that God is strong enough and loving enough to restore you;
- decide to turn control of your life and will over to God's care and control.

As you arrive at that decision, an obvious question remains. How does a person actually turn will and life over to God? How do you carry out the decision you made in Step 3? The answer is simple. You carry out the decision of Step 3 by going ahead and working the remaining Steps. If you keep working the Steps—applying them to your life—we believe you will discover that God has become real in your life, and you will find that He has helped you overcome your eating disorder.

The work of recovery begins with Step 4. Step 1 was only an admission of reality. You don't *do* anything by admitting what already is true. Step 2 is a willingness to trust. Again, it is an openness to the truth. Step 3 is a decision to commit yourself to Christ. Now, with His help, you can begin to take solid steps of recovery. The first of those practical actions is to write your inventory.

Most of us don't *feel* like writing down our inventories, but we do it anyway. We do it because writing promotes reflection and application.

What Your Inventory Is Not

Many people understand self-examination to mean either "self-absorption" or "self-condemnation." Step 4, however, refers to taking an inventory. A shopkeeper takes an inventory of his store so that he will know what he has in stock; what is damaged, outdated, and needs replacing; what he needs to order; and what new items need to be put in stock. A self-inventory is not a list of wrongs one has committed. An inventory is a thorough individual evaluation. It is a complete assessment of our good and bad traits, strengths and weaknesses, assets and liabilities, and how we use each.

immoral. –adj. Moral means having to do with both right and wrong. Immoral means only that which is wrong.

 Someone in a group said, "When I first came into program, I thought Step 4 meant I was to take a complete *immoral* inventory of myself." Use the information from the last paragraph to explain what the person meant by an "immoral" inventory.

_____

_____

The person referred to the idea of an inventory as self-condemnation. She thought the idea was to beat herself up by reviewing all the bad things she ever had done. She was surprised to learn that an inventory means an honest look at the good and the bad in her life.

✎ **In the following paragraph circle the benefits that come from taking a searching moral inventory.**

> Far from being a means of condemning yourself, or of putting yourself down, a *searching, courageous moral inventory* is a vehicle which can provide help for developing healthy self-esteem. It is also a plan for growth and maturity. It exposes hazards which may lead to a relapse. It highlights individual strengths and gifts you possess in your uniqueness as a person whom God has created—all of which will support your recovery. A moral inventory also helps you discover your weaknesses. Looking at the negative part of your personality and behavior is difficult if you tend to be a perfectionist.

The benefits of working Step 4 include building self-esteem, growing in maturity, warning you of relapse, seeing your strengths, and admitting your weaknesses. If you fear self-discovery, remember that God's design is for your healing. His perfect love for you will help you overcome your fears.

There is no fear in love; but perfect love casts out fear.
　　　　　　　　　–1 John 4:18

➡ **Before you continue, read the promise appearing in the margin. Stop and pray, thanking God that His love overcomes your fear. Ask Him to give you the power to be honest, open, and willing to work the Step.**

It takes courage to face the aspects you need to change about your personality and behavior. It may be equally difficult to accept your strengths and virtues. You may reject what is good and see only what you dislike about yourself. This is a destructive form of perfectionism.

He who conceals his transgressions will not prosper, but he who confesses and forsakes them will find compassion.
　　　　　　　　　–Proverbs 28:13

✎ **Read the proverb that appears in the margin. Describe how hiding your eating-disordered behaviors has given them more power over you.**

_____

_____

_____

Trying to hide your flaws—from others and from yourself—seems like a good solution. When you hide something about yourself from others, you usually invest a great amount of energy in maintaining appearances. As time passes, keeping the secret hidden consumes more and more of your attention and resources. Your "investment" in self-protection gives the secret more power over you. Secrecy also prevents you from facing squarely the consequences of your behavior. This leads to an inner sense of despair. Thus the cycle of addictive behavior continues. It goes from irresponsible act to denial to guilt and all over again. It is a vicious cycle leading eventually to self-destruction.

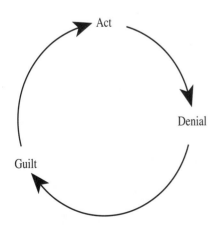

Notice the margin drawing of this vicious cycle. The cycle begins with stress in our lives. When the stress builds up to a certain level, we turn to some action that we discovered will relieve the stress. The action we turn to is our "drug of choice." For an alcoholic the stress reliever is alcohol. For some the action may be acting out sexually. For a compulsive overeater the stress reliever may be a chocolate cake or a dozen doughnuts. For the person suffering from bulimia the stress reliever may be a binge followed by guilt leading to a purge. For the anorexic the stress reliever may be to demonstrate control by avoiding food and turning to exercise instead.

After we have used our drug of choice, we feel guilty. The guilt brings on more stress. We deny the problem. Denial multiplies the stress. Eventually the stress drives us back to the behavior, and the cycle repeats itself.

In Step 2, you decided to seek God to restore your sanity through Jesus Christ. To replace denial with courageous honesty may be painful, but you gain control of your life again because honesty robs your character defects of the power that secrecy gives them. You now can fill with God's truth the emptiness which you tried to fill with compulsive food behaviors. This opens the door for freedom. Jesus said, *you shall know the truth, and the truth shall make you free* (John 8:32).

How Will God Respond to Your Honesty?

Because God is steadfast and consistent, you can depend on Him. When you write your inventory and then share it with Him, you will not tell Him anything new or unusual. Nothing about you is strange to Him.

✎ **Read the two Scriptures at left. According to 1 John 1:8-9, what two things does God do when we confess our sins honestly to Him?**

If we claim to be without sin, we deceive ourselves and the truth is not in us. If we confess our sins, he is faithful and just and will forgive us our sins and purify us from all unrighteousness.
                    –1 John 1:8-9, NIV

_____

According to Hebrews 4:15-16, what is Jesus uniquely able to do because He has lived in flesh like our own?

_____

For we do not have a high priest who cannot sympathize with our weaknesses, but one who has been tempted in all things as we are, yet without sin. Let us therefore draw near with confidence to the throne of grace, that we may receive mercy and find grace to help in time of need.
                    –Hebrews 4:15-16

When we confess, God is always faithful not only to accept our confession but also to forgive our sins and cleanse us from all unrighteousness. Because He has shared our experience, He can sympathize with us. He will not reject us. He will give mercy and grace to help us.

The Games We Play

Addictions are shame filled and shame driven. Think for a moment how the process works. Satan uses any number of methods—such as self-hatred because of abuse, low self-esteem, the desire for acceptance—to convince us that we need to use our drug of choice. Then when we have followed his cues, he accuses us. When we binge, purge, or starve, we feel temporary relief, but then we experience our original problems, compounded by the pain of shame. So Satan suggests that more of the behavior that caused the shame will relieve the pain. We become stuck in a shame-filled, shame-driven cycle.

The shame we feel leads us to act as if we are shameless. When we have had an eating disorder for any length of time, we become expert at playing games to temporarily shift the focus off the real problem. Unfortunately, these are games in which everyone loses, and the only way to win is not to play.

Here are some typical games you may have played at one time or another. Notice that each type of game is directly tied to one of the false beliefs and its related fear discussed in Step 2. Falling prey to Satan's lies led you to do whatever it took to "save face," shift the blame, or hide, even when hiding hurt you or others. Although you played the games to protect yourself and your ego from pain, greater pain resulted.

Game Type	Typical Games	False Belief	Alternatives
Self-defense	Dishonesty, Resentment	Fear of failure	Honesty, Forgiveness
Self-deception	Self-pity, False pride/ False humility	Fear of rejection	Gratitude, Humility
Self-delusion	Criticism, Destructive Anger	Fear of punishment; tendency to punish	Love, Constructive Anger
Self-distortion	Fear, Impatience, Impulsiveness	Sense of shame	Trust, Patience

Focusing outward

Notice the chart also lists the alternatives for the games—genuine, caring interactions with others. These interactions focus attention away from self and focus outward in redemption to others. Perhaps already you are beginning to see the Holy Spirit change you in these directions. Congratulations! The Bible contains this promise: "I am confident of this, that He who began a good work in you will perfect it until the day of Christ Jesus" (Philippians 1:6).

In the following lessons you will complete an inventory on each of the above character games and their alternatives. You will look for ways to change for the better with God's help.

> ## Key Concept for Lesson 1
> A moral inventory is an honest look at the good and the bad in my life.

 Pray and ask God how this concept can apply in your life. Now please review this lesson. What has God shown you that you can use?

_____

_____

➼ **Memorize this Step's memory verse:**
Let us examine and probe our ways, and let us return to the Lord.
–Lamentations 3:40

Dishonesty and Resentment

We make a searching, courageous moral inventory of ourselves.

If, however, you are fulfilling the royal law, according to the Scripture, "You shall love your neighbor as yourself," you are doing well.
–James 2:8

Key Concept:
Honesty and forgiveness are
essential to my recovery.

Someone in a group shared the following illustration. "I know that food is my drug of choice and that if the stress builds up too much, I will be tempted to use it. So I picture a big barometer that goes with me everywhere. The barometer measures the pressure in my life. Whenever I have a problem, tell a lie, indulge in a resentment, or hold on to self-pity or unresolved anger, the pressure reading in my barometer goes up. I know that if the pressure gets to a certain point, I will be tempted to use food to medicate my emotions, so my job is to keep the pressure down in the barometer. I keep the pressure down by working the Steps, especially the inventories."

The fear of failure leads to self-defense. Dishonesty and resentment are two ways people defend themselves. People with addictions find themselves trying to cover up their secrets by using any means possible. They try to keep up a front by lying, denying the truth, holding grudges—anything to shift the focus, anything to avoid facing the facts. Sadly, this form of supposed self-protection always backfires in time. It often destroys one's character, reputation, and loved ones.

More about Annie

Even when she was an inpatient, Annie had trouble distinguishing the truth from a lie when it involved her own treatment. Learning to eat using food exchanges was fun at first, until the nurse made Annie use normal serving sizes instead of the tiny ones she wanted. Annie still marvels at just how bizarre her behavior became. When she saw her skin-and-bones figure in the mirror, her mind still convinced her she was too fat. She even had herself convinced that she was one of the few people on earth who could live without food. She ate it only occasionally to keep people from bothering her. To make sure she never went back to that sick state of mind again, she keeps in close contact with her sponsor. Some day she hopes to be free enough to help someone else.

Do you remember times when a lie seemed like the truth to you? Can you see how important a sponsor is to help you stay on the road in recovery? Do you have a sponsor, yet? How often do you contact him or her?

Answer the following questions to see if you are being honest with yourself and others.

Hiding/Secretiveness

✎ **Do you try to make sure no one knows the "real you"? If so, explain what you do to cover up the things you wish to hide.**

_____

_____

_____

Masking

✎ Do you fear the thought of having others (even "significant others") know about your eating disorder? If so, explain why you have this fear.

_____

_____

_____

Excuse-making

✎ Do you sometimes look for others to blame, or seek to excuse yourself, rather than face up to a mistake, error, or sin you have committed? If so, how does this affect you and your relationships?

_____

_____

_____

Half-truths

✎ Describe an incident in which you've tried to protect yourself by telling only partial truths.

_____

_____

_____

Phoniness

✎ Do you try to impress others with the idea that you are someone or something other than who or what you really are, because you believe that your life otherwise would be considered unimportant or would have little meaning? If so, give an example and explain why you feel this way.

_____

_____

_____

Obvious dishonesty

✎ Complete the following inventory about blatant dishonesty.

Do you ever steal food or laxatives or steal money to buy them?
○ Yes ○ No

Do you ever eat then purge, but lie about it when you are asked?
○ Yes ○ No

Do you ever skip a meal then lie about it when asked? ○ Yes ○ No

Do you ever lie about how much food you have eaten? ○ Yes ○ No

Have you ever ordered enough food to feed five people, then lied and said it was for friends at home, when it actually was for your next binge? ○ Yes ○ No

Have you ever lied about where the grocery money went when you really spent it on food for binges or for laxatives? ○ Yes ○ No

O LORD, you have searched me and you know me. You know when I sit and when I rise; you perceive my thoughts from afar. You discern my going out and my lying down; you are familiar with all my ways. Before a word is on my tongue you know it completely, O LORD.
—Psalm 139: 1-4, NIV

✎ **Read Psalm 139:1-4. Does realizing that the Lord already knows everything about you—both good and bad—help you to be more honest? Why or why not?**

_____

_____

_____

Self-check on Resentment

Resentment is a refusal to let go of anger over some past harm or perceived injury. It is a highly destructive form of self-defense. It often is expressed as a desire to punish the person who offended you.

You will probably become like the very person you despise.

Resentment generally goes hand-in-hand with the abuse of people and things. Rather than keeping you at a distance from your target of resentment, you'll probably become like the very one you despise. You cannot focus continued emotional and mental energy on someone without picking up some of his or her traits. Resentment may cause you to neglect even the basic and important necessities for healthy life-styles and relationships. This may happen simply because you resent being told what to do (resistance to authority).

✎ **Do you sometimes use any of the following expressions of resentment? Check all that you have used.**

- ○ selective forgetfulness to punish
- ○ chronic lateness
- ○ gossip, slander, defamation
- ○ long-term nursing of anger
- ○ "justifiable" grudge-bearing
- ○ avoidance/silent treatment
- ○ self-righteous indignation
- ○ blame
- ○ plotting or seeking revenge/retaliation
- ○ sarcasm
- ○ unforgiveness
- ○ other _____

Self-check on Resentment

Holding grudges

✎ **Do you tend to hold grudges? Can you think of anyone you haven't yet fully forgiven? When will you? What will it take?**

_____

_____

_____

Sarcasm

✎ **Have you ever used sarcasm to hide your anger toward others? Explain.**

_____

_____

_____

Gossip, slander, defamation

✎ **Have you ever talked about the wrongs or misfortunes of others because you secretly were pleased about their problems? Explain.**

_____

_____

_____

Revenge   ✎ Have you ever looked for ways—subtle or overt—to "get even" with someone? Explain.

_____

_____

_____

Avoidance/silent treatment   ✎ Explain any incident in which you've given the "silent treatment" to someone with whom you've been angry. This may have involved punishing that person by refusing to talk with him or her.

_____

_____

_____

✎ Describe any other ways in which you've expressed resentment toward another person.

_____

_____

_____

✎ Mark any of the following authority figures toward whom you feel (or have felt) contempt.

     ○ Parent(s)   ○ Spouse
     ○ Boss/Supervisor   ○ Church leader
     ○ Government official   ○ School official
     ○ Other _____

Forgiveness: Reclaiming Damaged Relationships

Forgiveness is mercy triumphing over punishment. When you forgive, you give up your "right" to punish the one who offended you.

✎ **Carefully read the following paragraph. From the list of statements that follow the passage, check all the statements that are true according to the paragraph.**

True forgiveness is an informed decision to bear the pain of another's offense without demanding that he or she be punished for it. This does not mean you overlook or accept unacceptable behavior. The process of forgiving may include talking with the person who has hurt you about his or her behavior and/or allowing that person to experience any negative consequences the behavior produces. This enables the offender to understand at least some of the effects of the wrongdoing. However, pointing out another's faults or your willingness to forgive the person may not cause the offender to change his or her behavior or cause your relationship to change. Regardless of another person's response, you are **I am responsible**   responsible for forgiving anyone who offends you.

✎ **Check each statement that is true according to the paragraph you just read.**

     ○ 1. Forgiveness is a feeling.
     ○ 2. Forgiveness is a decision not to demand repayment of a debt.
     ○ 3. Forgiveness means I must overlook others' wrong behavior.
     ○ 4. Forgiveness means the other person does not have to face the consequences of his or her actions.
     ○ 5. Forgiveness means the other person will change his or her behavior.
     ○ 6. Forgiving is my responsibility and does not depend on the other person's response.
     ○ 7. Forgiving is my choice to stop torturing myself.

Did you note that most of the answers to the questions were false? Only 2, 6, and 7 are true. The other answers are commonly accepted false beliefs about forgiveness. Number 7 is true even though the paragraph didn't contain the statement. The wisest choice a person can make is to forgive, because resentment is self-destructive.

Three good reasons to forgive are:

• God commands you to forgive others through Jesus Christ. "And whenever you stand praying, forgive, if you have anything against anyone" (Mark 11:25).

• God through Jesus Christ has forgiven you. "And be kind to one another, tender-hearted, forgiving each other, just as God in Christ also has forgiven you" (Ephesians 4:32).

• An unforgiving spirit is self-destructive. Not forgiving often leads to suppressed hurt and anger. Repressing these powerful negative emotions affects every relationship you have and leads to bitterness, depression, and separation from others. This deadly combination can cause you to relapse into compulsive food behavior.

forgiveness–n. the act of giving up resentment of or claim to requital for an insult; to grant relief from payment of a debt; to pardon (Webster's)

When Wanda was a child, a relative sexually abused her. She vowed that she never would forgive her abuser. When a counselor confronted Wanda about her need to forgive, she said, "I'm never going to let him off that easy." The problem is "he" was not the one who was suffering; Wanda was. Refusing to forgive injures the one who carries resentment.

✎ **What people have offended you or harmed you? What did they do to you?**

Person	Offense
_____	_____
_____	_____
_____	_____
_____	_____
_____	_____

✎ What would it mean for you to release each person from the penalty he or she owes you?

Person   If I forgive . . .

_____   _____

_____   _____

_____   _____

_____   _____

Key Concept for Lesson 2
Honesty and forgiveness are essential to my recovery.

➔ Write three times in the margin this Step's memory verse.

✎ Pray and ask God how this concept can apply in your life. Now please review this lesson. What has God shown you that you can use?

_____

_____

LESSON 3

Self-pity and False Pride

We make a searching, courageous moral inventory of ourselves.

> *A man's pride will bring him low, but a humble spirit will obtain honor.*
> –Proverbs 29:23

Key Concept:
I continue to hurt myself with self-pity, false pride, and false humility.

In this lesson you will study self-pity and false pride/false humility—two more methods people use to defend themselves. Either method results in self-deception. In certain circumstances, you may attempt to fool yourself and others into thinking you are better than they are or worse than they are.

You may play these games for so long that you become completely deceived into believing that you are helpless, worthless, and pitiful. If others don't provide sufficient sympathy, you may wallow in paralyzing self-pity until they either finally feel sorry for you or totally reject you out of frustration and disgust. God wants us to replace these games with gratitude and genuine humility.

Self-pity: How to Be a Life-long Victim

Allow yourself to experience the pain essential to healing.

One of the most common causes of self-pity is a sense of being victimized by others. Without attention and care, the wounds continue to ache. Nothing is wrong with acknowledging the fact that you have been hurt. To allow yourself to experience the pain associated with the hurt is essential to healing, but when you let the experience drag out too long in your mind, you run the risk of falling into a "pity trap."

In a pity trap you see yourself as an innocent victim to the extent that you deny to others and to yourself your capacity for doing wrong. In extreme cases you may become emotionally paralyzed. You may blame others for your problems and for your depression. Self-pity may prompt you to control and manipulate others in an attempt to have them do for you what you need to do for yourself.

✎ **Take time to read carefully this list of common characteristics associated with self-pity. Check those you have thought, felt, or said.**

○ Projection: "I feel bad . . . it's your/his/her fault."
○ Denial: "I never did anything wrong."
○ Avoiding responsibility by reciting a long list of past hurts.
○ Avoiding responsibility by pleading physical illness or distress.
○ Reading the "whine list": "I can't." "I tried once before." "I never get anything right."
○ Controlling others by making them feel important. "You're the only friend I have." "You're the only one who understands me."

At one time or another all of us have employed some or most of the techniques in the list. Answer the following questions as honestly as you can to explore the hold self-pity has on your life. Remember that freedom comes through rigorous honesty.

Self-check on Self-pity

Denial

✎ **Do you ever refuse to acknowledge that you have done something wrong? If so, why?**

_____

_____

"Whine List"

✎ **Have you ever sought pity for your inability to achieve? Explain.**

_____

_____

Excuses: Physical

✎ **Have you relied on physical complaints or illnesses in order to escape responsibility? If so, explain.**

_____

_____

Excuses: Emotional ✎ Have you ever avoided taking responsibility for yourself because of past abuse or because of some other misfortune you've suffered? If so, how has this increased the burden you've carried?

_____

_____

Manipulation ✎ Have you loaded praise or thankfulness on another person—emphasizing how important he or she is to you—in order to get that person to take care of you or protect you? If so, explain.

_____

_____

Gratitude: Cure for the "Pity Party Blues"

As you work the Steps, you will experience many changes. You will become more thankful. You will realize that the changes you and other people are beginning to see in you result from God's intervention and from your courage.

Gratitude motivates you to share this news with other people. Also, as you start to feel better about yourself and become less preoccupied with your own well-being, you begin wanting to exercise responsibility and to share your resources with other people: your time, energies, talents, and sometimes even your finances. You may be surprised to discover that giving yourself to others brings great satisfaction. "Freely you received, freely give" (Matthew 10:8).

✎ **List the people, situations, and things for which you are thankful.**

_____

_____

✎ **Give an example of how gratitude helped you overcome a period of self-pity.**

_____

False Pride/False Humility: Two Sides of a Counterfeit Coin

Among the many ailments springing from eating disorders, false pride and false humility are among the most destructive. These are extreme perspectives in which you swing from feeling like the "general manager of the universe" to being "poor me." As one recovering person said: "Sometimes I think I am God, and the rest of the time I think I'm pond scum."

"Sometimes I think I'm God. Sometimes I think I'm pond scum."

False pride keeps recovery from happening because it is based on the notion that you don't need help from God or other people. You are self-sufficient. This emotional game usually includes an unwillingness to seek help; an unwillingness to be wrong and apologize; and an unwillingness to admit powerlessness over any habit, including an eating disorder.

devaluation–n. a lessening of value, status, or stature (Webster's)

False humility is self-**devaluation**. It is putting one's self down because of negative conclusions from past hurts. False humility is marked by self-condemnation, passive behavior, fear, and a sense of hopelessness and defeat.

In recovery, we replace our false pride and false humility with an accurate appraisal of our worth based on our value in God's eyes. The apostle Peter wrote, "You were not redeemed with perishable things like silver or gold . . . but with the precious blood, as of a lamb unblemished and spotless, the blood of Christ" (1 Peter 1:18-19).

Self-check on False Pride/False Humility

Superiority

✎ On what occasions have you thought or acted as if you were "the general manager of the universe"?

_____

_____

✎ Why do you think you've sometimes felt this way about yourself?

- ○ 1. I am better, smarter, and wiser than other people.
- ○ 2. I criticize anything less than perfect that I or others do.
- ○ 3. I secretly feel worth less than others, and I cover my feelings up by attempting to prove my worth.
- ○ 4. I become angry with others when they fail to measure up.
- ○ 5. I become angry with myself when others fail to measure up.
- ○ 6. Other _____

Hopelessness

✎ Give examples of situations in which you have you experienced fear, a sense of hopelessness, or defeat.

_____

_____

In what kinds of situations do you tend to act passively? Why do you think you become passive in those situations?

_____

_____

How have these feelings and actions affected you and your relationships?

_____

_____

Humility: Having the Mind of Christ

Humility is the opposite of pride and arrogance. People must be comfortable with themselves in order to practice humility. In the passage that appears in

When someone invites you to a wedding feast, do not take the place of honor, for a person more distinguished than you may have been invited. If so, the host who invited both of you will come and say to you, "Give this man your seat." Then, humiliated, you will have to take the least important place. But when you are invited, take the lowest place, so that when your host comes, he will say to you, "Friend, move up to a better place." Then you will be honored in the presence of all your fellow guests. For everyone who exalts himself will be humbled and he who humbles himself will be exalted.

–Luke 14:8-11, NIV

the margin Jesus told the story of the chief seats at the feast. In Jesus' day how people were seated at a banquet demonstrated their social importance.

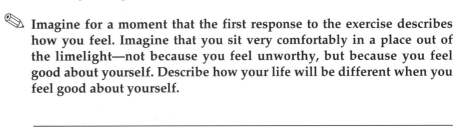 **Read the story that appears in the margin. Then check each of the following statements which are true of you.**

○ Taking the lowest seat is easy because I feel good about myself.
○ Taking the lowest seat would be very difficult for me.
○ I always take the lowest seat. I feel that I don't deserve better.
○ I would take the lowest seat but I would resent it.
○ Other _____

Humility begins with acknowledging that you are powerless over your eating disorder. It continues as you submit yourself to God daily. By working the Steps you are moving toward the time when the first response above will describe your feelings. With time, work, and support, you will reach the place that you feel comfortable with who you are. You will look in the mirror and see someone you respect and value.

Imagine for a moment that the first response to the exercise describes how you feel. Imagine that you sit very comfortably in a place out of the limelight—not because you feel unworthy, but because you feel good about yourself. Describe how your life will be different when you feel good about yourself.

_____

_____

As you continue to practice humility and to grow spiritually and emotionally, you may realize you need support from other people. When you feel out of sorts or are tempted to indulge in eating-disordered thinking or behavior, call on others or attend a support-group meeting. The fellowship you find there will help to meet the needs you once tried to fill with a food-related compulsion. By listening to other people who share your predicament, you realize that everyone—including you—has strengths and weaknesses. You realize that it's OK to be human and to be genuine with other people and with God.

Some have experienced abuse or neglect to the point that they fear loss of control. For them the idea of humility may sound like more of the old abuse.

Does the idea of being humble frighten or disgust you? If so, how and why?

_____

_____

Humble yourselves, therefore, under God's mighty hand, that he may lift you up in due time.
–1 Peter 5:6

Humility does not mean returning to an abusive situation. We are to humble ourselves "under God's mighty hand." Then we appropriately humble ourselves before other people as an expression of that love and trust in God. If the prospect of humility frightens you, remember the work you did in Step 2 on your concept of God. Little by little you can learn to trust your Heavenly Father to protect and care for you.

Describe how humility can be a sign of objectivity and strength.

_____

_____

 Describe how practicing humility can affect or now affects . . .

your life _____

_____

your relationship with God _____

_____

your relationships with other people _____

_____

> ### Key Concept for Lesson 3
> I continue to hurt myself with self-pity, false pride, and false humility.

 Pray and ask God how this concept can apply in your life. Now please review this lesson. What has God shown you that you can use?

_____

_____

→ Take five minutes to memorize this Step's memory verse:
Let us examine and probe our ways, and let us return to the Lord.
—Lamentations 3:40

LESSON 4

Key Concept:
I replace criticism and destructive anger with love, forgiveness, and honesty.

Criticism and Destructive Anger

We make a searching, courageous moral inventory of ourselves.

Do not associate with a man given to anger; or go with a hot-tempered man, lest you learn his ways and find a snare for yourself.
—Proverbs 22:24-25

Fear sometimes drives us to do destructive things, especially when that fear is based on the false belief that we are unworthy of love and deserve to be punished. The resulting fear that others will punish or criticize causes us to lash out at others in an effort to attack them before they attack us. Whether or not they really plan to attack us isn't the point: fear of punishment drives us to punish them first. We deflect the pain from ourselves and project it onto them.

With enough practice at this game, we eventually can delude ourselves into believing we always are right and others, who may question or criticize us, always are wrong. In essence, we play God. In time, we even may begin to enjoy picking at others, finding and exposing their faults, and punishing their wrongs—real or imagined. We may have left behind a number of victims of our sometimes cruel, vindictive anger.

Two emotional games

In this lesson, you will confront two particularly damaging emotional games you may have played: criticism and destructive anger. It may be a time of painful reflection, but the growth will be worth the pain.

➔ **Before you continue, stop and ask God to help you see the truth about this part of yourself. Pray for wisdom to know what to do about the truth you see and for a sense of His healing and forgiveness for all past failures.**

Criticism: Verbal Dissection

The criticism described here is not the constructive advice we offer to a friend. It is the negative judgment of others—and ourselves—that is rooted in pride and in our need to be perfect or to be perceived as perfect. Usually this criticism takes the form of verbal abuse, but sometimes it can be more subtle. It can be masked in sarcasm or silence.

We use criticism for many different reasons. One is that we see others as a reflection of ourselves, and criticizing them is a form of control to motivate them to conform to our standards.

We may put other people down to elevate ourselves. This usually results from a low sense of self-worth and from the belief that if we criticize others, we can make ourselves look better. Still another reason to criticize others is that it feels right; after all, those who fail *deserve* to be condemned and punished.[1]

Therefore, encourage one another, and build up one another.
        –1 Thessalonians 5:11

At other times we may be critical because we truly believe others need our guidance. We perceive that our correction will benefit them. Later, we are surprised to realize that these people avoid us because our habit of "correcting" has been more *de*structive than *con*structive to them.

The Scriptures emphasize loving others and building them up rather than tearing them down. In the verses appearing in the margin read how Paul and John described the attitude that ideally supports our interaction with others.

Beloved, let us love one another, for love is from God; and everyone who loves is born of God and knows God. Beloved, if God so loved us, we also ought to love one another.
        –1 John 4:7,11

Self-check on Criticism

✎ **Why do you criticize other people? What is your main motivation? What results do you expect? Check all the responses that apply.**

○ I feel better when someone else is the focus of blame.
○ I feel threatened when people don't do things well.

○ I fear criticism, so I criticize others before they can criticize me.
○ I am critical because others don't do their jobs well.
○ I'm only trying to help.
○ Other _____

✎ **In what ways do you communicate criticism?**

Communicating criticism

○ Sarcasm
○ Pointing out mistakes
○ Silence, with a raised eyebrow
○ "Helpful" suggestions
○ Snide remarks to others (gossip)
○ Other _____

✎ **How does a critical attitude affect your relationships, including your relationship with God?**

_____

_____

✎ **How do you feel about yourself when you criticize others?**

_____

_____

Love: the Healing Touch

When you think about love, you may think of the warm feelings, a funny sensation in the pit of your stomach, restlessness, and sense of anticipation you felt toward another person when "falling in love." Fortunately, love is more than emotional feelings experienced at the beginning of attraction. Feelings like these emotional ones tend to come and go.

Genuine love is a matter of choice and of action. John 3:16 says, "God so loved the world that He gave His only Son . . . ." Jesus said in John 15:13, "Greater love has no one than this, that one lay down his life for his friends." Titus 3:4-5 says: "But when the kindness of God our Savior and His love for mankind appeared, He saved us, not on the basis of deeds which we have done in righteousness, but according to His mercy, by the washing of regeneration and renewing by the Holy Spirit."

God's love for us is not based on His emotions but is demonstrated by His actions. As we grow in understanding His love and mercy, we increasingly will desire to demonstrate our love for Him and for others by actively obeying His commands.

You shall love the Lord your God with all your heart, and with all your soul, and with all your mind. This is the great and foremost commandment. The second is like it, You shall love your neighbor as yourself. On these two commandments depend the whole Law and the Prophets.

–Matthew 22:37-40

✎ **Read the Scripture that appears in the margin. Check the statement below which best describes Jesus' attitude toward love.**

○ Love is a matter of feelings.
○ Love includes both actions and emotions.
○ Behavior is what really counts.

Love is patient, love is kind, and is not jealous; love does not brag and is not arrogant, [love] does not act unbecomingly; it does not seek its own, is not provoked, does not take into account a wrong suffered, does not rejoice in unrighteousness, but rejoices with the truth; [love] bears all things, believes all things, hopes all things, endures all things. Love never fails.
–1 Corinthians 13:4-8

Jesus' words demonstrate that genuine love includes actions as well as feelings. The words of the apostle Paul appearing in the margin describe love in terms of actions.

 Place an *X* on the following scale to indicate where your own expression of love falls. Then place an *O* where you would like it to be.

All feeling/	Balanced feeling	All action/
No action	and action	No feeling

→ **Right now, ask God to help you achieve His ideal for your life in expressing love in both attitude and action. You may wish to include replacing criticism with love for others as a specific action.**

Destructive Anger: Human Cannonballs on the Loose

Anger is a God-given emotional response that everyone experiences. Anger can be a response to unmet expectations, irritation, or frustration when things don't go our way. We may show hostility when someone has a different opinion. Anger also can be a defensive response to a hurtful attack or to a real or perceived threat to our self-esteem or our well-being.

As with all other emotions, feeling angry is OK. What we do with the feeling of anger is another matter. Too often we use anger destructively rather than constructively. The apostle Paul indicated that we should express anger appropriately. See his thoughts at left. Appropriate expression of anger is limited in time and effect and is used to help rather than hurt people.

Be angry, and yet do not sin; do not let the sun go down on your anger, and do not give the devil an opportunity.
–Ephesians 4:26-27

Destructive anger can be expressed outwardly or inwardly. It can result in depression, suspicion, and a low sense of self-worth. Examples of destructive anger are verbal abuse—screaming, criticism, fault-finding—physical abuse, teasing, sarcasm, and in extreme cases, murder. Silence, neglect, and withdrawal also can be destructive expressions of anger.

Destructive anger can have catastrophic effects on your recovery. Expressed outwardly, it can alienate you from others and drive a wedge between you and God. Without relationships with God and others, you likely will return to your addiction to fill the void of emptiness in your life.

Anger turned inward also is very dangerous. As people with eating disorders, we already have a low tolerance for the burden of repressed anger. If we do not deal constructively with anger, we may return to compulsive behavior for relief from painful emotions.

 Read below about Barbara's struggle to replace anger with forgiveness. Then describe how Barbara learned to express her anger appropriately.

More about Barbara

Barbara had reached the point in her recovery that she knew she must forgive her father for years of sexual abuse. Her father died four years earlier, so her sponsor encouraged her to write a letter of forgiveness. Barbara wrote a long, long letter . . . more than 12 pages. She said, "I went over every detail and every wrong I could remember. Five evenings and a box of tissues later, I was finished. I put it aside for a few days because I didn't know what to do with it.

"Later, I picked it up again and read it. I remember thinking, *That's odd, I thought I had forgiven him,* but the letter seems so angry. I suddenly thought of several things to include that were positive. I added them to the letter.

"A few days later the same thing happened. I remembered more of the good times. After a month of on-again, off-again writing, revising and rewriting, I had my finished product. It didn't sound at all like my original letter. Oh, it told the truth about what happened, but the anger and blame were gone. I really did forgive my dad. In a little private ceremony with my husband and my two older children, I burned the letter. I knew that I finally was free from my bitterness."

✎ **Check all of the following statements that are true of Barbara's story.**

    ○ 1. Barbara was unable to forgive until she expressed her anger.
    ○ 2. Expressing her anger resulted in greater bitterness and resentment.
    ○ 3. Barbara was unable to forgive genuinely until she identified the extent of the offense.
    ○ 4. Long-held feelings changed when Barbara finally expressed her anger with the purpose of forgiving.
    ○ 5. Barbara just needed to forget the past.

Barbara's experience shows the importance of a decision to forgive coupled with appropriate expression of feelings and adequate time. Answers 1, 3, and 4 are all true.

Self-check on Destructive Anger

✎ **How would you describe yourself in the way you express anger? (Place an *X* along the following scale in the appropriate spot.)**

Slow simmer (Silent treatment)	Fireworks (Lots of heat; little damage)	Atomic bomb (Explosive; damaging)

✎ **What specific things do you frequently do when you express anger? Why?**

_____

_____

✎ **Do particular people or situations seem to trigger your anger? If so, describe those people or situations.**

_____

_____

✎ **In the box in the margin write one example of how destructive anger has affected you and your relationships.**

A time when my destructive anger affected me was—

_____

_____

_____

_____

_____

In recovery you will begin to discover ways in which you can channel anger into positive action. Because you are releasing your grip on denial, you more often can admit feelings of anger. You first can admit them to yourself and then to God.

He learned to express his emotions to God.

King David is a good illustration of how to deal in a positive manner with emotions like anger. David's half-crazed father-in-law, Saul, who then was ruler over Israel, continually attacked David before David began his reign as king. Saul wanted to kill David. Under constant attack, David had every reason to be defensive and angry. Yet David both honored Saul and gained victory over his potentially destructive emotions because he learned to express those emotions to God. You may wish to read more about this in 1 Samuel 26:1-25 and Psalms 42 and 58.

David used his anger constructively; it drove him to his knees. Once you can admit that you are angry, you can ask God for His direction in your response. You can call your sponsor or a friend who can look with a non-biased point of view at your situation. Then, if necessary, you can confront the offender with wisdom and strength.

Key Concept for Lesson 4
I replace criticism and destructive anger with love, forgiveness, and honesty.

✎ **Pray and ask God how this concept can apply in your life. Now please review this lesson. What has God shown you that you can use?**

____

____

➔ **Say this Step's memory verse aloud five times.**

LESSON
5

Fear and Impatience

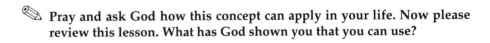

We make a searching, courageous moral inventory of ourselves.

> *Do not be afraid, little flock, for your Father has chosen gladly to give you the kingdom.*
>
> –Luke 12:32

Key Concept:
I replace fear and impulsiveness with trust and patience.

Satan tries to get people to accept another false belief—that they simply are products of their past and unable to change: *I am what I am. I am hopeless.*[2] Fear is one result of this false belief. The combination of impatience and impulsiveness is a second common result.

Fear: God's Warning System

Fear is a God-given emotional response to the awareness of danger. In proper perspective and in certain situations, fear is valuable. Fear prompts you to make decisions necessary for survival. You exercise fear wisely when you warn children to avoid playing with matches, to stay away from strangers, and to look both ways before crossing a street.

When we practice compulsive food behavior, however, fear usually controls our lives. Our response to it often is destructive. Fear blocks our ability to love, limits our social involvement, motivates us to avoid the risk of failure or rejection, and exposes our need to be in control. We schedule our lives around our food behaviors. Sometimes we hide food, our figures, and our behavior. Sometimes we lie about them. We do all of this in an attempt to gain control and security.

Even when we are in recovery, we still may be consumed by fear. We may be unable to sleep at night for fear of possible failure in our work or school performance. Afraid of failing, we may avoid anything that involves risk, including parties or other social situations which involve food. The fear of rejection may cause us to avoid meeting people and to avoid attending support-group meetings.

Feeling afraid is OK, but you do not have to allow this fear to consume you. Recovery gives you an opportunity to learn how to examine fear objectively and to use it constructively. Talking with a trusted friend about your fears to see if they're reasonable is helpful. Take your fears to God. He doesn't want you to be imprisoned by fear: "For God has not given us a spirit of timidity, but of power and love and discipline" (2 Timothy 1:7). His "perfect love casts out fear" (1 John 4:18).

"I'm afraid if I start eating I won't be able to stop."

"I'm afraid one bite will make me gain pounds."

Self-check on Fear

✎ **Which of these seems to have the greatest impact on you?**

_____ Fear of failure	_____ Shame: the fear of not
_____ Fear of rejection	being valued
_____ Fear of punishment	

✎ **How does fear control each of the following areas of your life? What are the results? (For example, fear of discovering cancer may cause you to put off going to a doctor. This could allow the disease to become more deadly.)**

	How fear controls you	What are the results?
Your attitudes		
Your actions		
Your relationships		
Your sense of freedom		

Trust: the Greatest Medicine of All

As we are released from the tyranny of our addiction, we develop the courage to acknowledge our fears and to move forward with our lives in spite of them. As we do, we exercise trust and discover truth.

Many of our fears are rooted in lies.

Many of our fears are rooted in lies. For example, you may have been convinced that you could not survive without your food behavior. Now you are learning that while recovery isn't easy, its benefits far outweigh the short-term gratification food—or the absence of it—once gave you. While that's the truth, you had to exercise some faith to find the truth.

You also needed faith when you placed your trust in Jesus Christ. Now you are discovering that He can do a better job of directing your life than you ever could have done alone. By developing trust in Him, you will begin to learn that you can afford to take the risks of getting to know some people and trying some new things. Fellowship helps your recovery. Remember this also: if a person rejects you, God still accepts you; if you fail, He still loves you.

Learn to trust God

You learn that because no human is consistent enough to merit your complete trust, you can learn to trust God completely and to trust people appropriately.

✎ **Go back to the last question you answered in the previous section about fear. Describe how trusting God can help you deal with fear in each of these areas.**

In your attitudes _____

_____

In your actions _____

_____

In your relationships _____

_____

In your sense of freedom _____

_____

Impatience and Impulsiveness: I Want What I Want—Now!

Impatience is a characteristic all addictions share. We have difficulty delaying gratification. We feel anxious as we wait impatiently for the three pizzas we ordered. We become angry while the person on the other side of the drive-through window slowly counts our change. Anxious to shed more pounds quickly, we take an entire box of laxatives only to wake up in the middle of the night in a cold sweat and with acute diarrhea.

Impatience carries over into our relationships. We bark orders. By our actions and attitudes we demand that others "shape up" and "get in line" NOW! We are impatient at work. We always hurry to meet deadlines. We hope to prove ourselves and hope to move to the top. Impatience leads to more anxiety and gives the eating disorder more power. Impatience carries over into other aspects of our lives. We spend money we don't have, steal food that isn't ours, and lie to those we love—all because we have little patience.

Self-check on Impatience and Impulsiveness

✎ **In what ways are you impatient or impulsive?**

_____

_____

✎ **What people and circumstances tend to bring out your impatience?**

People	Circumstances
_____	_____
_____	_____
_____	_____
_____	_____
_____	_____

✎ **Describe the consequences of impatience and impulsiveness in . . .**

your schoolwork/vocation: _____

your relationships: _____

your eating behavior: _____

Slow and Steady Wins the Race

One recovering Christian said, "Jesus does for me in a healthy way what my relationship to food did for me in a destructive way. Practicing my addiction calmed my fears, stabilized my feelings, and gave me the ability to cope. It did those things instantly but at a terrible price. Jesus is meeting those same needs, but He works more slowly. The difference is that with Christ I am learning to cope and to be proud of what He is accomplishing in my life. With my food addiction I felt progressively more ashamed and guilty. I am learning that the positive benefits of recovery are worth the wait."

Recovery provides an opportunity to learn patience.

Recovery provides an opportunity to learn patience. Gone is the need for an immediate escape and gratification the eating disorder once provided. Gone is the false sense of security when others act as rescuers and caretakers. The result is that we gradually recognize limitations and begin to slow down a little. We learn patience.

Developing patience

In recovery, you demonstrate patience each time you outlast an urge to binge, purge, or avoid a meal. You exercise patience when you begin to control your spending and other habits. You develop patience as you look for God's will and wait for His direction. Patience allows you to receive more enjoyment from others and to give more enjoyment to them.

Key Concept for Lesson 5
I replace fear and impulsiveness with trust and patience.

✎ **Pray and ask God how this concept can apply in your life. Now please review this lesson. What has God shown you that you can use?**

_____

_____

➙ **Memorize this Step's memory verse.**

Step Review

✎ **Step 4 says:** *We make a searching, courageous moral inventory of ourselves.* **Write in your own words what Step 4 means to you.**

_____

_____

_____

Describe how you plan to apply Step 4 daily to your life and recovery.

_____

_____

_____

Notes

[1]Robert S. McGee, *Search for Significance* LIFE Support Edition (Houston: Rapha Publishing, 1992), 11.
[2]Ibid.

Freedom Through Confession

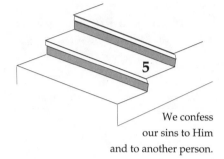

5

We confess
our sins to Him
and to another person.

A CAPTIVE OF FEAR

Carla's decision to surrender her eating disorder to God wasn't easy. In fact, she'd tried eight times in the last six months. But her determined effort was beginning to pay off. It had been more than a month since she had binged and purged.

For nearly two years she denied that she had a problem. She turned a deaf ear to concerned comments from friends and family. Finally a magazine story about a celebrity who had similar eating behaviors made her stop and think that what she was doing might not be normal. It took a long time, but eventually she admitted to God that her behavior was wrong and that she had been playing games with the truth. She really wanted to change now, and she began to make a conscious effort.

Something big stood in Carla's way: she feared being found out, admitting she was wrong for all these years, and having to face all the people she had hurt while she maintained her abnormal life-style. At first she experienced nervous tension, but soon she became physically ill at the very thought of having to reveal her past.

She had begun to date someone seriously. She knew she had to tell him, but the fear of rejection and of not being understood, accepted, and forgiven put a tremendous emotional and physical strain on her. The sleepless nights and the burning in her stomach were coming back. If only she could confide in someone . . . tell that person how she felt . . . trust him or her to accept her just as she was. (Read more about Carla on page 99.)

Step 5   *We admit to God, to ourselves, and to another person the exact nature of our wrongs.*

Memory verse   *Therefore, confess your sins to one another, and pray for one another, so that you may be healed.*

–James 5:16

Overview for Step 5

Lesson 1: Why Take the Fifth Step?
   Goal: You will define confession and describe four benefits that come from confession.
Lesson 2: Taking the Step, Part 1
   Goal: You will describe a key biblical teaching about confession.
Lesson 3: Taking the Step, Part 2
   Goal: You will make final preparation to share Step 5 with another person.

LESSON 1

Why Take the Fifth Step?

We admit to God, to ourselves, and to another person the exact nature of our wrongs.

> *But if we judged ourselves rightly, we should not be judged.*
> –1 Corinthians 11:31

Key Concept:
Taking Step 5 requires courage, but it pays great dividends.

You read Carla's story appearing on the unit page. Carla realized she needed to break the silence about her eating disorder. She began to attend a group where others modeled honesty. With great fear, she asked Nancy to be her sponsor. By the time she had progressed to Step 5 Carla knew she could trust Nancy. Carla wrote her Step 4 inventory, decided to tell Nancy her story even though she was afraid and nervous, and told her story to her sponsor. Carla broke the secrecy appropriately and is well on her way to a new life.

People working the 12 Steps almost always find two things to be true about Step 5. Of all the Steps, Step 5 is the most terrifying *before*—and the most freeing *after*—they take the Step. Many wonder later, *Why did it take me so long? If only I had known, I would have done this long ago.* The fear of blackmail is a powerful force. Most of us try to keep our "secret sins" hidden for fear that someone will expose us or someone will exploit the information about us. We may be unaware that our addiction has used the fear of exposure to maintain its control in our lives. Satan uses blackmail to rob us of the serenity God wants us to have and to keep us in slavery.

Our addiction has used the fear of exposure to maintain its control in our lives.

If you are like most people, you felt a sudden urge to protect your workbook and keep it confidential after you completed the exercises in Step 4. For the same reason, you may find it particularly difficult to admit your wrongs to God, to yourself, and to another person. Exposure can be threatening.

What Does It Mean to Confess?

It's one thing to confess to God, who already knows all about you, but quite another to confess to another person. Before finding out why confession to another person is necessary, read the meaning of **confess** printed in the margin.

confess–v. to speak the same thing, agree with, declare openly (Vine's)

 According to the definition, true confession to God includes which of the following? (Check all that apply.)

◯ 1. Revealing hidden things unknown to God
◯ 2. Being honest before God
◯ 3. Taking personal responsibility for my attitudes and actions
◯ 4. Telling God about another person's faults

True confession involves admitting to God what He already knows about me, being open and honest before Him, and taking personal responsibility for my sin. I cannot shock Him by revealing secrets He doesn't know. Answers 2 and 3 are parts of confession.

Someone may say, "God already knows everything about me. Why do I have to tell someone else?"

The Value of Confession

You will benefit four ways from breaking the silence by working Step 5.

- You will begin to experience genuine forgiveness.
- You will become capable of forgiving others.
- You will gain the ability to restore relationships with others—relationships you need for happy, effective living.
- You will remove an obstacle to the physical healing your body needs.

These four areas of benefit from confession will touch all aspects of your life—spiritual, mental, social, and physical.

Experiencing Forgiveness

The fact that God has forgiven you does not mean that you can experience that forgiveness. You still may be in slavery to feelings of guilt and shame.

Confess your sins to one another, and pray for one another, so that you may be healed.
–James 5:16

✎ **Read the verse in the margin. What three actions does James link together in the verse? On each of the lines below write a one-word description of the words James links. Then look for the practical application in Doug's story that follows.**

1. _____

2. _____

3. _____

More about Doug

For years Doug had been a committed Christian. He taught and served in his church. He genuinely loved the Lord. One problem remained a constant pain for Doug. It fueled his relapses and robbed him of his joy. No matter how much he accomplished, no matter how hard he tried, he never FELT forgiven. For as long as he could remember, Doug had felt that he was *worth less* than other people.

Because of his out-of-control eating, Doug joined the recovery group at his church. He never dreamed that he would be asked to talk to others about his secrets. Admitting his wrongs to God wasn't that difficult. Admitting them to himself was old hat for Doug. He constantly punished himself by reminding himself of his failings. But admitting the exact nature of his wrongs to another person—that simply was too much to ask.

Doug kept hearing others share the freedom and release they were experiencing by taking Steps 4 and 5. He finally could stand it no longer. He completed a written Step 4, and he made an appointment with his sponsor.

As Doug read the story about his life, he kept his head down. When he finished, he expected to hear his sponsor say, "Yuck, you are awful, and I never want to see you again." Instead, when Doug looked up, he saw a tear

Doug heard words of love and acceptance.

trickling down his sponsor's cheek. He heard words of love and acceptance. His sponsor understood and prayed for Doug, and Doug went away feeling more accepted and forgiven than ever before in his life. Now Doug encourages newcomers to work the Steps—especially Steps 4 and 5.

Did you note the connection in James 5:16 between confession, prayer, and healing? The most meaningful form of prayer is not a matter of religious words. It may be the blessing we give when we hear and accept another person's confession and when we together thank God for His cleansing and forgiveness. Did you see how the verse worked in Doug's life?

Many of us desperately need to experience forgiveness because deep-seated feelings of shame fuel our eating disorder. When we bring our hidden guilt and shame into the open with a sponsor, minister, counselor, or doctor— someone who has shown that he or she can be trusted—we somehow find it easier to receive forgiveness and experience freedom from the burden of our sins.

Extending Forgiveness to Others

The more you experience forgiveness, the more you will be able to forgive those who have hurt you. If you are honest with yourself, you may see that failing to forgive results from believing that you are morally superior—that as a victim, you have the right to go on accusing, despising, and denouncing those you refuse to forgive.

 Imagine that you are your food addiction—as if it were a living thing, perhaps a parasite. You must fight to stay alive and in control. Describe how you would use resentment and lack of forgiveness to maintain control.

_____

_____

Isolate and control

You may have noted that resentment stirs up many unpleasant emotions and memories. You could use that pain to drive your host to numb pain by returning to you—the addiction. The more you could isolate your victim, the greater control you could have in his or her life.

Restoring Our Relationships

Isolation is both a cause and a result of compulsive behavior. Addiction thrives on secrecy and aloneness. We avoid getting involved with others because we feel inferior to them or because we fear they will hurt us. To make up for these painful feelings, we turn for comfort to our food or our figure obsession.

Our obsessive behavior causes us to be anxious about the possibility that others will discover us. Anxiety then drives us further into the addiction. As a result, we feel the intense pain that accompanies loneliness and isolation. We have the powerful and unshakable feeling that we not only are alone in our struggle but that we also are odd, different, and unique in every bad way.

Something surprising happens when we disclose our harmful behavior to another human being. We learn that unacceptable patterns of behavior do not make us unacceptable people. We also learn that we are not so odd or different or unique after all! This is especially true if we summon the courage to share parts of our moral inventory with a therapy or support group.

Surprisingly, the thing we feared so much—disclosing what we considered to be our sheer awfulness—becomes the vehicle we need to end our desperate, aching loneliness and isolation. When we disclose ourselves to others and allow them to do the same with us, we obey the apostle Paul's words appearing in the margin.

Brothers, if someone is caught in a sin, you who are spiritual should restore him gently. But watch yourself, or you also may be tempted. Carry each other's burdens, and in this way you will fulfill the law of Christ.
—Galatians 6:1-2, NIV

Taking Step 5 is a channel for change and healing because it frees us from our old eating-disordered patterns of secret shame, secret compulsion, and isolation. In restoring damaged relationships, we not only open ourselves up again to receive help from others, we put ourselves in a position to experience the joy of giving help to those who need it.

Rebuilding Our Bodies

Our decision to forgive others and accept God's forgiveness directly affects our health. In Psalm 32, David testifies to unconfessed sin's powerful impact on his body.

When I kept silent about my sin, my body wasted away through my groaning all day long. For day and night Thy hand was heavy upon me; my vitality was drained away as with the fever heat of summer.
—Psalm 32:3-4

 Again, in Psalm 38, David shares the destructive power of sin on the human body. Read the passage below. Underline words that describe these effects.

Because of your wrath there is no health in my body; my bones have no soundness because of my sin. My guilt has overwhelmed me like a burden too heavy to bear. My wounds fester and are loathsome because of my sinful folly. I am bowed down and brought very low; all day long I go about mourning. My back is filled with searing pain; there is no health in my body. I am feeble and utterly crushed; I groan in anguish of heart. All my longings lie open before you, O Lord; my sighing is not hidden from you. My heart pounds, my strength fails me; even the light has gone from my eyes.
—Psalm 38:3-10, NIV

Circle the words in the passage above that you have experienced as a result of attempting to hide or cover your sin.

By God's grace, through the confession of our sin, we can begin to be released from sin's terrible consequences. By accepting forgiveness and forgiving others we free our minds and bodies to begin the natural healing processes God created.

Sometimes, as a result of long-term abuse, vindictive anger, or refusal to forgive, damage to the body is quite significant. If that is the case with you, trust God to do His will in your life. Remember that healing is a process and rarely occurs overnight. Though He may not immediately heal your body He always will give you the grace to meet each physical need.

> ### Key Concept for Lesson 1
> Taking Step 5 requires courage, but it pays great dividends.

➜ **Memorize this Step's memory verse, James 5:16.**

Taking the Step, Part 1

LESSON 2

Key Concept:
Understanding the biblical teaching about confession makes me willing to take Step 5.

We admit to God, to ourselves, and to another person the exact nature of our wrongs.

> *My enemies speak evil against me, "When will he die, and his name perish?"*
>
> –Psalm 41:5

Before going further in Step 5, understand that your confession does not make you forgiven. You are forgiven because Christ died to pay for your sins. Confession is a means for you to experience your forgiveness, not a way to obtain it. As an example look at what happened to King David, one of God's mightiest leaders, when he turned to God under the weight of unconfessed sin.

> Many of us immediately feel shame when we hear the word *sin*. Please understand that when the Bible talks of sin, it refers to the spiritual disease which afflicts every human being. God hates sin because sin harms the people He loves. Admitting to our sin is not shameful. Confessing our sin is honest and courageous. Pretending we have no sin is shameful.
>
> This material is intended to help you overcome shame. It is not intended to make you feel shame.

David: a Man After God's Heart

God called David, the shepherd, psalmist, and king of Israel, a man after His own heart (1 Samuel 13:14). But like all humans, David sinned. He committed what people would consider gross sins. He committed adultery. Then, to cover that sin, he arranged to have Bathsheba's husband killed (See 2 Samuel 11.)

 Complete the following checklist to compare your sin with that of King David. Check each sin of which you are guilty.

- ○ adultery
- ○ lying
- ○ betrayal of a loyal friend
- ○ premeditated murder

These were only four of the sins of King David, yet God called him "a man after My own heart." You probably did not check all four of the acts on the previous page. Even if you checked all four, God is just as loving and willing to forgive you as He was David.

Often we feel that we are different from others—that what we have done is unforgivable. We desperately need to bring some objectivity to our offenses. Yes, all sin is bad. It injures us and others. It grieves God. Unfortunately the most damaging thing may be the way Satan uses what we have done to tell us that we are unforgivable.

✎ **God not only forgave King David, He greatly loved him in spite of his sin. Is it reasonable to assume God will forgive you and that He loves you in spite of things you have done? ❍ Yes ❍ No**

What made David a man after God's heart was his attitude. He not only was sorry for his sin, but he confessed it, and then he repented (turned from it). Look at Psalm 32 to see the process of David's reconciliation to God:

How blessed is he whose transgression is forgiven, Whose sin is covered! How blessed is the man to whom the Lord does not impute iniquity, And in whose spirit there is no deceit!
–Psalm 32:1-2

✎ **Read Psalm 32:1-2 in the margin at left. What word does David use to describe the one whose transgression is forgiven?**

____

David describes as blessed the person who is forgiven. Blessed means happy, joyful—as when a person gets something wonderful and undeserved.

✎ **Describe what you think it would be like to FEEL forgiven and accepted.**

____

____

When I kept silent about my sin, my body wasted away Through my groaning all day long. For day and night Thy hand was heavy upon me; my vitality was drained away as with the fever heat of summer.
–Psalm 32:3-4

✎ **Read Psalm 32:3-4. What happened to David's body when he kept silent about his sin?**

____

What happens to your body when you keep silent about your eating disorder? Be specific.

____

____

____

Secrecy makes us feel isolated and alone. We become more depressed. The pain becomes greater. Confession is difficult and painful, but it brings blessing in the long run.

➔ **Look back to page 102, in which these verses were discussed. Review some of the effects of sin you've seen in your own life. Can you pray and thank God for giving you the courage to see this painful truth?**

I acknowledge my sin to Thee, And my iniquity I did not hide; I said, "I will confess my transgressions to the Lord"; and Thou didst forgive the guilt of my sin.

–Psalm 32:5

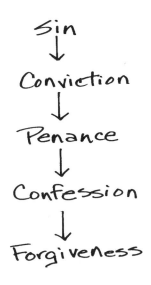

✎ **Read Psalm 32:5. What did David do about his sin?**

_____

What was God's response? _____

_____

David confessed his sin openly to God; that is, he agreed with what God already knew about him. And God forgave him.

Accepting Forgiveness: Part of Confession

All too often, Christians play a game of penance which they believe they must put themselves through before they can feel forgiven. Once convicted of a sin, they might plead with God for forgiveness and then feel depressed for a couple of days just to show that they really are sorry and deserve to be forgiven. They are attempting to *pay for their own sins* by feeling bad.

You cannot earn forgiveness by punishing yourself. Confession is simply an application of the forgiveness you already have in Christ. Accepting your forgiveness allows you to move on with the Lord and serve Him joyfully.

You may be preparing to confess your sins to God for the first time. If you need some help, you might use the prayer below as a guide.

> Dear Father,
> The Holy Spirit has shown me that I sinned when I (*name your sins of thought and action as specifically as possible*). Thank You that I am completely forgiven. I realize that You have declared me to be deeply loved, completely forgiven, fully pleasing, totally accepted, and a new creature—complete in Christ. Amen.

➛ **Stop and pray. Ask God to help you develop the habit of immediately confessing your sins to Him as soon as you commit them or recognize them. Thus you will minimize the amount of lost time in your fellowship with God and will maximize His work of healing in and through you.**

> ### Key Concept for Lesson 2
> Understanding the biblical teaching about confession makes me willing to take Step 5.

✎ **Pray and ask God how this concept can apply in your life. Now please review this lesson. What has God shown you that you can use?**

_____

_____

→ **Below write James 5:16 from memory. If necessary see page 98 to check the verse.**

_____

_____

LESSON 3

Taking the Step, Part 2

We admit to God, to ourselves, and to another person the exact nature of our wrongs.

> *He who conceals his transgressions will not prosper, but he who confesses and forsakes them will find compassion.*
>
> –Proverbs 28:13

Key Concept:
Keeping secrets results in slavery, while confession brings relief and joy.

Choosing a Good Listener

With a better understanding of what it means to confess your wrongs to God, you are ready to analyze the best way to complete Step 5 successfully. Begin by determining who will be the best person for you to talk with. Choosing a good listener is extremely important. In fact, make this choice only after you consider it prayerfully.

The following may help you in your selection process. Pray with these guidelines in mind for a person to hear you share your fifth Step.

1. Choose someone who has completed several years in recovery, or who at least is familiar with the 12 Steps, especially Step 5 and the issues involved in eating disorders. This person should see Step 5 as a crucial task. It can mean the difference between recovery and returning to an eating-disordered behavior. A person who is in a 12-Step program, especially for eating disorders, and who has spent some time in the program, will understand this Step's importance for you and your recovery.

2. Choose someone who can keep a confidence. The information you are preparing to disclose is very personal. Select someone who is completely trustworthy.

3. Choose an objective listener. This is not yet the time (it may never be) to talk openly with those who are emotionally involved with you and who may find that what you have to say is more than they can bear. Be considerate. Sharing is a responsibility.

4. Choose someone who may be willing to share personal examples from his or her own life with you. The person with whom you talk should be a good listener, but often through a two-way exchange you will find the acceptance you especially need right now.

List some people who might be good listeners for you.

_____

_____

Call the person you have selected and set a time to meet and talk. Your sponsor is an obvious choice. If you do not have a sponsor, tell your listener about your involvement in the 12-Step program. Explain that sharing your confession with him or her would be a major step in your recovery.

Give the person the opportunity to bow out graciously if he or she is uncomfortable and chooses not to listen. If that happens, simply select another listener.

Telling Your Story

Once you have found a good listener who has agreed to hear you, prepare your story. The process usually works best when you present it as a story—the story of your life.

Break the silence

Perhaps the best way to prepare is by taking some notes. Start from the very beginning and recall people, circumstances, and events that have affected you most along the way. You can, of course, refer back continually to Step 4 to help you recount all the significant things you have done—positive and negative—over the years.

When you finally sit down with the person you've chosen—your sponsor, pastor, counselor, physician, or trusted friend—you can read from your notes or refer back to them as an outline. This is up to you. The point is to get it ALL out—everything that is significant about your life that never has been said.

> **BOUNDARY ISSUE: Getting it all out does not mean all the sordid details. Notice carefully the wording of the Step. We admit _the exact nature of our wrongs_. The nature of our wrongs refers to their character or qualities.**

One final word of caution is in order as you write your story. Some people who take Step 5 are disappointed because they experience no immediate feelings of relief afterward. Some people feel guilty because they told the secrets they harbored so closely and so long.

Feelings do not determine the success of the Step.

Feelings do not determine the success of Step 5. The Step is successful when you disclose the significant events in your life which you need to share with another person. Think about this before you complete this Step so that you can be realistic in your expectations.

Finally, remember that this Step is for _you_. Regardless of whom you choose to share yourself with, realize that your purpose in taking this Step is not to please the listener but to gain healing for yourself.

Story Outline

The following outline will help you to write your story. You will need to use additional pages. Use as much paper and as much time as you need to do a thorough job, but do not feel that the Step must be done perfectly. Most people in recovery repeat this Step later when they become more aware of issues and circumstances in their lives.

✎ **What was your life like when you were a child? (Describe your relationships with your parents, brothers, and sisters).**

_____

_____

_____

_____

_____

How has your home life affected you?

_____

_____

_____

_____

_____

✎ **When did you first begin your compulsive eating behavior(s)?**

_____

_____

_____

_____

_____

✎ **Go back through the questions in Step 4. Explain in detail how your eating disorder has affected—**

Your self-esteem:

_____

_____

_____

Your relationships with your friends:

_____

_____

_____

_____

Your job or school:

_____

_____

_____

_____

Your health:

_____

_____

_____

_____

Your values:

_____

_____

_____

_____

Your relationship with God:

_____

_____

_____

_____

Congratulations on completing the writing of your story. As you share it, remember the truths of this unit: Keeping secrets brings slavery, while confession brings relief and joy. The Holy Spirit gives us power and encouragement to take Step 5.

but speaking the truth in love, we are to grow up in all aspects into Him, who is the head, even Christ.

–Ephesians 4:15

➜ Pray about each item you have just written. Surrender to God the memory and impact of each item in the list, whether they be good or bad. As you do so, draw a small cross beside each item. The cross indicates that Christ covered the item with His blood at Calvary.

➜ This is where you keep your appointment to tell your story to your chosen listener. Before you begin, pray and ask God to give you a clear mind and a humble spirit. Ask the Holy Spirit to help you speak the truth in love (Ephesians 4:15). Remember, you are *revisiting* your past, not *reliving* it. End by recognizing God's forgiveness and ongoing work in your life.

Key Concept for Lesson 3
Keeping secrets results in slavery, while confession brings relief and joy.

➜ Memorize this Step's memory verse.

Step Review

✎ **Step 5 says:** *We admit to God, to ourselves, and to another person the exact nature of our wrongs.* **Write in your own words what Step 5 means to you.**

_____

_____

_____

_____

Describe how you plan to apply Step 5 daily to your life and recovery.

_____

_____

_____

_____

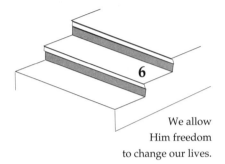

STEP 6

6

We allow
Him freedom
to change our lives.

Acting in Faith

GIVING UP ON PERFECTION

Sandy had been in treatment for several weeks. She originally thought her problem was anorexia alone. Now she was beginning to understand that her underlying problem was control. Sandy was a perfectionist. She thought, *If I can just do and be perfect, then people will love me.* Her eating disorder was an expression of her driving need to be perfect.

Sandy was ready to accept the fact that perfectionism was a problem. She was not ready for what came next. Her therapist assigned three of the other women in treatment to style Sandy's hair and apply her makeup. She said Sandy must allow each of the women to give her a makeover for one of three consecutive days, and Sandy must not change her "look" for the entire day. She told the three women to follow one guideline. They were to change Sandy's normally immaculate appearance.

The second day of the assignment Peggy was Sandy's makeup artist. To Sandy's horror she painted Sandy like a punk rocker. Worse still, she streaked her hair purple and orange—SPIKED. Sandy was horrified—and her parents were arriving for a visit. They were taking her out to a restaurant.

Sandy begged and pleaded, but her therapist wouldn't budge. "You told me you want to get well, so this is what you have to do," she said.

Sandy says her recovery took a giant step forward that day. Sandy obeyed orders. She learned that she didn't have to be perfect. She would live, even if she looked like a nightmare. Sandy is going to make it.

Step 6 *We commit ourselves to God and desire that He remove patterns of sin from our lives.*

Memory verse *Humble yourselves in the presence of the Lord, and He will exalt you.*
–James 4:10

Overview for Step 6 **Lesson 1: Becoming Willing to Obey**
Goal: You will recognize and surrender obstacles to your commitment to Christ.
Lesson 2: Positive Reasons to Obey
Goal: You will evaluate and choose six proper motivations for obedience.
Lesson 3: Harmful Reasons to Obey
Goal: You will evaluate and choose to avoid four improper motivations for obedience.
Lesson 4: Ownership and Conduct
Goal: You freely will choose the role of a servant of the Lord Jesus Christ.

Becoming Willing to Obey

We commit ourselves to God and desire that He remove patterns of sin from our lives.

> *Delight yourself in the Lord; And He will give you the desires of your heart.*
>
> –Psalm 37:4

Key Concept:
I experience fulfillment when God's desires become my desires.

The verse from Psalm 37 contains an important principle. The psalmist says "Delight yourself in the Lord." As a result God will give you the desires of your heart.

✎ **If I delight myself in the Lord, which of the following will be desires of my heart?**

○ 1. financial security;
○ 2. the love and acceptance of other people;
○ 3. happiness;
○ 4. fellowship with God;
○ 5. self-respect;
○ 6. God's approval.

Whoever wishes to save his life shall lose it; but whoever loses his life for My sake shall find it.
–Matthew 16:25

The principle the psalm contains is the paradox Jesus stated in the verse in the margin. When we seek financial security, acceptance by others, happiness, or even our own self-respect, we find frustration. But if our goal is God's approval and fellowship—if we delight in Him—He will give us the desires of our hearts. The catch is that the desires of our hearts no longer will be exclusively for the items listed by answers 1, 2, 3, or 5. The desires of our heart will be primarily for the items listed in answers 4 and 6.

Jesus used many ways to teach the principle behind Step 6. He taught and demonstrated that the key to life was to have the Father's will as our will. He knew the tragic results of being self-centered. When God's will is first in our lives, however, the results ultimately are positive.

When you can grasp this principle, you will begin to understand the power of Step 6. *We cannot overcome our addictions by our own will.* We cannot make ourselves do the things that are best for us. Step 6 is not a decision to accomplish something as much as it is a willingness to have God's priorities as our priorities. When our goal is to be happy, we are certain to fail in the end. When our goal is to love God and have a relationship with Him, He eventually gives happiness as a by-product.

Seek first His kingdom and his righteousness; and all these things shall be added to you.
–Matthew 6:33

Read Matthew 6:33 that appears in the margin. This is another way Jesus taught the same principle.

As we work Step 6 we seek to become persons who desire God's will. We work the Step knowing that we will experience victory to the degree that we can say with Jesus, "My food is to do the will of him who sent me" (John 4:34). We change our desires to match His desires by honestly facing reality and by overcoming false beliefs about God.

Why We Can't Stop Alone

Many of us with eating disorders share at least one common experience. Our friends and family members don't understand why we can't stop the harmful things we do to our bodies.

"Look, I don't understand," someone who knew about your disorder may have said. "Why don't you just stop this goofy behavior? It can't be *that* difficult." Indeed, when you tried to stop your actions in the past, you may have asked yourself the same question. *This really is bizarre behavior. Why can't I just make up my mind and knock it off?*

Changing our motivations

Then we discovered in Step 1 that we were powerless over our compulsion. We needed spiritual help to overcome our addictions. We examined our lives and confessed our sins. Now we recognize that we need God to change more than just our compulsive food behavior. Our very motivations need to be changed. We have grown accustomed to a way of thinking which stresses relief from pain over genuine change. In fact, most of us came to recovery to stop the pain rather than to make great changes in our values or ways of relating to others.

If we are honest with ourselves, we will recognize that we have long-established patterns of sinful behavior in our lives. We hang on to these patterns because they seem to meet important needs in our lives.

✎ **The following two paragraphs describe some of these patterns of behavior. Underline the two key forms of behavior the paragraphs described. Think about your life. Circle any phrase that describes an action you have done or are doing.**

People-pleasing means we need not risk confronting others with the truth. We can be "nice" and avoid the unpleasantness that often accompanies confrontation. Some of us are afraid of being close to people. We use our "niceness" as a way to please people and avoid the threat of confrontation or of intimacy.

These behaviors are my attempt to—

_____

_____

_____

_____

_____

_____

_____

Perfectionism often receives a lot of positive reinforcement in the workplace (never mind that it can drive you to destroy yourself as you relentlessly pursue the "perfect" body weight or size). In pursuit of perfection, we may blame others for past hurts and thereby feel superior to them. We may have learned to lie and steal and shield ourselves in secrecy to maintain our sense of control, and now the truth often is difficult to tell—even about things that have nothing to do with our eating behavior. It may be easier to lie than to tell the truth; to shoplift instead of pay, even when we have the money; to withdraw and hide from others instead of talking to them. These patterns of sin and others now are as impossible to conquer by willpower alone as our eating disorder was.

The two types of behavior were people-pleasing and perfectionism. Did you identify with such actions as avoiding confrontation, feeling superior, or learning to lie, steal, and keep secrets?

✎ **What need in your life is people-pleasing and/or perfectionism an attempt to meet? Write your answer in the margin box on the left.**

Don't Give in to Shame

Avoid falling into the trap of believing, *I am what I am. I cannot change. I am hopeless.*[1] God not only has promised us freedom, healing, and eternal life, but He has promised a changed life. This is the purpose of Step 6. As we place our lives in His hands and willingly agree that His ways are right, we allow Him to remove our self-destructive behavior patterns and to reform our will to match His will.

Our compulsive nature wants the "big fix."

This is not a one-time event. Our compulsive nature wants the "big fix" and wants it NOW! God is interested in our journey—in how we run the race. Even more important to Him is the runner, not the race. As we run, we grow and mature. And as we run, God perfects us in Himself. But the course of the race itself is a lifetime journey. Step 6, then, is not just a step along the way, but it is a commitment to a new way of life and a continued surrender to the Lord of life.

Fears About God

We may experience difficulty trusting God because we fear Him. Many people who have eating disorders have one or more of the seven attitudes about God that follow.[2] These faulty views often prove to be powerful obstacles to commitment to God.

We think God chooses us only to use us.

1. God is mean. Many people do not believe God has their best interests at heart. They think He chooses us only to use us. They serve Him through an increasing number of activities out of fear that He will punish them if they don't please Him.

✎ **What about you? Do you ever have this fear? If so, who or what convinced you that God wants to use and abuse you?**

_____

_____

2. God demands too much. Some fear they'll never measure up to the extremely high expectations of the Christian life. A double-edged sword motivates them. They fear failure to meet every Christian standard, and they feel guilt for having failed. They may give lip service to grace and forgiveness, but they experience demands and expectations.

✎ **What about you? Do you ever have this fear? If so, who or what convinced you that God demands too much?**

_____

_____

3. I'm already trying as hard as I can; what more can I do? When we feel guilt for inadequately meeting the demands of our harsh, strict concept of God, we soon find ourselves also feeling anger. Unfortunately, we often turn this anger against ourselves, a friend, a family member, or the church. Why? Because we believe that *no one* can express anger toward God or can admit feeling anger toward God.

✎ **What about you? Do you ever have this fear? If so, who or what convinced you that God cannot tolerate your anger?**

_____

_____

_____

More about Annie

Annie had been a perfectionist for as long as she could remember. She thought God was the ultimate perfectionist. She felt that He would not accept anything less than absolute perfection, and she believed He certainly would not tolerate anger. Annie was in a terrible double bind. She was angry about many things in her life, but she could not express anger because she feared that God would reject her.

One day Annie's sponsor gave her a most unusual assignment. She said, "I want you to read Jeremiah 20:7-18, and I want you to do what Jeremiah did."

✎ **Read Jeremiah's words that are printed in the margin. What was Jeremiah feeling? What did he do with his feelings?**

_____

_____

O Lord, you deceived me, and I was deceived; you overpowered me and prevailed. I am ridiculed all day long; everyone mocks me. Cursed be the day I was born! May the man who brought my father the news who made him very glad, saying, "A child is born to you—a son!" May that man be like the towns the Lord overthrew without pity. May he hear wailing in the morning, a battle cry at noon. For he did not kill me in the womb, with my mother as my grave, her womb enlarged forever. Why did I ever come out of the womb to see trouble and sorrow and to end my days in shame?
—Jeremiah 20:7,14-18

Annie read the passage and discovered that Jeremiah was feeling depressed and angry. She was amazed to find that he expressed his anger not only to God but at God. Annie began to understand her sponsor's point. If God is able to take Jeremiah's anger—and still love him, then just maybe God could take Annie's anger as well.

4. I don't want to lose control of my life. We live our lives attempting to control every detail, activity, and emotion. We encounter great internal difficulty when we try to turn control of our lives over to another person—even to the Lord.

✎ **What about you? Do you ever have this fear? If so, who or what convinced you that you must never "lose control" of your life?**

_____

_____

5. God will make me into something "weird." We already are lonely people. We feel distant and alienated from others who are supposed to be close family or friends. When we hear stories of those who stand for Christ and who suffer ridicule or rejection, we are not drawn to the Christian life. We feel neither safety nor assurance in such a choice. We fear that if we really become committed to God, He will send us as a missionary to some far-off place or will make us do all the things we hate.

✎ **What about you? Do you ever have this fear? If so, who or what convinced you that God will make you into something weird?**

_____

_____

6. I only earn worth by serving God. You've been reading about the fears that push us away from God and from the Christian life. This is the other side of that coin. Some Christians with eating disorders see serving God as a means of earning security and worth. Rather than backing away from extreme kinds of commitment, they plunge headfirst into Christian activities. They hope God and others will give them recognition of their value and worth as persons. They feel the same fears as those listed above, but their thirst for approval drives them to take risks others won't take. They do this to become acceptable to others and to God.

✎ **What about you? Do you ever have this fear? If so, who or what convinced you that you only earn worth by serving God?**

_____

_____

7. If God loves me, He won't ask me to do anything difficult. We sometimes read the Scriptures selectively. We pick out passages that soothe, and we overlook passages that prompt guilt feelings. We may focus entirely on one aspect of God's character such as His love and never hear the balance or see the larger perspective of biblical teachings.

A larger perspective

✎ **What about you? Do you ever have this fear? If so, who or what convinced you that God won't ask you to do anything difficult because He loves you?**

_____

_____

✎ **Reread your responses to the seven fears you've studied today. Use those thoughts to write a prayer to God about how you feel and what you need to share with God about your fears.**

_____

_____

_____

_____

```
┌─────────────────────────────────────────────┐
│            Key Concept for Lesson 1           │
│   I experience fulfillment when God's desires become │
│   my desires.                                 │
└─────────────────────────────────────────────┘
```

✎ **Pray and ask God how this concept can apply in your life. Now please review this lesson. What has God shown you that you can use?**

_____

_____

Humble yourselves in the presence of the Lord, and He will exalt you.

–James 4:10

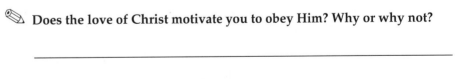

✎ **Copy the words of James 4:10 three times to help you memorize this Step's memory verse.**

_____

_____

_____

_____

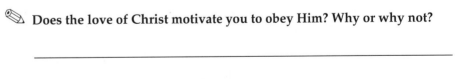

LESSON 2

Key Concept:
Appropriate motivations lead me to faithful and loving service.

If you love Me, you will keep My commandments. . . . He who has My commandments and keeps them, he it is who loves Me; and he who loves Me shall be loved by My Father, and I will love him, and will disclose Myself to him.

–John 14:15,21

For the love of Christ controls us, having concluded this, that one died for all, therefore all died; and He died for all, that they who live should no longer live for themselves, but for Him who died and rose again on their behalf.

–2 Corinthians 5:14-15

Positive Reasons to Obey

We commit ourselves to God and desire that He remove patterns of sin from our lives.

> *Do not let sin reign in your mortal body that you should obey its lusts.*
> –Romans 6:12

God bases His love and acceptance on His grace—His unmerited favor—not on our ability to impress Him through our good deeds. If He accepts us on the basis of His grace and not our deeds, why should we obey God? According to scriptural principles, at least six proper motivations for obedience exist. In this lesson, you will examine these six motivations.

1. Christ's love motivates us. Our obedience to God expresses our love for Him. We love because He first loved us and at the cross clearly demonstrated His love for us. (See the verses at left.) This great motivation is missing in many of our lives because we really don't believe that God loves us unconditionally. We expect His love to be based on our ability to earn it.

Our perceptions are the basis for how we experience God's love. If we believe that He is demanding or distant, we will not experience His love and tenderness. We either will be afraid of Him or angry with Him. Our concept of God is the basis for all our motivations. As we grow in understanding His unconditional love and acceptance, we increasingly will want our lives to bring honor to the One who loves us so much.

✎ **Does the love of Christ motivate you to obey Him? Why or why not?**

_____

_____

2. Sin is destructive. God's plans for my life always are for my good. Disobeying God always causes pain and hurt, although the pain may be delayed or disguised. Satan has blinded us to the painful, damaging consequences of sin. Sooner or later sin always will result in some form of destruction.

Sin is destructive in many ways. Emotionally, it brings guilt, shame, and fear of failure or punishment. Mentally, we spend our time and energy thinking about our sins and rationalizing our guilt. Physically, it contributes to a number of illnesses. Relationally, it separates us from others. Spiritually, we grieve the Holy Spirit, lose our testimony, and break our fellowship with God.

✎ **Think of a time you have disobeyed God and experienced painful consequences. Below write a summary of that experience. In your summary include what you can learn from the experience.**

_____

_____

Satan is the master deceiver. He whispers promising suggestions to us. When these thoughts first enter the mind, they speak only about pleasure and never about sin's devastating consequences. When such an occasion happens to you, would it help to remember the example you wrote above? ○ Yes ○ No

If so, why? _____

_____

> My son, do not regard lightly the discipline of the Lord, nor faint when you are reproved by Him; for those whom the Lord loves He disciplines.
>
> –Hebrews 12:5-6

3. The Father's discipline trains us. If sin is so destructive, why doesn't God do something about it? The answer is, He does. He lovingly but firmly disciplines His children. See what the verse at left says about disobeying God. Discipline is not punishment. Punishment is venting one's anger about an offense. Discipline is training. God is training us to live effectively and to obey Him for His glory and our good. That God disciplines us is a proof that we belong to Him. The following chart shows the profound difference between discipline and punishment:

Punishment vs. Discipline		
	Punishment	**Discipline**
Source:	God's wrath	God's love
Purpose:	To avenge a wrong	To correct a wrong
Relational result:	Alienation	Reconciliation
Personal result:	Guilt	A righteous life-style
Directed toward:	Non-believers	His children

Jesus took all our punishment on the cross; we no longer have to fear punishment from God for our sins. We seek to obey out of love and wisdom. When we sin and are disciplined, we can remember that God corrects us in love so that we may be like Christ.

God corrects us in love so that we may be like Christ.

4. God's commands for us are good. God gives commands to protect us from the harm of sin and to lead us to a life of effective service and victory. Many people view God's commands only as restrictions on their lives. We need to see these commands as guidelines which God gives us that we may live life to the fullest. God's commands are holy, right, and good. They have value in themselves. To choose to obey God and follow His commands always is best.

✎ **Check all the reasons why God's commands for you are good.**

○ 1. He knows the complete results of an action.
○ 2. He loves me and has my best interest at heart.
○ 3. He doesn't want me to have any fun.
○ 4. He wants to protect me from harm.
○ 5. Only He knows what joys await my faithfulness.
○ 6. His purpose is to develop my character.

Avoid trying to use legalism and your own efforts to keep God's commands. That leads to bitterness, condemnation, and rigidity. The Holy Spirit will give you power, joy, and creativity as you trust Him to fulfill the commands of God's Word through you. All the answers were correct—except answer 3.

5. God will reward our obedience. Our self-worth is not based on our performance and obedience, but our actions make a huge difference in the quality of our lives and in our impact on others. Disobedience results in spiritual poverty; it short-circuits intimate fellowship with God, causes confusion and guilt, and robs us of spiritual power and the desire to see people won to Christ. Obedience enables us to experience His love, joy, and strength. It also enables us to minister to others, to endure difficulties, and to live for Him. We are completely loved, forgiven, and accepted apart from our performance, but how we live is very important!

How we live is very important!

✎ **Which of the results of disobedience mentioned in the paragraph above have you experienced in your life?**

_____

Which were most painful? _____

_____

Which of the benefits of obedience are you enjoying? _____

_____

6. Christ is worthy. Our most noble reason for serving Christ simply is that He is worthy of our love and obedience. Each time we choose to obey, we express the righteousness of Christ. Our performance, then, reflects who we are in Him. We draw on His power and wisdom so that we can honor Him.

✎ **Write in the margin the six reasons you have just read for being willing to have Christ as Lord of our lives. Review the chapter if necessary.**

Now go back and rank your list from the most important to the least important. Be prepared to share with your group or sponsor your results.

Six Reasons to Obey

1. _____
2. _____
3. _____
4. _____
5. _____
6. _____

Key Concept for Lesson 2
Appropriate motivations lead me to faithful and loving service.

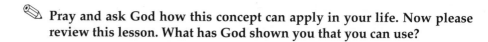 Pray and ask God how this concept can apply in your life. Now please review this lesson. What has God shown you that you can use?

_____

_____

Memorize this Step's memory verse:
Humble yourselves in the presence of the Lord, and He will exalt you.

–James 4:10

Harmful Reasons to Obey

<table>
<tr><td>

LESSON

3

</td></tr>
</table>

Key Concept:
My wrong motives lead to false obedience, bitterness, and resentment.

We commit ourselves to God and desire that He remove patterns of sin from our lives.

> *But the goal of our instruction is love from a pure heart and a good conscience and a sincere faith.*
>
> –1 Timothy 1:5

Unfortunately higher, purer, motives alone do not always motivate us. Sometimes lower motivations like fear or even greed drive us. We begin to obey to feel accepted or to earn self-worth. We attempt to maintain an image of performance in front of God and people. Jesus repeatedly emphasized that He not only is concerned about *what* we do but also about *why* we do it. The Pharisees obeyed many rules, but their hearts were far from God. Motives are important! The following are poor motives for obeying God and their possible results:

1. Someone may find out. We may obey God because we fear what others will think of us if we don't. Allen visited prospects for his church because he feared what his Sunday School class would think if he didn't. Karen contributed to the employee benevolence fund at her office. She feared what her friend, the fund drive chairperson, would think if she didn't.

Basing our behavior on others' opinions is not wise. Times will occur when no one is watching. Our desire to disobey eventually may exceed the peer pressure to obey. Once someone finds out we've sinned, we no longer may have a reason to obey. The biggest problem with this type of obedience is that it isn't obedience at all. It is purely self-interest.

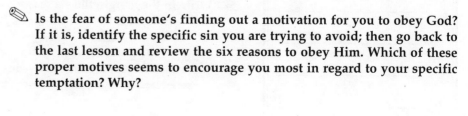 Is the fear of someone's finding out a motivation for you to obey God? If it is, identify the specific sin you are trying to avoid; then go back to the last lesson and review the six reasons to obey Him. Which of these proper motives seems to encourage you most in regard to your specific temptation? Why?

_____

_____

2. God will be angry with me. We sometimes obey God because we think He will get angry with us if we don't. We have discussed the difference between God's discipline and punishment, but we will state this again: God disciplines us in love, not anger. His response to our sin is grief, not condemnation.

Hank was afraid that God would "zap" him if he did anything wrong, so he performed for God. He lived each day fearing God's anger. As you might expect, Hank's relationship with the Lord was cold and mechanical. God doesn't want us to live in fear of His anger but in response to His love. Living in response to His love produces joyful obedience instead of fear.

God doesn't want us to live in fear of His anger but in response to His love.

→ **Pray and ask God to show you ways you can change this feeling of unhealthy fear. Take time to recall what you have been learning in recovery.**

✎ **Now write as many ways as possible that you can change your attitude toward God from an unhealthy fear to a healthy love and respect.**

_____

_____

You may have written such answers as: *I can be honest and voice my feelings and complaints to God; I can meditate on Scripture and on Jesus' love and sacrifice for me; I can write about my feelings; I can share feelings honestly with another person.*

3. I couldn't approve of myself if I didn't obey. Some people obey rules in an attempt to live up to standards they've set for themselves. In doing this they are not yielding their lives to a loving Lord. They are trying to avoid the feeling of shame that occurs when they don't meet their own standards. These people primarily are concerned with do's and don'ts. Instead of an intimate relationship with God, they see the Christian life as a ritual—as a life emphasizing rules. If they succeed in keeping the rules, they become prideful. They compare themselves with others. They hope others will accept them because they are a little bit better than someone else.

Emphasizing rules

Philip was reared in a strict church family. His family taught him that cursing is a terrible sin. All of Philip's friends cursed, but he never did. He secretly thought that he was better than his friends. The fact that God wants pure language is not the reason Philip refrained from cursing. He refrained from cursing because he was compelled to live up to his own standards. Philip needed to base his behavior on God and His Word, not on his own standards.

✎ **What things are you not doing because you couldn't stand yourself if you did them? What are you doing to obey God with the motivation to meet your own standards?**

_____

_____

_____

God gave us His commands because He loves us. As we obey Him, we are protected and freed to enjoy life more fully.

4. I'll obey to be blessed. God doesn't make bargains. If our only motive to obey is to be blessed, we simply are attempting to manipulate God. Our underlying assumption is, "I've been good, so bless me." It's true that we will reap what we sow. It's true that obedience keeps us within God's plan for our lives, but our decision to obey never should be based solely on God's rewards.

Brian went to church so that God would bless his business, not because he wanted to worship God. Penny chose not to spread gossip about Diane because she told God that she wouldn't tell anybody about Diane if He got her the promotion she wanted.

Bargaining with God

✎ **Have you ever bargained with God and said, "I'll obey You if You'll 'fix' me?"** ○ Yes ○ No

We reason that if we are "fixed," we will be able to serve God and be freed from having to deal with a particular problem or temptation. God sometimes has something important to teach us through our weakness. The apostle Paul three times begged the Lord to remove a "thorn," or difficulty, from him. Read in the margin how the Lord responded to him.

✎ **Christ has freed us from the bondage of sin so that we can respond to Him in obedience. We have discussed six reasons the Bible tells us to be involved in good works. As a review, fill in the key words from those reasons.**

My grace is sufficient for you, for power is perfected in weakness. Most gladly, therefore, I will rather boast about my weaknesses, that the power of Christ may dwell in me. Therefore I am well content with weaknesses, with insults, with distresses, with persecutions, with difficulties, for Christ's sake, for when I am weak, then I am strong.
–2 Corinthians 12:9-10

1. Christ's _____ motivates us to obey Him.

2. Sin is _____.

3. The Father's _____ trains us.

4. His commands for us are _____.

5. God will reward our _____.

6. Christ is _____.

You will find the answers on pages 117-119.

The Lord never said everything had to be perfect in our lives for us to follow Him. He said, "If anyone wishes to come after Me, let him deny himself," (In the context of this passage, "denying yourself" means giving up your selfish desires.) "take up His cross daily, and follow Me" (Luke 9:23). This doesn't mean we should stop working to rid ourselves of our difficulties. We can express our feelings about them to the Lord and with others as appropriate. Then we are to act in faith on His Word.

We don't have to deny the difficulties we have in life, but spiritual growth, character development, and Christian service must not be held hostage by them. God has given each of us a will, and we can choose to honor the Lord in spite of our difficulties.

We can choose to honor the Lord in spite of our difficulties.

As you become aware of your motives, you may think, "I've never done anything purely for the Lord in my whole life!" You may feel a sense of pain and remorse because you've had inappropriate motives.

Try not to shame yourself for your past attitudes—we all have them. Instead, realize that the Lord wants you to make godly choices today so that you can enjoy the benefits of those decisions in the future. Then ask the Holy Spirit to help you develop an intensity about these choices.

Beloved, now we are children of God, and it has not appeared as yet what we shall be. We know that, when He appears, we shall be like Him, because we shall see Him just as He is.

–1 John 3:2

As the verse at left indicates, your motives won't become totally pure until you see the Lord face to face. The more you grow in your understanding and relationship with Him, the more you will desire to honor Him with your love, loyalty, and obedience.

 Recognizing the great reasons for obedience, please write your own statement showing that you intend to grow in your willingness to follow Christ. It will provide you with direction and be your own "pledge of allegiance to Jesus."

_____

_____

Key Concept for Lesson 3
My wrong motives lead to false obedience, bitterness, and resentment.

Memorize this Step's memory verse:
Humble yourselves in the presence of the Lord, and He will exalt you.

–James 4:10

LESSON 4

Key Concept:
As a bond-servant I am owned by my Master.

Ownership and Conduct

We commit ourselves to God and desire that He remove patterns of sin from our lives.

> *Do you not know that when you present yourselves to someone as slaves for obedience, you are slaves of the one whom you obey, either of sin resulting in death, or of obedience resulting in righteousness*
>
> –Romans 6:16

An Important Principle

You will find your growth, the control of your emotions, your faithful obedience, and your choice of proper motives for obedience much more natural, and even easier, if you can accept one all-important principle. It is the principle of ownership—the issue of who owns you. The constant struggle between sin and righteousness, between victory and defeat, is mainly a battle about who—Christ or you—is master or owner of your life.

Or do you not know that your body is a temple of the Holy Spirit who is in you, whom you have from God, and that you are not your own? For you have been bought with a price: therefore glorify God in your body.

–1 Corinthians 6:19-20

✎ **According to the verse in the margin, who bought you? What was the price? Whose were you before that purchase?**

_____

_____

Before you became a Christian, you were a slave to sin—sold into slavery to sin, as the apostle Paul puts it (Romans 7:14). God, at great cost, redeemed you, or "bought you back," and set you free. The cost was the sacrifice of His own Son on the cross. He paid the price of any claim sin had on you.

Accepting the fact of Christ's ownership frees you to trust Him with your life and provides courage to act in faith. While trusting in Christ as Lord the apostle Peter was able to do the impossible.

Peter answered Him and said, "Lord, if it is You, command me to come to You on the water." And He said, "Come!" And Peter got out of the boat, and walked on the water and came toward Jesus.

–Matthew 14:28-29

✎ **Read the Scripture in the margin. Peter asked what seemed to be impossible. What seemingly impossible request would you like to bring to Jesus?**

_____

Obedience is faith in action. Trust Him as your Lord to take responsibility for your requests and for your life. Step out in faith.

✎ **Under the ownership and lordship of Christ, you are asked to glorify God in your body (1 Corinthians 6:20). List six ways you can do that. Put a star (★) by one you'll start this week.**

1. _____   4. _____

2. _____   5. _____

3. _____   6. _____

List two troublesome areas in your life that still need work. Present them to the Lord so that He might receive glory by helping you. (Do not be discouraged if you attempt to do this more than once. Keep on asking, acting, and trusting God for the outcome.)

You recognize that your compulsion has robbed you of life and has cheated you of the life that should have been yours, but in recovery, you discover the gift of new life.

The comedian Jack Benny performed a routine in which a mugger demanded at gunpoint, "Your money or your life!" Benny, whose comedian character centered around his supposed extreme tightness with money, always got a laugh as he stalled and mulled over this demand and finally answered, "Don't rush me! I'm thinking, I'm thinking!" How well we could identify with this in our compulsions, because we could not bring ourselves to consider what we thought were the horrors of life without our addiction. In recovery, we learn that life is worth living, for God has given us infinite worth and meaningful purpose for a full life. In Step 7 we will discover some new means for experiencing the transformation necessary to enjoy that life.

Life with our addiction is merely struggling to survive. Life without our addiction is real living.

```
┌─────────────────────────────────────────────┐
│                                               │
│          Key Concept for Lesson 4             │
│      As a bond-servant I am owned by my Master. │
│                                               │
└─────────────────────────────────────────────┘
```

✎ Pray and ask God how this concept can apply in your life. Now please review this lesson. What has God shown you that you can use?

_____

_____

➜ Memorize this Step's memory verse:

Humble yourselves in the presence of the Lord, and He will exalt you.

–James 4:10

Step Review

✎ Step 6 says *We commit ourselves to God and desire that He remove patterns of sin from our lives.* Write in your own words what Step 6 means.

_____

_____

_____

_____

Describe how you will daily apply Step 6 to your life and recovery.

_____

_____

_____

_____

_____

_____

Notes

[1]McGee, Robert S., *Search for Significance* LIFE Support Edition (Houston: Rapha Publishing, 1992), 11.

[2]Pat Springle, *Untangling Relationships: A Christian Perspective on Codependency* (Houston: Rapha Publishing, 1993), 156-157.

STEP
7

Ready for Change

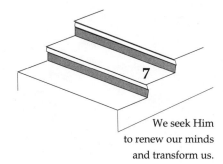

7

We seek Him
to renew our minds
and transform us.

CHALLENGED AND GROWING

Once again Cathy's sponsor challenged her. Jan told Cathy to read some material on the Steps and then to write in her own words what Step 7 means.

Jan wasn't satisfied with Cathy's first answer. She kept sending Cathy back to the Step until Cathy began to see a crucial difference between her purposes and God's purposes.

Finally Cathy wrote, "Step 7 is not just about asking God to help me. It is about grace. Grace is undeserved. I am powerless. Step 7 does not mean God lends me power so I will no longer be powerless—so I can go on struggling with my compulsions with God's help. Step 7 is about the end of the struggle. I have been asking God to help me to be perfect and to gain others' approval. I was asking the wrong question and praying the wrong prayer. I now realize that I need God to do the work. I can begin to accept myself. I can 'Let Go and Let God.'"

Jan smiled as she listened to Cathy read the words. *She's going to make it yet*, Jan thought.

Step 7   *We humbly ask God to renew our minds so that our sinful patterns can be transformed into patterns of life and health and righteousness.*

Memory verse   *And do not be conformed to this world, but be transformed by the renewing of your mind, that you may prove what the will of God is, that which is good and acceptable and perfect.*

–Romans 12:2

Overview for Step 7   **Lesson 1: The Grace Step**
Goal: You will identify why you need a renewed mind.
Lesson 2: The Performance Trap
Goal: You will determine the negative effect of trying to gain a sense of worth through your performance, and you will describe the solution.
Lesson 3: The Approval Addict
Goal: You will learn about the negative effect of an addiction to approval, and you will describe the solution.
Lesson 4: The Blame Game
Goal: You will study the negative effect of habitual blaming, and you will describe the solution.
Lesson 5: Shame
Goal: You will evaluate the negative effect of low self-esteem, and you will describe the solution.
Lesson 6: Taking the Step
Goal: You will describe three practical actions necessary to work this Step.

LESSON 1

Key Concept:
A solid, biblical, belief system is the key to my healthy behavior.

The Grace Step

We humbly ask God to renew our minds so that our sinful patterns can be transformed into patterns of life and health and righteousness.

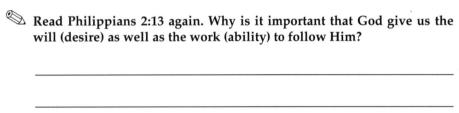

for it is God who is at work in you, both to will and to work for His good pleasure.

–Philippians 2:13

In Step 1 we discovered that we are powerless. In Step 7 we begin to apply God's power to our situation. Philippians 2:13 above describes grace in a distinctive way. God gives us both the desire and the power to do His will. God's grace creates a renewed mind so we can be rid of our self-destructive patterns.

✎ **Read Philippians 2:13 again. Why is it important that God give us the will (desire) as well as the work (ability) to follow Him?**

_____

_____

We often define grace as God's unmerited favor. It is His free, undeserved gift of loving and accepting us. God's gift includes the desire and the power to follow Him. We do not naturally desire what is best. We do not, on our own, have the ability to do God's will.

Why Do I Need My Mind Renewed?

Distorted thinking

We need our minds renewed because we think in a distorted manner. Theology tells us that sin has damaged every aspect of our lives—our thinking, feeling, and acting. This is called depravity. This Step is designed to help us see that damage and to ask God to correct it.

An ox knows its owner, And a donkey its master's manger, But Israel does not know, My people do not understand.
                    –Isaiah 1:3

✎ **The Scriptures in the margin speak about our depravity. Read them, and then answer the questions:**

Who is smarter, a "dumb" animal or us in our sin? _____

What has sin done to our understanding? _____

_____

What has it done to our heart or our emotions? _____

walk no longer just as the Gentiles also walk, in the futility of their mind, being darkened in their understanding, excluded from the life of God, because of the ignorance that is in them, because of the hardness of their heart; and they, having become callous, have given themselves over to sensuality, for the practice of every kind of impurity with greediness.
                    –Ephesians 4:17-19

_____

What has it done to our behavior? _____

_____

You are of your father the devil, and you want to do the desires of your father. He was a murderer from the beginning, and does not stand in the truth, because there is no truth in him. Whenever he speaks a lie, he speaks from his own nature; for he is a liar, and the father of lies.

–John 8:44

And do not be conformed to this world, but be transformed by the renewing of your mind, that you may prove what the will of God is, that which is good and acceptable and perfect.

–Romans 12:2

Although the Spirit of Christ lives within us, our minds tend to dwell on worldly thoughts instead of on God's truth. Our understanding has been darkened, our hearts have been hardened, and our behavior has become impure and greedy. We have become more foolish than the animals.

 What does the first passage in the margin say about the source and nature of our behavior?

_____

As the second passage in the margin states, God's goal is to renew our minds and transform our lives. Satan's goal is to keep us in darkness with our minds unrenewed so that our lives won't be transformed. The ugly truth is that we are depraved. John 8:44 says Satan is the source of our behavior and we are naturally like him. Sin shapes our thoughts, our actions, and our feelings.

Sin in our lives occurs largely because of our distorted belief system. The following diagram shows this process:

Most of the time we act because of habit rather than because of clear choices. Our thoughts, feelings, and actions mostly are habit. They result from learned behavior. We all must deal with a variety of situations in life. Between our situation and our thoughts, emotions, and actions is a filtering system—our beliefs. Here is an example:

> Todd doesn't seem to like the job I do. My belief is that my worth comes from doing a good job and being approved by others. I begin to think depressing thoughts about myself. This causes me to feel bad about myself. I find myself bingeing to soothe my frayed emotions.

As long I believe my worth is based on performance and approval, I always will be stuck. Habit is almost impossible to change without confronting and changing the underlying belief system.

As (a man) thinks within himself, so he is.

–Proverbs 23:7

Our beliefs represent our deepest, most basic thoughts. They affect the way we feel, the way we perceive others and ourselves, and ultimately, the way we act. They determine whether we will live according to God's functional truth or the world's dysfunctional value system.

 Below check the response which shows the root from which our habits originate.

O 1. our thoughts
O 2. our actions
O 3. our beliefs
O 4. our emotions

Our beliefs (number 3) are the basic attitudes from which spring our habits of thinking, feeling, and acting.

🖉 **Check all of the following that are false basic beliefs:**

False beliefs

○ 1. I must gain the approval of others to feel good about myself.
○ 2. I cannot change, I am hopeless.
○ 3. I am feeling depressed because I failed to meet expectations.
○ 4. I must meet certain standards to feel good about myself.
○ 5. Those who fail are unworthy of love and deserve to be punished.

🖉 **Which approach is more likely to succeed: confronting and replacing the basic false belief, or continually battling with the habits? Why?**

_____

_____

In your opinion, upon which do we usually concentrate most—the dysfunctional beliefs or the habits they produce?

_____

If you checked numbers 1, 2, 4, and 5, you were correct. Answer 3 is a feeling that grows out of the false belief that my worth is determined by my performance. In my opinion, people usually concentrate on habitual thoughts, feelings, and actions. They seldom deal with the genuine problem—a false belief system.

How False Beliefs Run and Ruin Our Lives

Our beliefs represent the filters through which we interpret the situations we encounter. Some of these interpretations are conscious reflections; however, most are based on unconscious assumptions—habits. These beliefs trigger thoughts, which in turn lead to emotions, which drive actions.

How our filters work

False Beliefs

If we use the truth of God's Word as the base for what we believe about ourselves, we likely will have a positive sense of self-esteem. However, as we mentioned in Step 2, Satan has deceived most of us by convincing us that:

Our Self-Worth = Performance + Others' Opinions

🖉 **The four false beliefs serve as a summary of the many lies Satan tells us. Here and on the next page we again list these beliefs for you. To what extent do they affect you? Estimate the percentage, from zero to 100 percent, which you think indicates how much you live by each belief.**

_____% *I must meet certain standards in order to feel good about myself.*
_____% *I must have the approval of certain others* (boss, friends, parents) *to feel good about myself. If I don't have their approval, I can't feel good about myself.*
_____% *Those who fail are unworthy of love and deserve to be punished.*

_____% *I am what I am. I cannot change. I am hopeless.* In other words, I am the sum total of all my past successes and failures, and I'll never be significantly different.

In your work on this Step you will examine how each of those false belief systems operates in your life. Remember from Step 2 that for each of the false beliefs God has a life-changing truth.

✎ **Read the two lists below. The first contains the four basic false beliefs. The second contains four of God's truths. At the left of each false belief write the letter of the corresponding truth.**

Beliefs, consequences

_____ 1. *I must meet certain standards to feel good about myself*: results in fear of failure; perfectionism; being driven to succeed; manipulating others to succeed; withdrawing from healthy risks for fear of failing.

_____ 2. *I must have the approval of certain others to feel good about myself*: results in fear of rejection; becoming a people-pleaser; being overly sensitive to criticism; withdrawing from others to avoid disapproval.

_____ 3. *Those who fail, including me, are unworthy of love and deserve to be punished*: results in fear of punishment; a tendency to punish others; blaming self and others for personal failure; withdrawing from God and fellow believers; being driven to avoid punishment.

_____ 4. *I am what I am. I cannot change. I am hopeless*: results in feelings of shame, hopelessness, apathy, inferiority; passivity; loss of creativity; isolation, withdrawing from others.

A. *Propitiation*, which means we have the capacity to experience God's love deeply because we no longer will fear punishment or punish others. Results include: increasing freedom from the fear of punishment; patience and kindness toward others; being quick to forgive; deep love for Christ (1 John 2:2).

B. *Justification*, which means we are completely forgiven and fully pleasing to God. Results include: increasing freedom from the fear of failure; desire to pursue the right things: Christ and His kingdom; love for Christ (Romans 5:1).

C. *Regeneration*, which means we have been made brand new, complete in Christ. Results include: no longer experiencing the pain of shame; Christ-centered self-confidence; joy, courage, peace; desire to know Christ (Colossians 1:21).

D. *Reconciliation*, which means we are totally accepted by God. Results include: increasing freedom from the fear of rejection; willingness to be open and vulnerable; ability to relax around others; willingness to take criticism; a desire to please God no matter what others think (2 Corinthians 5:18).

These four basic truths are the foundation on which we can build an effective, Christ-honoring life. The responses are 1. B, 2. D, 3. A, 4. C.

Key Concept for Lesson 1
A solid, biblical, belief system is the key to healthy behavior.

Please pray and ask God how this concept an apply in your life. Now please review this lesson. What has God shown you that you can use?

_____

_____

<table>
<tr><td>

LESSON

2

</td></tr>
</table>

Key Concept:
I am completely forgiven by God and am fully pleasing to Him.

The Performance Trap

We humbly ask God to renew our minds so that our sinful patterns can be transformed into patterns of life and health and righteousness.

> *knowing that a man is not justified by the works of the Law but through faith in Christ Jesus, even we have believed in Christ Jesus, that we may be justified by faith in Christ, and not by the works of the Law; since by the works of the Law shall no flesh be justified.*
>
> –Galatians 2:16

The false belief that I must meet certain standards in order to feel good about myself results in a fear of failure. Take the following test to determine how strongly this belief affects you.

Fear of Failure Test

✎ **Read the statements below. Then, from the top of the test, choose the term which best describes your response. Put in the blank beside each statement the number above the term you chose.**

1	2	3	4
Always	Sometimes	Seldom	Never

_____ 1. I avoid participating in some activities because I am afraid I will not be good enough.

_____ 2. I become anxious when I sense I may fail.

_____ 3. I worry.

_____ 4. I have unexplained anxiety.

_____ 5. I am a perfectionist.

_____ 6. I feel I must justify my mistakes.

_____ 7. I feel I must succeed in some areas.

_____ 8. I become depressed when I fail.

_____ 9. I become angry with people who interfere with my success and who make me appear incompetent.

_____ 10. I am self-critical.

_____ Total (Add up the numbers you placed in the blanks.)

My score means—

Interpreting Your Score
If your score is . . .

34-40
God apparently has given you a very strong appreciation for His love and unconditional acceptance. You seem to be free of the fear of failure that

plagues most people. (Some exceptions exist: Some people who score this high either are greatly deceived or have turned off their emotions as a way to suppress pain. Examine your heart and talk to your group members to see if these exceptions apply to you.)

28-33
The fear of failure rarely controls your responses or does so only in certain situations. Again, people who are not honest with themselves represent the major exceptions to this statement.

Fear of failure

22-27
A sense of failure and fear of criticism is a cause of pain in your life. As you reflect on many of your previous decisions, you probably will find that you can relate many of them to this fear. The fear of failure also will affect many of your future decisions unless you act directly to overcome this fear.

16-21
The fear of failure forms a general backdrop to your life. Probably, few days exist in which this fear does not affect you in some way. Unfortunately, this fear robs you of the joy and peace your salvation is meant to bring.

10-15
Experiences of failure dominate your memory. They probably have caused you to experience a great deal of depression. These problems will remain until you take action. In other words, this condition will not simply disappear. You need to experience deep healing in your self-concept, in your relationship with God, and in your relationships with others.

Effects of the Fear of Failure

Remember from the last lesson the following diagram:

We interpret situations through our belief system. This results in a cycle of thoughts, feelings, and actions. The key beliefs behind the fear of failure are our self-imposed standards. Fear of failure stems from the false belief, *I must meet certain standards in order to feel good about myself.*

In *Search for Significance* LIFE Support Edition, author Robert S. McGee tells the story about how he experienced the fear of failure during his teenage years. During those years he practiced basketball a lot and became a good player. In the process he learned that he could attempt many maneuvers when he practiced on the court or when he played basketball with friends.

But during a game when he felt intense pressure, he was afraid to do those same maneuvers. "I now realize that same fear has prevented me from attempting things in several other areas of my life," he wrote. "Although God has enabled me on many occasions to conquer this fear, I still struggle with the risk of failing. This story may surprise some people who know me and who think of me as a successful person." Success does not reduce the amount of fear of failure we experience in our lives.[1]

> ✎ Think of a situation in which your performance did not measure up to the standard you had set for yourself. Try to remember what thoughts and emotions arose because of that situation. What action did you take in response to those emotions? Read the example below, then write your thoughts.
>
> Situation: I failed to make a sale.
> Standard: I must meet my quota to feel good about myself.
> Thoughts: I'm a failure. I'll never make my quota. I'll never get promoted. I'll probably be fired any day now.
> Emotions: Fear, anger, depression.
> Actions: I avoided my boss for three days. I yelled at my wife and kids. I took out my anger on them.
>
> Situation: _____
>
> Standard: _____
>
> Thoughts: _____
>
> Emotions: _____
>
> Actions: _____
>
> _____

✎ **Do you see any of the following patterns at work in your emotions and actions? Check all that apply:**

- ○ avoiding failure at all costs by attempting only things in which I feel offer limited risk of failure.
- ○ spending time around those who are not a threat to me.
- ○ avoiding people who by their greater success make me feel like a failure.
- ○ feeling angry at those who stand in the way of me meeting my standards and goals.
- ○ blaming myself or others for my inability to meet my standards.
- ○ others_____

Most of us have become experts at avoiding failure.

If we believe that our self-worth is based on our success, we will try at all costs to avoid failure. Most of us have become experts at avoiding failure. We attempt only those things in which we are confident of success. We avoid activities in which the risk of failure is too great. We spend time around people who are not a threat to us. We avoid people who, either by their greater success or by their disapproval, make us feel like failures. We have trained ourselves very well!

✎ **Do you have to be successful in order to feel good about yourself?**
○ Yes ○ No

What would you have to be or do to feel like you are a success?

_____

When we evaluate ourselves by our performance, we ultimately lose no matter how successful we are. As we answer the previous question, many of us discover that even reaching our goals would not make us feel successful.

 In the following paragraph underline two additional dangers of living by the lie of performance-based self-worth.

The gospel is about relationships, not regulations.

Meeting certain standards in order to feel good about ourselves also causes us to live a rules-dominated life. We know people who have a set of rules for everything and who always place their attention on their performance. They miss the joy of walking with God. The gospel is about relationships, not regulations. The opposite danger is feeling good about ourselves because we are winning the performance game. We can't afford to mistake this pride for positive self-worth. God can bring about circumstances to stop us from trusting in ourselves. God intends to bring us to Himself through prayer and through studying His Word so that we can know, love, and serve Him. Sometimes He will allow us to fail so that we will look to Him instead of to ourselves for our security and significance. Before becoming upset that God would allow you to experience failure, remember that any life less than God intended is a second-class existence. He loves you too much to let you continue to obtain your self-esteem from the empty promise of success.

 What do you think the writer meant when he wrote the verse appearing in the margin? Write your own version of the verse:

It is good for me that I was afflicted, That I may learn Thy statutes.

–Psalm 119:71

_____

_____

The two dangers that appear in the paragraphs above are: a rules-dominated life and pride in our seeming success. My own version of the psalm read: "God loves me so much that He is willing to allow me to learn from experiencing my failure and inadequacy. Failure can lead me to the joy of a love and trust relationship with Him."

God's Answer: Justification

The solution

Impute means to credit something to one's account. My sins were imputed to Jesus, and His righteousness was imputed to me. God loves us and has provided a solution to the nightmare of the performance trap. That solution is called *justification*. Someone explained the meaning of *justified* very simply. God makes me "JUST as IF I'D" never sinned. As a result of Christ's death on the cross, our sins are forgiven and God has imputed Christ's righteousness to believers. Christ has justified us. Therefore, we are fully pleasing to God.

Some people have trouble thinking of themselves as being pleasing to God because they link pleasing so strongly with performance. They tend to be displeased with anything short of perfection in themselves, and they suspect that God has the same standard. The point of justification is that we never can achieve perfection on this earth, yet God loves us so much that He appointed His Son to pay for our sins. God credited to us His own righteousness, His perfect status before God.

✎ **What does it mean to be justified?** _____

He made Him who knew no sin to be sin on our behalf, that we might become the righteousness of God in Him.

–2 Corinthians 5:21

Justification is one of the central messages of Scripture. 2 Corinthians 5:21 at left is an example. We have not pulled out a couple of isolated passages to prove a point. Literally hundreds of passages all through the Bible teach this liberating truth. If you have accepted Christ, God considers you just as holy and righteous as the Lord Jesus Himself because He has taken your sins and placed His righteousness in its place.

✎ **Read this statement:** *I am completely forgiven by God and am fully pleasing to Him.* **How does being justified and having Christ's righteousness lead you to the conclusion reached in that statement?**

_____

_____

This doesn't mean that our actions don't matter and that we can sin all we want. Our sinful actions, words, and attitudes make the Lord sad, but our status as beloved children remains intact.

Taking sin seriously

Some people may read these statements and become uneasy. They may believe that we are not taking sin seriously. As you will see, we are not minimizing the destructive nature of sin. We are trying to make sure we see Christ's payment on the cross as very, very important.

Visualize two ledgers like the ones appearing below. On one is a list of all your sins; on the other, a list of the righteousness of Christ. In the left column write your name and list some of your sins.

All _____'s (your name) Sins	All Christ's Righteousness

Now go back to the right column and list some of Christ's wonderful characteristics, such as His love, faithfulness, holiness, and kindness.

God transferred our sin to Christ and His righteousness to us.

Now exchange names on the ledgers. Mark out the name of Christ and write your name in place of Christ's. Mark out your name and write His name in place of yours. This represents an example of justification: transferring our sin to Christ and His righteousness to us. In 1 Corinthians 5:21 Paul wrote "He (God) made Him (Jesus) who knew no sin to be sin on our behalf, that we might become the righteousness of God in Him."

Please pray and ask God how the concept you just read can apply in your life. Now please review this lesson. What has God shown you that you can use?

_____

_____

LESSON 3

Key Concept:
I am totally accepted by God.

The Approval Addict

We humbly ask God to renew our minds so that our sinful patterns can be transformed into patterns of life and health and righteousness.

> _For am I now seeking the favor of men, or of God? Or am I striving to please men? If I were still trying to please men, I would not be a bondservant of Christ._
>
> –Galatians 1:10

Living by the false belief that I must be approved by others to feel good about myself causes fear of rejection. We cannot be free to serve Christ as long as this fear makes us conform our attitudes and actions to others' expectations. Take the following test to determine how strongly you fear rejection.

Fear of Rejection Test

 Read each of the statements below. Then, from the top of the test, choose the term that best describes your response. Put in the blank beside each statement the number above the term you chose.

1	2	3	4
Always	Sometimes	Seldom	Never

_____ 1. When I sense that someone might reject me, I become anxious.

_____ 2. I spend lots of time analyzing why someone was critical or sarcastic to me or ignored me.

_____ 3. I am uncomfortable around those who are different from me.

_____ 4. It bothers me when someone is unfriendly to me.

_____ 5. I am basically shy and unsocial.

_____ 6. I am critical of others.

_____ 7. I find myself trying to impress others.

_____ 8. I become depressed when someone criticizes me.

_____ 9. I try to determine what people think of me.

_____ 10. I don't understand people and what motivates them.

_____ Total (Add up the numbers you have placed in the blanks.)

My score means—

Interpreting Your Score
If your score is . . .

34-40
God apparently has given you a very strong appreciation for His love and unconditional acceptance. You seem to be free of the fear of rejection that plagues most people. (Some exceptions exist: Some people who score this high either are greatly deceived or have turned off their emotions as a way to suppress pain. Examine your heart and talk to your group members to see if these exceptions apply to you.)

28-33
The fear of rejection controls your responses rarely or only in certain situations. Again, the only major exceptions are those who are not honest with themselves.

22-27
Emotional problems you experience may relate to a sense of rejection. Upon reflection you probably will relate many of your previous decisions to this fear. The fear of rejection also will affect many of your future decisions unless you take direct action to overcome that fear.

16-21
The fear of rejection forms a general backdrop to your life. Probably few days go by in which this fear does not affect you in some way. Unfortunately, this robs you of the joy and peace your salvation is meant to bring.

10-15
Experiences of rejection dominate your memory and probably cause you to experience a great deal of depression. These problems will persist until you take definitive action. In other words, this condition will not simply disappear; time alone cannot heal your pain. You need to experience deep healing in your self-concept, in your relationship with God, and in your relationships with others.

In the margin list a specific instance in which a relative, friend, or boss withheld approval or used criticism, silence, or sarcasm to make you do what this person wanted you to do. Then describe how you felt in this situation.

 We need great courage to face the results of fear of rejection in our lives. Circle from the following paragraph the words or phrases that describe patterns you identify in your life:

When we have felt the pain of rejection, our fear of going through it again can affect us profoundly. Sometimes people see emotional pain as a sign of weakness, and since we have not learned how to deal with it, we avoid it. We deny our pain by stuffing or ignoring it. To try to gain approval we do tasks we hate. Some of us can't say no for fear others will reject us. Others of us become passive. We withdraw from people and avoid decisions or actions which others might criticize. Our goal usually is to avoid rejection by not doing anything which might be objectionable.

Evaluating our self-worth by what we and others think about our performance leads us to believe that any time our performance is unacceptable, we are unacceptable as well.

I felt rejection when—

_____

_____

_____

How I felt when it happened:

_____

_____

_____

✎ **Do you identify in your life any of the following results of fear of rejection? Check all that apply:**

○ being easily manipulated
○ being hypersensitive to criticism
○ defensiveness
○ hostility toward others who disagree with me
○ superficial relationships
○ exaggerating or minimizing the truth to impress people
○ shyness
○ passivity
○ nervous breakdown
○ other _____

Virtually all of us have internalized the following sentence into our belief system. We hold to it with amazing strength:

I must have the acceptance, respect, and approval of others in order to have self-worth.

This is the basic false belief behind all peer pressure. Several of the characteristics in the checklist and paragraph above have affected my life. Underlying all of them is the idea in the sentence above. That sentence is so powerful because it is partly true. I do need acceptance from outside myself. We make the mistake of trying to get this acceptance from people who don't have what we need and wouldn't give it if they did. We need to learn to get our acceptance, respect, and approval from our loving Lord and then from healthy believers.

We try to get acceptance from people who don't have what we need and wouldn't give it if they did.

Have you ever been in a relationship in which what someone said to you "sounded" like praise, but it "felt" like rejection?

✎ **Read carefully the following and answer the question: "How can praise be a form of rejection?"**

Rejection often is a subtle thing. We easily can see the rejection in criticism, sarcasm, and silence. Praise also can serve as a form of manipulation and rejection, although this may be more difficult to see. When the purpose of praise is to get us to do what someone wants, it is a subtle but powerful form of rejection. Many of us fall prey to this manipulative praise because we so desperately want to be appreciated and will do whatever it takes to get it from others.

✎ **How can praise be rejection?** _____

_____

How do you feel when people praise you only to manipulate you?

_____

We may use praise as a form of manipulation. Our motive is to influence people to do something we want them to do. If you realize that you manipulate others through praise, confess it as sin and choose to seek their good instead of your goal.

God's Answer: Reconciliation

reconcile-v. to restore to friendship or harmony; to settle or resolve differences (Webster's)

namely, that God was in Christ reconciling the world to Himself, not counting their trespasses against them, and He has committed to us the word of reconciliation.
                    –2 Corinthians 5:19

And although you were formerly alienated and hostile in mind, engaged in evil deeds, yet He has now reconciled you in His fleshly body through death, in order to present you before Him holy and blameless and beyond reproach.
                    –Colossians 1:21-22

He saved us, not on the basis of deeds which we have done in righteousness, but according to His mercy.
                    –Titus 3:5

God's answer to the pain of rejection is **reconciliation**. Christ died for our sins and restored us to a proper relationship with God. We are both acceptable to Him and accepted by Him. We are not rejected! We are His. The verse at left from 2 Corinthians at left explains this.

When God chose to redeem us He did not go part way. He did not make us partially righteous because of our poor performance. The blood of Christ is sufficient to pay for all sin. Because of His blood, we are holy and righteous before God, even in the midst of sin. This does not minimize the destructiveness of sin. It glorifies the sacrifice of Christ. We are restored to a complete and pure love relationship with God.

We may neglect this teaching more than we may neglect any other in Scripture. The passage from Colossians at left says it plainly. Enjoy those last words. God sees us as holy and blameless and beyond reproach at this very moment. This is not merely a reference to our future standing; it describes our present status as well. We are totally accepted by God. God received us into a loving, intimate, personal relationship the moment we placed our faith in Christ. We are united with God in an eternal and unbreakable bond (Romans 8:38-39). Knowing that no sin can make a Christian unacceptable to God is faith in a pledge sealed with the Holy Spirit (Ephesians 1:14).

Since our relationship with God was bought entirely by the blood of Christ, no amount of good works can make us more acceptable to Him. Read Titus 3:5, which appears in the margin. Because Christ has reconciled us to God, we can experience the incredible truth that we are totally accepted by and acceptable to God.

✎ **Review the last two paragraphs and look for reasons to thank God for reconciling you to Himself. Write a prayer thanking Him for totally accepting you.**

_____

_____

_____

As in the last lesson, this truth is a central theme of Scripture.

What can we do when we have failed or when someone disapproves of us? We can learn to use the truth in this lesson and say:

> "It would be nice if _____ (my boss liked me, I could fix the refrigerator, my complexion were clear, James had picked me up on time, or _____), but I'm still deeply loved, completely forgiven, fully pleasing, totally accepted and complete in Christ."

This statement doesn't mean that we won't feel pain or anger. We can be honest about our feelings. The statement simply is a quick way to gain God's perspective on what we experience. It is not magic, but it enables us to reflect on the truth. We can apply this truth in every difficult situation, whether it involves someone's disapproval, our own failure to accomplish something, or another person's failure.

✎ **On the lines below, write the following statement: I am deeply loved, completely forgiven, fully pleasing, totally accepted, and complete in Christ.**

_____

_____

_____

Now go back and read the statement three times. Cathy's sponsor assigned her to look in the mirror and read that truth to herself each day for a month. Cathy said it was the most difficult thing she ever did. Today Cathy gratefully acknowledges that this statement was a key to changing her life.

➔ **Memorize the truth in the above statement and begin to apply it in your situations and relationships.**

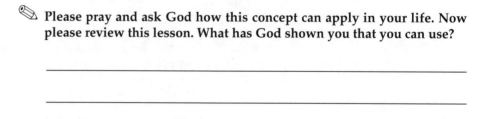

Key Concept for Lesson 3
I am totally accepted by God.

✎ **Please pray and ask God how this concept can apply in your life. Now please review this lesson. What has God shown you that you can use?**

_____

_____

_____

LESSON 4

The Blame Game

Key Concept:
I am deeply loved by God.

We humbly ask God to renew our minds so that our sinful patterns can be transformed into patterns of life and health and righteousness.

> *He has not dealt with us according to our sins, Nor rewarded us according to our iniquities.*
>
> –Psalm 103:10

The false belief that *those who fail, including me, are unworthy of love and deserve to be punished,* is at the root of our fear of punishment and our tendency to punish others.

Take the test on the next page to determine how much this lie influences you.

Fear of Punishment/Punishing Others Test

 Read each of the following statements. Then, from the top of the test, choose the term that best describes your response. Put in the blank beside each statement the number above the term you chose.

1	2	3	4
Always	Sometimes	Seldom	Never

_____ 1. I fear what God might do to me.

_____ 2. After I fail, I worry about God's response.

_____ 3. When I see someone in a difficult situation, I wonder what he or she did to deserve that situation.

_____ 4. When something goes wrong, I tend to think that God must be punishing me.

_____ 5. I am very hard on myself when I fail.

_____ 6. I find myself wanting to blame others when they fail.

_____ 7. I get angry with God when someone who is immoral or dishonest prospers.

_____ 8. I am determined to make sure others know about it when I see them doing wrong.

_____ 9. I tend to focus on the faults and failures of others.

_____ 10. God seems harsh to me.

_____ Total (Add the numbers you have placed in the blanks.)

My score means—

Interpreting Your Score
If your score is. . .

34-40
God apparently has given you a very strong appreciation for His unconditional love and acceptance. You seem to be freed from the fear of punishment that plagues most people. (Some exceptions exist: Some people who score this high either are greatly deceived or have turned off their emotions as a way to suppress pain. Examine your heart and talk to your group members to see if these exceptions apply to you.)

28-33
The fear of punishment and the compulsion to punish others control your responses rarely or only in certain situations. Again, the only exceptions are those who are not honest about how strongly these matters affect them.

22-27
When you experience emotional problems, they may have to do with a fear of punishment or with an inner urge to punish others. Upon reflection you probably can relate many of your previous responses to this fear. The fear of punishment and/or the determination to punish others also will affect many

Take direct action of your future responses unless you take direct action to overcome these tendencies.

16-21
The fear of punishment forms a general backdrop to your life. Probably few days go by that the fear of punishment and the tendency to blame others do not affect you. Unfortunately, this robs you of the joy and peace your salvation is meant to bring.

10-15

Experiences of punishment dominate your memory. You probably have suffered a great deal of depression as a result. This condition will not simply disappear; time alone cannot heal your pain. You need to experience deep healing in your self-concept, in your relationship with God, and in your relationships with others.

The Fear of Punishment and Tendency to Punish Others

A wife spent her hour in the counselor's office attempting to show that a marital problem was all her husband's fault. When it was time for her husband's appointment, he tried to prove that she was to blame. People often are more interested in avoiding blame and pinning it on someone else than they are in solving problems.

 Using the example of the couple above, explain the meaning of the slogan appearing in the margin.

_____

_____

An addict is someone who would rather be in control than be happy.

We seem to believe that we deserve blame for our shortcomings and that others deserve the same. You may have written that we would rather be in control by proving something isn't our fault than solve the problems and have the pain taken away.

 Pretend that you are captain of the school debate team. Your subject is "Why blaming doesn't work." Draw from the paragraphs below and from your own knowledge and experience to list all the facts you can to support your argument. As you read, circle items you can use.

We have been conditioned either to accept personal blame or to blame somebody else when our performance is unsatisfactory. You may think that this false belief does not affect you at all—but it probably does. Do you generally have an urge to find out who is at fault when something fails?

Rather than evaluating our problems objectively, we tend to defend ourselves. We sometimes do this by attacking others. The more we criticize other people, the more defensive they become, and the less likely they are to admit their errors, especially to us. Criticism can lead to a counterattack from both sides, and pretty soon it's like a volleyball game, with each person intensifying the pace while returning blame to the other person's side.

The blame debate

Points for the debate—Why blaming doesn't work: _____

_____

Some of us have learned to accept blame without defending ourselves. Under his wife's constant condemnation Tom was becoming an emotional zombie. Instead of fighting back he kept thinking, "Yes, Suzanne's right. I am an incompetent fool." He was like a worn-out punching bag.

I listed some of the following as arguments why blaming doesn't work:

- It leads to defensiveness.
- It builds walls instead of solving problems.
- It creates more denial because I can't risk being wrong.

Both self-inflicted punishment and the compulsion to punish others result from the false belief: *Those who fail are unworthy of love and deserve to be punished.*

God's Answer: Propitiation

propitiation–n. describes what happened when Christ, through His death, became the means by which God's wrath was satisfied and God's mercy was granted to the sinner who believes on Christ

God's plan for us is centered in the cross. At the cross, God poured out His wrath against sin. To understand His plan we can look at what **propitiation** means. Propitiation is difficult to define because it brings together the following four concepts:
1. God is holy.
2. His holiness leads to the necessity of justice—His actions must be expressions of justice. He must punish sin.
3. God lovingly chose to provide a substitute—His beloved Son took the punishment our sins deserved.
4. As a result, God's justice is satisfied—no more punishment is required.

✎ **Write the number of the appropriate part of propitiation in the blanks following the parts of the following paragraphs. I have done the first one for you.**

a. # __1__ The problem with our sinfulness is that God is absolutely holy, pure, and perfect. Absolutely nothing is unholy in Him.

b. #_____ Therefore, since God is holy, He can't overlook or compromise with sin.

c. #_____ It took one sin to separate Adam from God. For God to condone even "one" sin would instantly defile His holiness.

d. #_____ The Father did not escape witnessing His Son's mistreatment: the mocking, the scourging, and the cross. He could have spoken and ended the whole ordeal, yet He kept silent.

e. #_____ Confronted with the suffering of His Son, God chose to let it continue so that we could be saved. What an expression of love!

f. #_____ God loves you, and He enjoys revealing His love to you. He enjoys being loved by you, but He knows you can love Him only if you are experiencing His love for you.

g. #_____ Propitiation means that His wrath has been removed and that you are deeply loved!

h. #_____ God is holy, and therefore He must punish sin. But He loves us and therefore provided a substitute to take the punishment we deserve.

Jesus has satisfied completely the righteousness of God so God's only response to us is in love. I answered the exercise: a. 1, b. 1, c. 2, d. 2, e. 3, f. 3, g. 3, h. 4.

By this the love of God was manifested in us, that God has sent His only begotten Son into the world so that we might live through Him. In this is love, not that we loved God, but that He loved us and sent His Son to be the propitiation for our sins.
–1 John 4:9-10

✎ **Read the verse at left. Does the Father love you?** ○ Yes ○ No
How do you know He loves you?

_____

Do you feel loved? ○ Yes ○ No
Explain _____

Try to recall an experience in which you felt someone loved you. That person cared about you and wanted to be with you. You didn't have to perform; just being you was enough. The thought of that person selecting you to love was intoxicating. He or she loved you, and that love was soothing to you and satisfied many of your inner longings. If a person's love can make us feel this way, consider how much greater fulfillment the heavenly Father's love can bring. We can't truly appreciate the Father's love unless we realize that it goes beyond any experience of being loved by another man or woman. If you've never felt that kind of love from a person, God wants you to feel it from Him.

Many of us have a distorted concept of the heavenly Father. We believe that God is thrilled when we accept Christ and are born into His family. But many of us also believe that He is proud of us for only as long as we perform well, and that the better we perform, the happier He is with us.

> Many, O LORD my God, are the wonders which Thou hast done, And Thy thoughts toward us.
> –Psalm 40:5

In reality, as the Scripture at left indicates, not a moment goes by that God isn't thinking loving thoughts about us. We are His children, and we are special to Him because of Christ! Propitiation, then, means Jesus Christ satisfied the Father's righteous condemnation of sin by His death. The Scriptures give only one reason to explain this incredible fact: God loves you!

Applying the Principle to Others

The more we understand God's love and forgiveness, the more we will be willing and able to forgive others. If we think about it, the things that others do to us all are trivial compared to our sin of rebellion against God that He graciously has forgiven. This is why Paul encouraged the Ephesian Christians to forgive each other just as God in Christ also has forgiven you—completely and willingly (Ephesians 4:32).

> And be kind to one another, tender-hearted, forgiving each other, just as God in Christ also has forgiven you.
> –Ephesians 4:32

 Do you have trouble forgiving some sins, or even personality differences, in others? If so, list them and confess to God your lack of forgiveness.

_____

_____

How do these compare to your sins that deserved God's wrath but that received the payment of Christ's substitutionary death?

Key Concept for Lesson 4
I am deeply loved by God.

 Stop and pray. Ask God how this concept can apply in your life. Now please review this lesson. What has God shown you that you can use?

_____

_____

LESSON 5

Shame

We humbly ask God to renew our minds so that our sinful patterns can be transformed into patterns of life and health and righteousness.

> *And now, little children, abide in Him, so that when He appears, we may have confidence and not shrink away from Him in shame at His coming.*
> –1 John 2:28

Key Concept:
I am complete in Christ.

Read again the story of Cathy's experience with Step 7, on page 126. Cathy realized that her problem was not that her performance and appearance were inadequate. The problem was basing her self-worth on her performance and appearance at all. Making that mistake led to a fourth false belief: *I am what I am. I cannot change. I am hopeless.*

The fourth false belief binds people to the hopeless pessimism of poor self-esteem. Take the following test to establish how strongly you experience shame.

Shame Test

✎ **Read each of the following statements. Then, from the top of the test, choose the term that best describes your response. Put in the blank beside each statement the number above the term you chose.**

1	2	3	4
Always	Sometimes	Seldom	Never

_____ 1. I often think about past failures or experiences of rejection that have occurred in my life.

_____ 2. I cannot recall certain things about my past without experiencing strong, painful emotions (such as guilt, shame, or anger.)

_____ 3. I seem to make the same mistakes over and over again.

_____ 4. I want to change certain aspects of my character, but I don't believe I ever can successfully do so.

_____ 5. I feel inferior.

_____ 6. I cannot accept certain aspects of my appearance.

_____ 7. I am generally disgusted with myself.

_____ 8. I feel that certain experiences basically have ruined my life.

_____ 9. I perceive of myself as an immoral person.

_____ 10. I feel I have lost the opportunity to experience a complete and wonderful life.

_____ Total (Add the numbers you have placed in the blanks.)

My score means—

Interpreting Your Score
If your score is. . .

34-40
God apparently has given you a very strong appreciation for His love and unconditional acceptance. You seem to be free of the shame that plagues most

people. (Some exceptions exist: Some people who score this high either are greatly deceived or have turned off their emotions as a way to suppress pain. Examine your heart and talk to your group members to see if these exceptions apply to you.)

28-33
Shame controls your responses rarely or only in certain situations. Again, the only major exceptions are those who are not honest with themselves.

22-27
Emotional problems you experience may relate to a sense of shame. When you think about some of your previous decisions, you may relate many of them to your feelings of worthlessness. Feelings of low self-esteem may affect many of your future decisions unless you take direct action to change those feelings.

16-21
Shame forms a generally negative backdrop to your life. Probably, few days go by when shame does not affect you in some way. Unfortunately, this robs you of the joy and peace your salvation was meant to bring.

10-15
Experiences of shame dominate your memory and probably have caused you to experience a great deal of depression. These problems will remain unless you take definite action. In other words, this condition will not simply disappear one day; time alone cannot heal your pain. You need to experience deep healing in your self-concept, in your relationship with God, and in your relationships with others.

Effects of Shame

Shame comes from our own negative estimate of 1) our past performance; and/or 2) our physical appearance. Shame leads to the false belief: *I am what I am. I cannot change. I am hopeless.*

Even when others don't know of our failure, we assume their opinion of us is poor.

Shame often results from instances of neglect or abuse and then is reinforced by failures in our performance or "flaws" in our appearance. Even when others don't know of our failure, we assume their opinion of us is poor, and we adopt what we think their opinion might be.

✎ **Study the paragraph above and check all of the following statements that are part of the paragraph:**

    ❍ 1. My perception that I am physically imperfect adds to my sense of shame.
    ❍ 2. Feeling shamed becomes a habit so that I feel others disapprove of me even when they really approve.
    ❍ 3. My shame will decrease if I can improve my performance enough.
    ❍ 4. Shame may begin when I am ignored or mistreated.
    ❍ 5. Christians are wrong to feel shame.
    ❍ 6. The feeling that I have failed feeds my sense of shame.
    ❍ 7. The only way to be rid of shame is to experience love and acceptance.

The paragraph makes clear four critical issues concerning shame. Shame comes from not being loved and accepted—usually very early in life. The feeling that our performance and appearance is flawed feeds our sense of shame. Once shame has become our habit, we shame ourselves. Answers 3, 5, and 7 were not in the paragraph. Answer 3 is a lie because working harder will not remove my feeling of shame. Answer 5 is a more damaging lie; we cannot get rid of our shame by dumping still more shame on ourselves. Answer 7 is the truth. The only way to change the habit of shaming myself is to replace it with love and acceptance. I can get that love and acceptance from the Lord and from healthy believers. The answer simply wasn't in the paragraph.

✎ **Describe an incident in your life for which you felt shame for your addictive behavior.**

____

____

Did the shame cause you to improve or did the shame drive you into depression and more eating-disordered or other behavior?

____

Shame fuels our compulsions and assures our failures.

We so easily fall for the performance lie, "If only I could make myself feel ashamed enough, I would be motivated to succeed." The truth is that the shame fuels our compulsions and assures our failures.

➔ **Stop to pray. Ask God to remind you each time that you try to shame yourself into better behavior. Ask Him to replace your shame with the awareness that you are loved, accepted, and absolutely perfect in His eyes.**

Shame and Performance

If we base our self-worth on our performance long enough, our past behavior eventually becomes the sole basis of our worth. We see ourselves with certain character qualities and flaws because that's the way we have always been. We then include Satan's lie, "I always must be what I have been and live with whatever self-worth I have, because that's just me," in our belief system.

We then risk going to one of two extremes. Some of us act out our low self-worth through false humility, and we become self-abusers. Others go to the opposite extreme and become arrogant.

✎ **Describe a time when you have gone to one of the two extremes of acting out low self-worth or of abusing yourself.**

____

____

True humility is an accurate appraisal of our worth in Christ.

We may think that humility is belittling ourselves, but true humility is an accurate appraisal of our worth in Christ. Because of our sin we deserved God's righteous condemnation, yet we receive His unconditional love, grace, and righteousness through Christ. We are deeply loved, completely forgiven, fully pleasing, totally accepted, and complete in Him. Thankfulness, generosity, kindness, and self-confidence constitute true humility! Arrogant persons are striving to fill the hole in their souls by appearing strong and independent. They only make matters worse by driving people away.

Shame and Appearance

Another aspect of poor self-concept relates to personal appearance. Most of us have some aspect of our appearance that we wish we could change but can't. Are you angry with God for the way He made you? Can you ever be thin enough to be satisfied with your appearance? Do you compare your appearance to that of others? If you do, at some point in your life you will suffer because someone prettier, thinner, stronger, or more handsome always will be around. Even if you are beautiful or handsome, you still will suffer because you will fear losing your good looks—the basis of your self-worth.

Are you angry with God for the way He made you?

✎ **Check all of the following you feel when you consider your physical appearance.**

- ○ I hate the way I look.
- ○ I am grateful that God made me like He did.
- ○ I am more beautiful/handsome than others.
- ○ I am unhappy with _____ about my appearance.
- ○ My appearance makes me feel that I am worth more/less than others.

If we insist on valuing our worth by our appearance and performance, sooner or later God will graciously allow us to see the futility of that struggle. God created our need for a sense of significance. However, He knows we never will come to Him until we find the importance of people's opinions to be empty and hopeless. At that point we can turn to Him and find comfort and encouragement in the truths of His Word.

God's Answer: Regeneration

God created an answer to shame. His answer is unique and powerful. He makes you a new you. He makes me a new me. Imagine that you are guilty of all manner of crimes. The police come to your home to arrest you, but just before they break down the door, God works a miracle. He turns you into . . . SOMEBODY ELSE! That is the miracle of regeneration. God recreates us. He changes our identity.

✎ **The miracle described above is real. Through your relationship with Jesus Christ, you are a new person. Think of a time in your life when you were shamed, ridiculed, or ignored. With the awareness that you are a different person, write below what you would say to yourself.**

Jesus answered and said to him, "Truly, truly I say to you, unless one is born again, he cannot see the kingdom of God."

–John 3:3

_____

_____

Therefore, if any man is in Christ, he is a new creature; the old things passed away; behold, new things have come.

–2 Corinthians 5:17

✎ **Read the two Scriptures appearing in the margin. Write below the key words the passages use to describe regeneration.**

_____

Did you note the words *born again* and *new creature*? To the person who shamed you wouldn't it be fun to say, "I'm terribly sorry, but you must be talking about somebody else. She doesn't live here anymore"?

The problem is that many of us rationalize away the practical power of regeneration by thoughts like this, *"Well, yes, God did make me brand new in the past, but I've sinned since then. I'm not brand new any more."*

✎ **Read the words of the apostle Paul to the Ephesians—remember, these were Christians to whom he was writing. The words are printed in the margin. Write below what you think Paul meant by the command, "put on the new self."**

put on the new self, which in the likeness of God has been created in righteousness and holiness of the truth.
    –Ephesians 4:24

_____

_____

_____

If you looked in the Bible, you found that Ephesians 4:23, the verse before Ephesians 4:24, tells us to *be made new in the attitude of our minds.* "Putting on the new self" means to make choices to act in ways that are consistent with our new identity in Christ. We are to train our minds to reflect the fact that we are new creatures.

✎ **Read Lamentations 3:22-23 appearing in the margin. How do you feel about the promise that God's mercies are *new every morning*?**

It is of the Lord's mercies that we are not consumed, because his compassions fail not. They are new every morning; great is thy faithfulness.
    –Lamentations 3:22-23

  ○ hopeful   ○ doubtful
  ○ afraid   ○ relieved
  ○ joyful   ○ other _____

Jeremiah recognized that only God's continuing mercy keeps God from punishing us for our sin. His mercy is certainly as great toward His children as it is toward lost persons. One of His expressions of mercy is regeneration. Moment by moment He continues to make us new.

> ### Key Concept for Lesson 5
> I am complete in Christ.

✎ **Please pray and ask God how this concept can apply in your life. Now please review this lesson. What has God shown you that you can use?**

_____

_____

✎ **Write from memory Romans 12:2.**

_____

_____

LESSON

6

Key Concept:
I can cooperate with God as He renews my mind.

New options for life

Taking the Step

We humbly ask God to renew our minds so that our sinful patterns can be transformed into patterns of life and health and righteousness.

> *Finally, brethren, whatever is true, whatever is honorable, whatever is right, whatever is pure, whatever is lovely, whatever is of good repute, if there is any excellence and if anything worthy of praise, let your mind dwell on these things.*
>
> –Philippians 4:8

In this Step you examined in detail the effects of the key false beliefs. You have considered the truths you need for recovery. Now you can do the work necessary to apply these truths. That work includes: making a Truth Card, exposing ungodly thoughts, and identifying and stopping the bargaining process.

Speaker and author Earnie Larsen compared our habits to a ravine washed out by desert rains. For years we have thought, felt, and acted in certain ways. When the rains fall, the water naturally runs in the same channel. The false beliefs are the channels for our guilt, shame, and dysfunctional behaviors. Now we want to change our behavior, thinking, and feeling. When the pressure builds up, we naturally will fall back into the old channels. We can decide what is more healthy behavior and begin to scratch out a new channel. When the rains come, much of the water still will run in the old ditches, but with time and persistence, we will make new paths.[2]

✎ **Write your own statement of the message in the story of the ravine and the desert rain.**

_____

_____

_____

We begin to scratch out that new channel by repeatedly feeding our mind with the truth. Here is an exercise in how to do just that: make a Truth Card.

A simple three-by-five-inch card can be a key factor in helping you base your self-worth on the liberating truths of the Scriptures. To make the Truth Card, use a three-by-five-inch card. On the front, write the following truths and their corresponding verses from Scripture.

- I am deeply loved by God (1 John 4:9-10).
- I am completely forgiven and fully pleasing to God (Romans 5:1).
- I am totally accepted by God (Colossians 1:21-22).
- I am a new creation, absolutely complete in Christ (2 Corinthians 5:17).

On the back of the card, write out the four false beliefs.

Carry this card with you at all times. For one month, each time you do a routine activity, like drinking your morning cup of coffee or tea, look at the

Let the word of Christ richly dwell within you, with all wisdom teaching and admonishing one another with psalms and hymns and spiritual songs, singing with thankfulness in your hearts to God.

–Colossians 3:16

front side and slowly meditate on each phrase. The Scripture at left tells us how we are to meditate on God's Word. Thank the Lord for making you into a person with these qualities. By doing this exercise for the next month, you can develop a habit of remembering that you are deeply loved, completely forgiven, fully pleasing, totally accepted, and complete in Christ.

If you have not already done so, memorize the supporting verses listed on the card. Look in your Bible for other verses that support these truths. Memorize them. Doing this will establish God's Word as the basis for these truths. Also memorize the false beliefs. The more familiar you are with these lies, the more you can recognize them in your thoughts. Then, as you recognize them, you more readily can replace them with the truths of God's Word.

Exposing Ungodly Thoughts

Habitual lies

One reason the lies we believe are so destructive is because they are habitual rather than conscious. We have a running conversation with ourselves, often without even realizing it. When we make a mistake, we begin to call ourselves names. Our thoughts reveal what we really believe, yet it is difficult for most of us have difficulty being objective in our thinking simply because we haven't trained ourselves to be. We usually let any and every thought run its course in our minds without analyzing its worth.

We need to develop the skill of identifying thoughts that reflect Satan's deceptions. Then we can reject those lies and replace them with scriptural truth.

✎ **As a first step in developing this skill, write down your thoughts in response to the four truths we've examined. For example, you might respond to the truth that you are fully pleasing to God by thinking, "No, I'm not! I mess up all the time, and to be fully pleasing, I'd have to be perfect!" When we see it written out, we more easily recognize that response as a lie. Write your own personal response, not necessarily what you may believe is the "correct" response.**

I am deeply loved by God: _____

_____

_____

_____

_____

I am completely forgiven and fully pleasing to God: _____

_____

_____

_____

_____

I am totally accepted by God: _____

_____

_____

_____

_____

I am complete in Christ: _____

_____

_____

_____

_____

_____

Thoughts that contradict these truths are lies. Reject them and replace them with passages of Scripture to reinforce the truth in your mind. We have listed some passages on which to reflect.

Propitiation: Matthew 18:21-35; Luke 7:36-50; Romans 3:25; 8:1-8; Colossians 3:12-14; Hebrews 2:17

Justification: Romans 3:19-24; 4:4-5; 5:1-11; Titus 2:11-14; 3:4-7

Reconciliation: John 15:14-16; Romans 5:8-10; Ephesians 2:11-18

Regeneration: 2 Corinthians 5:17; Galatians 5:16-24; Ephesians 2:4-5; 4:22-24; Colossians 3:5-17

As we become increasingly aware of the battle within us between the Spirit and the flesh, as we identify false beliefs that prompt sinful behavior and renew our minds with the truth of God's Word, we can confidently ask God to remove our sinful patterns of behavior. We can begin to live in His resurrection power. It is true that we never will be sinless until we reign with Him in His kingdom, but as we grow in Him, we will sin less.

Identifying and Changing Bargaining Behavior

When we see how our lives are damaged, we often respond by trying to bargain with ourselves, with our families, and with God. After learning about dysfunctional families, Christy quickly saw those painful effects in her own life. She asked a friend, "How can I get my father to love me?"

✏ Pretend that you are Christy's friend. How might you respond to her question?

_____

_____

_____

Secure in the Lord

Her friend explained, "Christy, it's not up to you to get your father to love you. It's up to you to be secure in the Lord, whether or not your father ever loves you."

Bargaining takes many shapes and forms, but its goal is to get other people to change by offering some change in ourselves. We'll say, "I'll be a better husband to her," or "I won't nag him any more, then he'll love me the way I want to be loved."

We can come up with all kinds of "deals" to get people to love us, but bargaining still is not totally objective. The responsibility still remains on us alone, and we still believe the best about the other person. Believing the best about others usually is good and right. But when a person by months and years of irresponsible, manipulative behavior proves he or she is pathological, then believing the best is naive and foolish.

Loving unconditionally

Bargaining expresses hope—hope that the other person will change and give us the love and worth that we need. But it is a false hope. Observing objectively leads us to a painful but honest conclusion: We need to give up the vain hope that the other person will change and will give us what we need. Giving up doesn't sound very godly, but it is. Giving up reflects reality. It involves abandoning the idol of pleasing others and having them love and accept us as the way to win self-worth. Actually, it is an act of worship to the Lord. It is loving the other person unconditionally whether or not they ever change.

The Awkwardness of Change

Expect wide mood swings

Many of us will experience wide swings in feelings and behavior during these early stages of growth. As we take the cap off our emotions for perhaps the first time, we may feel more hurt, anger, and fear than we ever thought possible. We may become afraid of how intense our emotions are, and we may put the cap back on until we have more courage to experiment again with these feelings. We also may feel more joy and freedom and love than ever before. We may cry for the first time in years. We may feel loved and comforted for the first time ever. We may ask hundreds of questions, or we may become more introspective than we've been before. These wide swings in mood and behavior are understandable. Don't try to clamp them; instead, realize that surges of emotion are perfectly understandable for one who has repressed them for years. Be patient.

Key Concept for Lesson 6
I can cooperate with God as He renews my mind.

✎ Please pray and ask God how this concept can apply in your life. Now please review this lesson. What has God shown you that you can use?

_____

_____

_____

Step Review

✎ Please review this Step. Pray and ask God to identify the Scriptures or principles that are particularly important for your life. Underline them. Then respond to the following:

Restate Step 7 in your own words: _____

_____

_____

_____

What do you have to gain by practicing this Step in your life?

_____

_____

_____

Reword your summary into a prayer of response to God. Thank Him for this Step, and affirm your commitment to Him.

_____

_____

_____

_____

Notes
[1]Robert S. McGee, *Search for Significance* LIFE Support Edition (Houston: Rapha Publishing, 1992), 48.
[2]Earnie Larsen, *Stage II Recovery*, E. Larsen Enterprises, Inc., 1990.

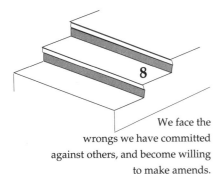

STEP 8

We face the wrongs we have committed against others, and become willing to make amends.

Forgiveness and Amends

WRITING HIS AMENDS LIST

After an hour Doug lifted his head. Tears were rolling gently down his cheeks. Writing this amends list was more difficult than he thought, but already he could see it would be worth the effort. Doug was creating a list of individuals he had wronged while he practiced his eating disorder. His list was complete with descriptions of the offenses. His sponsor asked him to record on one side of the paper all the people and offenses for which he needed to ask forgiveness. On the other side of the paper he was to record all the people and offenses he needed to forgive. Already Doug had filled three pages and hadn't yet made it to the second part of the assignment.

He listed Mrs. Whitworth, who made insensitive remarks about his weight. At a church dinner she said, "It looks like you need two chairs to sit there, honey." He realized he shouldn't have replied with sarcastic remarks.

He listed his mother. "It hurt to think of all the lies and deceptions I put her through, even though we both knew what was happening."

Then he wrote, "Bobbi. I grew up with her. She knew me like a book, but I put up a front just the same. We had talked about marriage a couple of times . . . just talked. We used to be able to talk about everything until I started to get worse. Funny how you seem to hurt the people you love the most . . . ."

As the list grew, Doug thought, *I didn't realize that my behavior affected so many people.* Through the pain he also began to feel a sense of hope. He would do what was necessary. He wanted to be well, to respect himself, and to honor Christ.

Step 8   *We make a list of all persons who have hurt us and choose to forgive them. We also make a list of all persons we have harmed, and become willing to make amends to them all.*

Memory verse   *And just as you want people to treat you, treat them in the same way.*
—Luke 6:31

Overview for Step 8   **Lesson 1: People to Forgive**
Goal: You will accept responsibility for forgiving others.
Lesson 2: Forgiving Others
Goal: You will describe the negative consequences of failing to forgive.
Lesson 3: Taking the Step Part 1
Goal: You will make a list of people to forgive.
Lesson 4: Taking the Step Part 2
Goal: You will make a list of the people you have harmed.

People to Forgive

We make a list of all persons who have hurt us and choose to forgive them. We also make a list of all persons we have harmed, and become willing to make amends to them all.

> *The wise woman builds her house, but the foolish tears it down with her own hands.*
> –Proverbs 14:1

Key Concept:
My refusal to forgive is self-destructive.

Forgiveness means that we choose to give up our self-proclaimed "right" to blame others.

Step 8 involves writing two lists of people: those we have harmed—to whom we owe amends—and those we need to forgive because they have harmed us. Proverbs 14:1 powerfully applies to the issue of forgiving. By refusing to forgive we harm ourselves. We tear down the house in which we must live.

Up to this point we have used eating-disordered behavior as part of our strategy to repress or deny strong emotions like fear and anger and to prevent them from causing pain in our lives. Unfortunately, it didn't always work—we still got hurt. We hid our true feelings. For years we nursed grudges, hatred, jealousy, and secret anger. Bottled-up emotions grew. Those strong emotions supported our addiction. The process of recovery requires that we deal with hidden or denied feelings. Forgiveness means that we choose to give up our self-proclaimed "right" to blame, condemn, find fault, punish, and retaliate against others.

 A list of methods we often substitute for forgiveness appears below. Check each method which you have used or currently are using.

- ○ 1. Forgetting an offense or pretending it never happened;
- ○ 2. Trying to bury the pain or avoid the issues by binging or purging the rage away;
- ○ 3. Punishing your offender by passive-aggressive forms of revenge, like procrastination, the "silent treatment," or starving yourself.

Rather than pretending the offense never happened or burying the pain by practicing our addiction, we learn in recovery to deal with the offense as it is—raw, ugly, and painful. Instead of secretly punishing the offender, we learn to put aside our pride and deal with the offender in humility. We gain freedom from the burden of remembering the offense. We allow everyone involved to settle the issue and get on with their lives.

As long as we hold a grudge against another person for his or her offense—no matter how long ago it happened—we carry the full impact of the offense. Many hurting people go to their graves needlessly bound by the chains of past injuries because they failed to forgive! If any of this strikes a painful nerve within you, pay close attention to the exercises in this Step. Along with the inner working of the Holy Spirit, the exercises will help you experience freedom from the tyranny of a bitter, unforgiving spirit.

We insist we are "fat" when we actually are near death from starvation.

Ironically, we often act out through our addictions the feelings we try to deny.
- Some of us eat compulsively. We consciously or unconsciously blame ourselves for the offenses of others.
- We think obsessively about our body weight.
- We insist we are "fat" when we actually are near death from starvation.

Perhaps what we really feel is all the extra weight of the anger against the ones who did us wrong. Perhaps we desperately try to purge the anger and shame that we have from being hurt by people in our past. In any of these cases, we carry a heavy burden.

Our unwillingness to forgive others also blocks our ability to experience God's forgiveness. This compounds the deep feelings of shame and self-hatred and strengthens the old cycles of performance, perfectionism, and hopelessness. Step 8 helps us to seek liberation from this slavery!

The thought of Step 8 may frighten you. Your mind already may be racing to Step 9, where you actually will begin to make amends; however, the purpose of Step 8 simply is to identify those people to whom you need to make amends. By making your list, you will clarify your responsibilities in your relationships with others. Work the Steps one at a time!

You may want to avoid the responsibility to forgive. You may think that your response to someone else was exactly what he or she deserved. Read the words appearing in the margin from the apostle Paul to the Roman Christians.

Never pay back evil for evil to anyone. Respect what is right in the sight of all men. If possible, so far as it depends on you, be at peace with all men. Never take your own revenge, beloved, but leave room for the wrath of God, for it is written, "Vengeance is Mine, I will repay," says the Lord.

–Romans 12:17-19

✎ **Which of the following statements do you think most accurately describes what Paul meant by to *be at peace with all men*?**

○ 1. Never argue with anyone.
○ 2. Let others always have their way.
○ 3. Settle disagreements as quickly as possible.
○ 4. Don't let anyone walk over you.

Arguments and disagreements with others are normal and may be justified or even necessary. But the broken peace between people that results should be repaired as quickly as possible. Although all issues may not be resolved, and disagreements may remain, forgiveness and restoration of fellowship are better than bitterness and hatred. The physical, emotional, and spiritual toll of unforgiveness is just not worth it. The answer in the exercise is number 3.

✎ **How would your life be different if you allowed God to take care of your grievances, rather than trying to take revenge on someone else yourself?**

_____

_____

_____

_____

Forgiveness

One of the benefits we experience from Step 5 is acceptance. Once we have experienced acceptance from another person, we more easily can accept and forgive other people. In fact, our ability to love and forgive is directly related to how much we have experienced love and forgiveness. As Christ said, "he who is forgiven little, loves little" (Luke 7:47). The reverse also is true.

In the past we found it easier to block out or temporarily repress feelings of resentment against others. We waited for the right moment to get revenge. We buried the painful emotions so deeply that we no longer recognized them as resentments.

Do you simply not like to be around some people? Do you have a difficult time looking some people in the eye? Do you get angry every time you even think of certain people? The following exercise is designed to help you see the need to forgive others and accept the responsibility to do so when necessary.

In Matthew 18:21-35 Jesus told the story of the unmerciful servant. He said a king called in a servant who owed him 10,000 talents. The talents were measures of money. Depending on whether the talents were of silver or gold, the value of the debt was between $20 million and $300 million (Unger's Bible Dictionary). The servant was unable to pay, so the king forgave him the debt. Then the servant found one of his fellow-servants who owed him a very small amount of money. The servant who had just been forgiven the huge debt grabbed his fellow-servant and began to choke him. "Pay back what you owe me!" he demanded. Read the rest of the parable which appears in the margin.

 Was it possible for the first servant to pay back the $20 to $300 million that he owed? ○ **Yes** ○ **No**

Likewise, before you trusted Christ, how great was your debt to God for your sin? Was it possible for you ever to repay it?

_____

The debt of the first servant—like our debt of sin—was beyond any hope of payment. Yet the man who the king graciously forgave so much refused to forgive even a small debt.

 Write your own statement of the meaning of the parable.

_____

_____

You could have stated the meaning of the parable in one of many ways. You may have written that since God forgave you of so much, you are responsible to forgive others.

 God wants you to forgive others to the same degree He forgave you. Circle all the terms below that describe how God has forgiven you.

1. fully and completely	7. until I sin again
2. after much begging	8. without reservation
3. at personal cost	9. with little concern
4. after becoming sinless	10. in spite of my sin
5. without earning it	11. after earning it
6. without deserving it	12. after deserving it

Being offended by others is a frequent experience in life. You may go through periods when it seems that almost everybody is letting you down. You are hurt by both your experience of the offense and your reliving it over and over

His fellow servant fell to his knees and begged him, "Be patient with me, and I will pay you back." But he refused. Instead, he went off and had the man thrown into prison until he could pay the debt. When the other servants saw what had happened, they were greatly distressed and went and told their master everything that had happened. Then the master called the servant in. "You wicked servant," he said, "I canceled all that debt of yours because you begged me to. Shouldn't you have had mercy on your fellow servant just as I had on you?" In anger his master turned him over to the jailers to be tortured, until he should pay back all he owed. This is how my heavenly Father will treat each of you unless you forgive your brother from your heart.
–Matthew 18:29-35, NIV

Why make a list?

Deal with offenses

in your mind. In fact, the first pain of the wrong usually amounts only to a small fraction of the total hurt. To avoid being offended is impossible, but you can avoid most of the pain if you will learn to deal quickly and completely with offenses rather than mentally reliving them countless times. Failing to forgive others is a sure way of cutting the flow of God's power in your life. Unforgiveness brings about many negative consequences which you will examine later in this Step. Answers number 1, 3, 5, 6, 8, and 10 describe God's way of forgiving.

> ## Key Concept for Lesson 1
> My refusal to forgive is self-destructive.

✎ **Pray and ask God how this concept can apply in your life. Now please review this lesson. What has God shown you that you can use?**

_____

_____

And just as you want people to treat you, treat them in the same way.

–Luke 6:31

The suggested memory verse is printed in the margin. Repeat it five times. In the space in the margin attempt to write the verse from memory.

➥ **Ask God to help you make this verse a reality in your life in a way that you could unmistakably point others to Christ. Commit yourself to working through this Step as fully as you can in the power of His Spirit.**

LESSON 2

Key Concept:
Failing to forgive others can cause me to injure myself again and again.

Forgiving Others

We make a list of all persons who have hurt us and choose to forgive them. We also make a list of all persons we have harmed, and become willing to make amends to them all.

> *I am writing to you, little children, because your sins are forgiven you for His name's sake.*
>
> –1 John 2:12

Even though God has forgiven us, we seem to forget about this fact when we decide how we will treat others. We inflict punishment on those around us—and on ourselves—by refusing to forgive them. We add up all the times someone has wronged us and all the things we don't like about the person.

Much of the material in this lesson comes from *Search for Significance* LIFE Support Edition.[1] When you have completed *Conquering Eating Disorders* you may wish to participate in a *Search for Significance* group to develop a more Christ-centered sense of self-worth.

Reasons We Don't Forgive

We often fail to forgive others (and ourselves) because we don't think it's possible to forgive. We forget how God graciously has forgiven all of our sins through Christ's death, and we come up with reasons we can't forgive.

✎ **The following represent many of the countless excuses we make for our unwillingness to forgive ourselves and others. Write the letter of the matching reason in the left margin beside each of the case studies below.**

a. the person never asked for forgiveness

b. the offense was too great

c. the person won't accept responsibility

d. I simply don't like the person

e. the person did it too many times

f. the person isn't truly sorry

_____1. Grant's wife left him for another man, and Grant was bitter toward his wife. Her infidelity was too great a sin for him to forgive.

_____2. Janet's mother emotionally abused Janet as a child. Her mother never has admitted her harsh treatment of Janet. Janet refuses to forgive her mother.

_____3. John pulled a practical joke on you. His prank caused you to be late for class, and your professor refused to accept your paper because you didn't turn it in on time. John doesn't see anything wrong with a little joke. Oh, he made some rather insincere statements about being sorry, but he still thinks the incident was hilarious.

_____4. Darrell knew he made you angry when he deliberately didn't invite you to his Christmas open house. He never asked you for forgiveness. You decide to withhold forgiveness until it's requested.

_____5. Candy's husband stayed out late playing cards every Friday night for three years. Some nights he didn't come home at all. "Forgive that jerk? Look how many times he's wronged me!" Candy exclaimed.

_____6. Cindy just plain didn't like Martha, who constantly was trying to make Cindy look bad at work. Every emotion in Cindy called for getting back at her co-worker. She certainly wasn't interested in forgiving her.

✎ **Which of the above reasons has kept you from forgiving in the past? Below, describe how that reason interfered with your ability to forgive.**

_____

_____

_____

_____

_____

_____

Possible answers include 1. b, 2. c, 3. f, 4. a, 5. e, 6. d.

✎ Here are more of the excuses we make for our unwillingness to forgive ourselves and others. Again, write the letter of the matching reason in the left margin beside each of the case studies.

a. I've found an excuse for the offense.

_____1. George's best friend, Hal, swindled George out of $10,000. George's mind raced through times he had been generous to Hal. Hal had carefully planned the swindle. George felt he never could forgive the planned betrayal.

b. Someone has to punish the person.

_____2. Ben excused himself for slandering Steve by pointing out how Steve had offended him. He felt justified in lying to destroy Steve's reputation. Forgiving him might mean Ben would have to be nice to this scoundrel.

c. The person did it deliberately.

_____3. Shirley had been cold for two weeks to Greg, who had offended her. She would forgive him, all right—as soon as she was through punishing him.

d. Something keeps me from forgiving.

_____4. Steve knew he should forgive Joe, but something kept him from it. He told others that the devil kept him from having a forgiving spirit toward Joe, but Steve showed no signs of trying to resist Satan, either.

e. If I forgive, I'll have to treat the offender well.

_____5. Mary thought she had forgiven her brother for his cruelty to her when they were children, but during arguments between the two, Mary kept bringing up past incidents. When Mary and her brother were together, it seemed that she always was stewing about these past misdeeds.

f. I'll forgive but I won't ever forget.

_____6. Hank behaved irresponsibly. His wife, Sally, attempted to forgive him by placing the blame on his mother, who babied Hank even after he was grown. Sally thought she had forgiven Hank when really she had just excused him.

✎ With which of the above case studies do you most readily identify? Below, describe a situation in which the excuse used in that case study has kept you from forgiving.

_____

_____

_____

_____

_____

Possible answers include 1. c, 2. e, 3. b, 4. d, 5. f, 6. a.

When We Don't Forgive

When we fail to forgive others, our lives and our relationships suffer. Let's take a look at some problems in our lives that stem directly from a lack of forgiveness.

• **Stress:** Sarah announced to the group that her husband did not deserve to be forgiven. She vowed that she wasn't going to forgive him even if it meant her life. It turned out that it did. Sarah died of kidney failure which physicians said was related to the extreme stress under which she lived. She wanted to kill her husband, but in reality, she caused her own death.

Many people experience extreme stress because they hold inside bitterness and anger. Their stress occurs because they have not forgiven. In the margin write about a time when you have experienced physical illness because of the stress of unforgiveness.

• **Self-inflicted Reinjury:** Robert recalled this incident: "As I drove home, I saw flashing through my mind the face of a guy I played basketball with in college. He was a great enemy of mine. He was one of the few people I ever met whom I truly wanted to punch out. I began to remember the unkind things he did to me. Soon anger started creeping up inside of me. I had not thought about this fellow for years, and I'm sure that he doesn't remember me at all. Yet my reliving this event caused me a lot of pain. I had not properly dealt with it in the beginning."

• **No More Love:** "I don't know if I can ever love someone again" is a frequent complaint from those offended by someone about whom they care deeply. Our deepest hurts occur at the hands of those we love. One way we deal with the pain of being offended is simply to withdraw, refusing to love anymore. We often make this unconscious decision when we have not adequately dealt with an offense. We desperately may want to love again but feel that we are incapable of it. Refusing to experience love and feeling unable to love are devastating conditions.

✎ **Which of these three problems stemming from lack of forgiveness do you most readily spot in your life? Describe it here.**

_____

_____

• **Bitterness:** Emotions trace their lines on our faces. We think others don't notice what's going on inside us, but even the casual observer usually can detect our anger. Kristin recalled seeing a neighbor go through difficulties in her marriage. Hatred was so much a part of the neighbor's life that her face became permanently snarled. Kristin described the neighbor as still having that ugly look on her face. Unforgiveness produces ugliness of all sorts.

• **Perpetual Conflict:** A husband and wife, both of whom had been married previously, received counseling several years ago. Having been hurt in their first marriages, each anticipated hurt from the present spouse. At the smallest offense each reacted as if the spouse were about to deliver the final blow. This husband and the wife constantly were on the defensive. They protected themselves from the attacks they imagined their mate would deliver. Having been offended in the past, they anticipated more hurt in the present and the future. They reacted in a way that perpetuated the conflict.

• **Walls that Keep Others Out:** Many of us refuse to experience love from those who love us. We often may become anxious and threatened when personal intimacy becomes possible. Jane hoped and prayed that her husband

---

Describe a time in which stress from a past wrong someone has done to you made you physically ill.

_____

_____

_____

_____

Has failing to forgive put an ugly snarl on your face?

Frank would come to know the Lord. She thought that if he were a Christian, he would be more loving toward her and toward their children. One day Frank accepted Christ. His life began to change. He paid more attention to Jane and started spending time with her and the children. He was sensitive and loving. Was it a dream come true? Instead of rejoicing, Jane deeply resented Frank for not changing sooner! *If Frank is able to love us like this now, then he's always had the ability,* she thought. She also felt confused and guilty about her anger.

Hiding behind a wall of unforgiveness is a lonely experience.

Jane's anger was a defense mechanism to keep distance between Frank and herself. The closer they might get, the more pain she might experience if he reverted to his old ways. She never really had forgiven Frank, so the bricks of unforgiveness were stacked to form a wall that kept him from getting too close. Hiding behind a wall of unforgiveness is a lonely experience.

✎ **Do you see any of these results of unforgiveness in your life? Review these last three results of unforgiveness; think about them for a few moments. Describe below a time this problem has affected you.**

____

____

____

We have looked at what happens to us when we don't forgive. God loves us and expects us to care about ourselves because we are His creation. When we abuse our bodies and our emotions by not forgiving, we are not living the way God wants us to live. Not forgiving also hinders our relationships with others—our brothers and sisters in Christ about whom God cares deeply. We can choose to stop acting in a way that harms ourselves and others.

➔ **Stop and pray, asking God to help you forgive others and to help you remember that forgiving others is a part of His plan.**

Key Concept for Lesson 2

Failing to forgive others can cause me to injure myself again and again.

✎ **Pray and ask God how this concept can apply in your life. Now please review this lesson. What has God shown you that you can use?**

____

____

Write from memory Luke 6:31. Look on page 155 to check your memory work.

____

____

Taking the Step, Part 1

We make a list of all persons who have hurt us and choose to forgive them. We also make a list of all persons we have harmed, and become willing to make amends to them all.

> *Whenever you stand praying, forgive, if you have anything against anyone; so that your Father also who is in heaven may forgive you your transgressions.*
>
> –Mark 11:25

Key Concept:
Forgiving is counting the debt paid in full.

Sometimes we think that forgiveness is like a large eraser that wipes our offenses off the books. God never has forgiven like this. For each offense He demanded full payment. This is the reason for the cross. Christ has paid for our sins in full.

Christians have a special ability to forgive because they can forgive as God does. God has forgiven us fully and completely. We, of all people, know what it is like to experience unconditional forgiveness. As a result, we in turn can forgive those around us. Think of it this way: I will not have to forgive anyone else for anything that can compare with what Christ already has forgiven me for doing.

And be kind to one another, tender-hearted, forgiving each other, just as God in Christ has forgiven you.
–Ephesians 4:32

We can look at others' offenses in a different light when we compare them to our sin of rebellion that Christ has forgiven completely. Read the verse appearing in the left margin about what Paul said regarding this kind of forgiveness.

 List 10 things for which you are glad God in Christ has forgiven you. This can prompt you to be willing to forgive everyone who has done wrong to you.

1. _____
2. _____
3. _____
4. _____
5. _____

6. _____
7. _____
8. _____
9. _____
10. _____

➜ Stop and pray, thanking God for forgiving you for the matters you mentioned above.

Your Book of Forgiveness

The exercise on the following pages will help you to recognize any lack of forgiveness in your life and will help you move toward a life-style of forgiving others just as God in Christ has forgiven you. It is not a mechanical formula but a living opportunity to exercise a life-changing power. Forgiving is one of the many awesome responsibilities God has given His children. It is holy work not to be taken lightly.

Write the headings listed on this page on a separate sheet of paper. In the appropriate spaces, complete the information requested below. Add to this forgiveness guide when you need to and refer to it frequently, focusing on the forgiveness and not the offenses.

- **Persons to be forgiven:** List everyone who participated in the offense.
- **Offense:** Describe in some detail an event which caused you pain.
- **Date:** When did the offense take place?
- **Reasons for not forgiving:** Go through the summary of reasons for not forgiving. Which ones apply?

As an act of your will, and with God's help, choose to forgive. Remember the complete forgiveness you have in Christ.

At the conclusion of the exercise, use the prayer provided at the end of this lesson (or use your own) as an exercise of faith for each offense.

Below is an example of the guide.

People to Be Forgiven	My brothers, Harry and Frank	_____ _____ _____ _____
Offense	Refusing to have anything to do with me	_____ _____ _____
Date	1974 - 1981	_____
Reasons for Not Forgiving	1, 2, 4, 5, 9	_____ _____ _____ _____

Prayer of Forgiveness

Dear Lord,
I forgive _____ (name) for _____ (offense) on the basis that you have forgiven me freely and have commanded me to forgive others. I have the capacity to do this because Christ has completely forgiven me. I do not excuse this person's offense in any way, nor do I use any excuse for not forgiving. Thank You, Lord Jesus, for helping me to forgive him (her). I also confess that I have sinned by using the following excuses for not forgiving: _____ (name any). Thank You for forgiving me and for helping me to have victory in this important area of my life. Amen.

Key Concept for Lesson 3
Forgiving is counting the debt paid in full.

 Review today's lesson. Name at least one thing God wants you to do in response to this study. Ask Him for the grace to help you do it.

_____

_____

LESSON 4

Key Concept:
I begin to make amends by writing a list.

Taking the Step, Part 2

We make a list of all persons who have hurt us and choose to forgive them. We also make a list of all persons we have harmed, and become willing to make amends to them all.

> *God has not given us a spirit of fear, but of power and of love and of a sound mind.*
>
> –2 Timothy 1:7, NKJV

This lesson is designed to prepare you to ask forgiveness of and to make amends to the people you have offended. The task before you is simply to list their names and the offenses. Don't get ahead of yourself on this Step.

You probably do not know for certain whether or not you need to make amends to certain individuals. Sometimes you may feel you need to make amends when you really don't need to. For now, make your list. You will determine in Step 9 how to deal with each situation. Use additional paper and refer to Step 4 as often as necessary. Use the following guidelines as you write your amends list.

Questions to Ask in Filling Out Your List of Offenses

- From whom did I cheat or steal?
- What promises and/or confidences did I break (sexual infidelity, lying, sharing something told to me in confidence) and whom did I hurt or betray?

Whom did I harm?

- For whom did I cause pain by missing family obligations (birthdays, anniversaries) or other special days or commitments?
- What social responsibilities (laws, commitments) did I break or avoid, and who was harmed by my actions?
- What financial obligations did I avoid or wrongly create, and who was harmed or inconvenienced by my behavior?
- What have I done to harm those with whom I have worked?
- What harm have I caused by my eating-disordered behavior (refer to the "sanity list" in Step 2 for help), and whom did I harm?
- To whom have I neglected to show gratitude?
- Who was victimized by my anger, resentment, blame, or fear?

My List of Offenses

People I Have Harmed	How I Harmed Them
_____	_____
_____	_____
_____	_____
_____	_____
_____	_____
_____	_____
_____	_____

A clearer view

As she grew closer to Christ, Annie's outlook on life improved. Like the view of a climber ascending a mountain, Annie's view of her world became wider and clearer. Once a slave to perfectionistic thoughts and actions, she began to feel God's forgiveness and loving acceptance. She had beaten herself to exhaustion on a never-ending, self-defeating treadmill of critical attitudes toward others, constant weight checks, intense exercise sessions, purging, and starving. Still she never felt accepted or perfect.

Annie tells how she "had been a real Christian for eight months. I say 'real' because I had tried to be one for a long time by pleasing church people and God. I had become a physical and emotional wreck trying to be perfect, though I didn't know it at the time. As a genuine child of God, I began to feel real love for the first time I could remember.

"A passage in the Bible clarified my drive for perfection and my hatred toward those who had hurt me. In my old warped thinking I would have taken this passage to mean I had to be perfect to be a child of God. Now I see an entirely different meaning. We become perfect in God's eyes through Jesus. We then begin to understand God's true nature, receive His grace and forgiveness, and learn to give that same forgiveness to ourselves and others. We are most like God—closest to His perfection—when we forgive and love our enemies. If we are our own worst enemies, then we need most to forgive ourselves."

You have heard that it was said, "You shall love you neighbor, and hate your enemy." But I say to you, love your enemies, and pray for those who persecute you in order that you may be sons of your Father who is in heaven. Therefore you are to be perfect, as your heavenly Father is perfect.
                    –Matthew 5:43-45, 48

 Read Matthew 5:43-45, 48, appearing in the margin, the passage about which Annie was speaking. According to the passage, what is an evidence that we are children of our Father who is in heaven?

By this all men will know that you are My disciples, if you have love for one another.
                    –John 13:35

Love shows that we belong to God. Love can be demonstrated toward fellow believers (John 13:35) or toward our enemies (Matthew 5:44-45). Love also is evidence before the world that God sees us as perfect in His eyes.

For I am confident of this very thing, that He who began a good work in you will perfect it until the day of Christ Jesus.
—Philippians 1:6

 Read Philippians 1:6 appearing in the margin. Achieving perfection by performance is not the focus of the passage in Matthew. The focus is Christ in you. How real is that truth to you? On the scale below, place an X where you think you are between striving for perfection in your own power and allowing God to perfect you in His power.

Striving in my own power   Letting God perfect me in His power

You may find yourself marking the scale much farther to the left than you would like. Your goal eventually can be to reach the point of trusting God to such a degree that you will let Him be in charge of changing your life. Wherever your honest reply was above, you can move toward the ability to relax the self-criticism and trust God to work.

➥ **Take time to pray. Thank God for His gift of acceptance—for seeing you as perfect because of the shed blood of His Son. By faith, claim His strength and His love as you commit to love and forgive others, not by perfectionistic self-effort, but by surrendering to His loving control.**

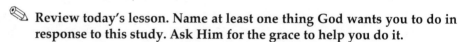

Key Concept for Lesson 4
I begin to make amends by writing a list.

 Review today's lesson. Name at least one thing God wants you to do in response to this study. Ask Him for the grace to help you do it.

Step Review

 Please review this Step. Pray and ask God to identify the Scriptures or principles that are particularly important for your life. Underline them. Then respond to the following:

Restate Step 8 in your own words: _____

_____

_____

Reword your summary into a prayer of response to God. Thank Him for this Step, and affirm your commitment to Him.

_____

_____

Notes
[1]McGee, Robert S. *Search for Significance* LIFE Support Edition (Houston: Rapha Publishing, 1992), 129-130.

STEP 9

Making My Amends

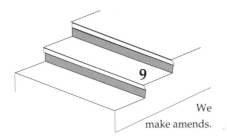

9

We make amends.

CONFRONTING THE PAST

This was it . . . the biggie. Barbara's sponsor had instructed her to begin with her smaller amends. She said Barbara would build the strength and faith to make the more difficult ones. Barbara had followed that advice. She felt much stronger and better about herself as she thought of the relationships she had mended.

Now it was time for the amend Barbara feared most. During the darkest days of her bulimic behavior, Barbara regularly stole from a grocery store. At first she merely ate some food items from her shopping cart. Later she ate most of the contents of boxes and returned the boxes to the shelves. Finally she hid packages of laxatives in her purse.

Barbara had money to pay for the items, but money wasn't the reason she stole. She stole because of the way people looked at her when she checked out with all her junk food and her little pink laxative pills. Stealing seemed easier than risking discovery of her addiction.

Now Barbara was prepared to make her amends. She walked into the store thinking about signs she had seen: "Shoplifters will be prosecuted to the full extent of the law."

With resolve Barbara walked through the automatic doors. She asked for the manager. As she walked into the office, Barbara said, "My name is Barbara. I have stolen items from your store. I've come to do whatever is necessary to make up for my actions." Read more about Barbara on page 177.

Step 9   *We make direct amends to such people where possible, except when doing so will injure them or others.*

Scripture   *If therefore you are presenting your offering at the altar, and there remember that your brother has something against you, leave your offering there before the altar, and go your way; first be reconciled to your brother, and then come and present your offering.*
—Matthew 5:23-24

Overview for Step 9

Lesson 1: The Benefits of Amends
   Goal: You will describe some of the benefits that come from making amends.

Lesson 2: The Skill of Confrontation
   Goal: You will develop a plan for confronting someone you have wronged or who has wronged you.

Lesson 3: Taking the Step
   Goal: You will begin to make amends.

The Benefits of Amends

We make direct amends to such people where possible, except when doing so will injure them or others.

> *See that no one repays another with evil for evil, but always seek after that which is good for one another and for all men.*
>
> –1 Thessalonians 5:15

Key Concept:
Step 9 requires faith and courage, but it pays great dividends.

amends–n. compensation for a loss or injury (Webster's)

Step 9 picks up where Step 8 left off—preparing to make amends as appropriate and to restore wounded relationships. In this Step you will design and carry through your amends.

Many benefits await you if you are willing to make amends to those you have hurt and to deal appropriately with those who have hurt you. Making amends will release you from the control the people you have offended have over your life. Think about people you have been avoiding—those whom you've been dodging, hoping they won't see you, or those you've been excluding altogether from your circle of friends. Have you ever considered that your guilt and fear are controlling you and are keeping you from the life God wants you to have?

Released from prison

When you make amends, you are released from the emotional prisons of your past. This is true whether or not the other person accepts your amend. This releases you from the fear that someone will discover something about you that you don't want known. As you probably know, this fear could haunt and control you for the rest of your life if you don't confess it.

Making amends will enable you to enjoy fellowship with others—an important key to your continued recovery. Secrecy and isolation supported your eating disorder. Restoring relationships replaces adversaries with friends who may add their own healing touch or word to your rehabilitation. This process may start with a simple act of forgiveness, request for forgiveness, or restitution.

✎ **What do you fear most about making amends?**

_____

Do you think this is a realistic fear? Why or why not?

_____

_____

Are you willing to lay aside this fear and make amends even though it may be painful to do so?

_____

What possible joys might result from making amends? _____

_____

To which of these do you most look forward? Why? _____

_____

Correcting Problems in Faith

Those of us with an eating disorder are perfectionists in ways unique to us. We tend to be overly responsible about catering to the needs we perceive in others. We sometimes even assume responsibility for their sins! We each are somewhat like the man who read a classified ad which specified, "Only responsible people need apply." He decided that this must be him, because no matter where he went, he felt responsible if anything went wrong.

Discernment required

Step 9 requires real discernment. We may find ourselves trying to "make amends" to some bewildered people we never offended. Many of us have such sensitive consciences that we tend to blame ourselves for things we have not even done and for things that were not wrong or harmful to begin with. We may stir up trouble with people who were not aware of our offense but who react quite negatively when they find out.

Step 9 is another good place to seek help from our sponsors. Someone who is mature and familiar with the program of recovery can help us "check our thinking." Again, a sponsor should be someone whose relationship with God is more mature than is our own. Ideally, this person will have spent a minimum of one year in recovery (preferably from eating disorders) and will have worked through the 12 Steps, or at least through Step 9. A person like this usually can provide the objectivity we need to determine whether or not we need to make amends, and if so, to whom.

Step 9 calls for direct amends. Direct not only means face-to-face but it means that we are open, honest, and to the point, rather than seeking to excuse or minimize our wrongdoings or trying to manipulate a favorable response from the person to whom we are trying to make restitution.

Make a complete change

Perhaps the most important point of Step 9 is understanding that "making direct amends" does not refer only to making restitution to those we have wronged in the past. It means learning how to be open, honest, and straightforward in all of our relationships. We are not simply dealing with the past here. We are beginning to make a complete change in the way we relate to others—both in the present and the future.

Why is this necessary? Part of our eating disorder has involved isolation, secrecy, private shame, and attempts to manipulate others to gain or keep their approval. We manipulated our bodies to win or maintain others' approval or to keep our distance from them. We were endless people-pleasers, never violating the unspoken code not to tell others the truth even when it needed to be told. Instead, we stuffed and swallowed our emotions of anger and resentment, never really speaking up when we needed to—both for our benefit and for theirs.

We probably still cringe at the word *confrontation*. We think that it means some brutal, ugly scene we want to avoid at all costs. We may think it's easier to say nothing about an offense, a hurt, a loss, than to speak up and run the risk of an argument or other emotional contest. But confrontations, properly and

confrontation–n. a face-to-face meeting (Webster's)

Better is open rebuke than love that is concealed. Faithful are the wounds of a friend, but deceitful are the kisses of an enemy.
–Proverbs 27:5-6

carefully used, can be productive means to set things right by bringing long, overdue attention to and discussions focused on problem solving, instead of focused on face-saving or revenge. In order to see this more clearly, take a closer look at what confrontation really involves.

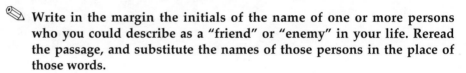 **Read Proverbs 27:5-6 which appears in the margin. Below rewrite it in your own words.**

_____

_____

How would you define *friend* and *enemy* as used in this passage?

_____

_____

The friend mentioned in the passage is someone who is willing to tell the truth—even if that truth is painful. The enemy mentioned in the verse takes the easy way out and tells you what you want to hear.

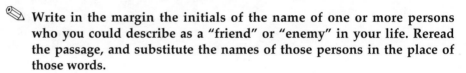 **Write in the margin the initials of the name of one or more persons who you could describe as a "friend" or "enemy" in your life. Reread the passage, and substitute the names of those persons in the place of those words.**

Most of us label others as friend or foe on the basis of whether or not they support our goals (or our habits, cravings, wants, etc.). If they stand in our way, they are enemies. In the same way most of us are afraid that we will lose the acceptance we crave from others if we confront them honestly. We are afraid that someone will perceive us as "attacking" the person if we are open, honest and direct with him or her. We therefore need to learn what it means to confront as opposed to attack, because these words have very different meanings.

Confrontation does not mean attack. It means to face someone with the facts as we see them and to open a dialogue. The purpose is to solve problems. Faith is a key in understanding and using confrontation. Left uncorrected, a situation may fester into an ugly life-scarring wound, but confronted in faith, it can lead to restoration and redemption. Proverbs 27:6 says, "faithful are the wounds of a friend."

Key Concept for Lesson 1
Step 9 requires faith and courage, but it pays great dividends.

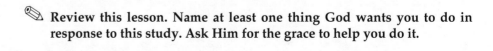 **Review this lesson. Name at least one thing God wants you to do in response to this study. Ask Him for the grace to help you do it.**

_____

➡ In faith, thank God that He will show Himself strong in this area of your life, and will help you to correct any longstanding unresolved relationships. Begin praying for the people you will confront in love in the last lesson of this Step.

The Skill of Confrontation

We make direct amends to such people where possible, except when doing so will injure them or others.

> *He who rebukes a man will afterward find more favor than he who flatters with the tongue.*
>
> –Proverbs 28:23

Key Concept:
Solving problems through honest confrontation is an important recovery skill.

Jan amazed Cathy. Cathy never had experienced anything like it. When a problem occurred Jan went directly to Cathy, pulled up a chair, looked Cathy in the eye, and spoke the truth. Cathy wasn't used to this direct approach. In Cathy's experience people did everything but tell the truth and solve problems. They smiled, said nothing was wrong, and talked behind your back. They said things were OK when they weren't. Cathy discovered that Jan had the life skill of confrontation, and Cathy was beginning to think confrontation wasn't such a bad thing after all.

This lesson provides a model for simple and effective confrontations for many situations. It presents guidelines and examples to help you develop your own approach to confronting both those who have wronged you and those you have wronged. Not designed as a foolproof formula of success, it nevertheless is founded on the hope that God will restore those relationships that were damaged in your past. This lesson lays the foundation for the next one, in which you actually confront someone in love, in an attempt to gain forgiveness, repair a wounded relationship, or make amends for a past offense.

Repair a relationship

Principles to Guide Confrontations

Use the following guidelines to direct your attitudes and actions regarding confrontation. Begin to memorize this simple outline: confrontations have a goal, a focus, an initiator, and limits.

1. **Rule number one:** Appropriate confrontations have a goal.

 Read the Scripture appearing in the margin, and state below in general terms the goal of confrontations.

If your brother sins against you, go and tell him his fault between you and him alone. If he hears you, you have gained your brother.

–Matthew 18:15

_____

The goal of the confrontation is to restore the relationship—to *gain your brother.*

2. Rule number two: Appropriate confrontations have a focus.

 According to Matthew 18:15, what is the general focus of appropriate confrontation?

_____

The appropriate focus of confrontation is the offense, not the offender. The point is not to place blame but to solve problems.

3. Rule number three: Someone initiates a confrontation; confrontations do not initiate themselves.

 Some passages of Scripture say that the offender is to take the initiative to make amends. In Galatians 6:1 and Matthew 18:15 who initiates the confrontation, the one who committed the offense or the one who was offended?

_____

Brethren, even if a man is caught in any trespass, you who are spiritual, restore such a one in a spirit of gentleness; each one looking to yourself, lest you too be tempted.

–Galatians 6:1

Each of us at one time or another has thought, "It's the other person's problem. Let him or her do something about it!" Such thinking is a luxury we cannot afford. We have our recovery to think about. The passages above instruct the one who was offended to initiate healing.

- Be the first to offer or request forgiveness or to make amends.
- Be humble in your confrontation; you could be wrong!
- Be gentle in your confrontation; you could be next!
- Be firm, but show mercy, forgiveness, and love. Love covers a multitude of sins (1 Peter 4:8).
- Listen as well as talk; you may learn something.

Gossiping to others is not appropriate confrontation.

4. Rule number four: Confrontation is to be between only specific individuals. Gossiping to others is not appropriate confrontation.

 According to Galatians 6:1 and Matthew 18:15, what persons should be involved in the initial confrontation?

_____

Both Jesus and the apostle Paul were very clear. Confrontation is initially to be between the two parties involved.

- Make quiet and private your efforts at reconciliation and making amends.
- Attempt face-to-face meetings whenever possible, but use letters or phone calls, if necessary; do not fax notes or send postcards, which invite inspection by others.
- Be willing to meet the other person on his or her "turf" if it is safe to do so.

ISSUE ALERT
All the principles about confronting problems do not mean God intended that we put ourselves in danger. If someone in your life is violent or physically abusive, we urge you to get counsel. The priority is your safety.

Using the principles, guidelines, and Scripture references found on the previous page, write a definition of confrontation.

Your definition may have elements of the following: A confrontation occurs when one person goes to another who has committed an offense against her, draws attention to the offense (without accusing or attacking the offender), and makes it plain that she seeks to enlist the cooperation of the offender to resolve the issue(s) or problem(s), with a goal of rebuilding and strengthening the relationship. It involves acting in love and in truth and accepting the wrongdoer while revealing the unacceptability of her performance.

Models of Confrontation

Practice with a sponsor or a trusted friend before you confront.

Below are two ways to confront: the right way and the wrong way. Practice your own version with your sponsor or a trusted friend before you actually use it to make amends with someone; your sponsor or friend may give you a few pointers on how your attempt comes across. Make sure your friend is familiar with the principles of confrontation.

The Wrong Way

Goal: Dave really hurt me when he said those nasty, rotten things to me. I want him to be really sorry for that! If I let him know how hurt I am, then he will hurt, too.

Focus: I really want to hurt Dave. He is a bad person because of what he did!

Initiator: I will give Dave the "cold shoulder" and the "silent treatment" while I tell everyone else how much he hurt me. Then he'll come crawling and beg for forgiveness.

Participants: I'll tell everyone I can whine to and get to be on my side, so that Dave can have M.H.P. (Maximum Humiliation Potential).

Conclusion: This action will hurt Dave so badly that it will kill our relationship. But, who needs him, anyway?

True to my expectation, Dave is humiliated and angered over the treatment I gave him and said he never wants to see me again. He said something else, too. He told me that this wasn't the end of it. What did he mean by that?

The Right Way

Goal: Dave said some things which really offended me. I'm hurt. I am very angry, but for the sake of our relationship I need to resolve this with him.

Focus: I want to be open, honest, and direct with Dave, and I especially want to find out if I might have contributed in some way to this problem. I want to concentrate on the offense, not attack Dave.

Initiator: I want to go to Dave right away. He may not even know that he's offended me, or if he does, he might want to take steps with me to repair our relationship.

Participants: This is just between Dave and me. If I complain to other people, I only will damage Dave's reputation and offend him for sure. Just in case, though, I will talk this out with my (counselor/sponsor/someone else who is objective and uninvolved), just to make sure I'm doing the right thing.

Conclusion A: Dave and I talk about the matter. After pointing out what happened and its impact on me, he learns about an area of sensitivity in my life and apologizes. I may learn about some important issues between us about which previously I was unaware.

Conclusion B: Dave says that he doesn't want anything more to do with me and that he wanted to hurt me in the first place. I'm hurt by the loss of this relationship but am aware that God loves me deeply, is fully pleased with me, totally accepts me, and that I am absolutely complete in Christ. This knowledge will help me to pursue new relationships confidently and enable me to forgive Dave (although I may never see him again).

ISSUE ALERT

In committed relationships such as marriage, the conclusion should be to establish a healthy identity and healthy boundaries in the context of the relationship if possible. If you are in a particularly difficult marriage relationship, you may want to talk with your sponsor, group facilitator, pastor, or a counselor about how to set healthy boundaries.

You cannot do anything to make others like you.

Surprised by Outcome B? Remember that relationships are risky. People can reject you—and you can reject them! You are not obligated to like other people any more than they are obligated to like you. You cannot do anything to make others like you. When you perform to win others' approval, the best you get is approval of your performance, not you.

Healthy patterns of relating—instead of our old, addictive game plan, can govern our future encounters with others.

✎ **Try the new pattern for yourself. First, describe an offense you wish to correct, then use the model you just learned to show how you plan to deal with it.**

Offense: _____

_____

_____

Your Plan of Action

Goal: _____

_____

Focus: _____

_____

Initiator: _____

_____

Participants: _____

_____

We cannot control the outcome of the situation, even when we confront appropriately. But we can approach the issue in a manner which is healthy, both for ourselves and the other person, and we can trust God for the results. Our actions can contribute to a desired outcome, but we cannot control others' decisions. We can accept their decisions—just as we want them to accept our decisions—without letting them control us.

Key Concept for Lesson 2
Solving problems through honest confrontation is an important recovery skill.

✏️ **Review this lesson. Name at least one thing God wants you to do in response to this study. Ask Him for the grace to help you do it.**

_____

_____

➜ **Memorize the suggested memory verses. Do you know of anyone you need to be reconciled to, as commanded in this passage? Make a commitment to make amends with this person, in obedience to the instruction of Christ presented here.**

➜ **In faith, thank God for whatever happens as a result of your obedience.**

If therefore you are presenting your offering at the altar, and there remember that your brother has something against you, leave your offering there before the altar, and go your way; first be reconciled to your brother, and then come and present your offering.
–Matthew 5:23-24

LESSON 3

Key Concept:
Life change comes when I take action and make my amends.

Taking the Step

We make direct amends to such people where possible, except when doing so will injure them or others.

Blessed are the peacemakers, for they shall be called sons of God. Matthew 5:9

Barbara came into the meeting with a new spring in her step. When her time to share arrived, she was bubbling. She said, "If I had known what a relief it would be, I would have worked Step 9 long ago. It's like the story of the little boy beating his head against the wall. When his mother asked why he did this,

I had no idea being free of this guilt could feel so good.

he replied, 'Because it feels so good when I quit.' I had no idea it could feel so good to be free of this guilt I've been carrying around."

Now you will begin to put into action the plans you have made to make amends. Commit yourself to follow through at the earliest opportunity. If possible, make the arrangements today. Whether you are confronting today or at a later date, some last words of instruction and encouragement are in order.

Step 9 involves two types of amends—amends we owe others because we have wronged them and confrontations in which we need to stand up for our values. We all are different. Most of us find one type of amend far more difficult than the other. Apologizing for our wrong actions is second nature for some of us, but it is extremely difficult for us to stand up for our values. Others of us find it easy to assert our rights, but we find it difficult to admit we are wrong.

 Which is more difficult for you—to admit your wrong actions or to confront a person who has offended you?

_____

Here is a painful but useful rule of thumb. Whichever type of amend you find most difficult is probably the one you need most to practice.

Words to Avoid

To sum up, let all be harmonious, sympathetic, brotherly, kindhearted, and humble in spirit; not returning evil for evil, or insult for insult, but giving a blessing instead. "Let him who means to love life and see good days refrain his tongue from evil."
–1 Peter 3:8-10

Although you cannot control others' decisions and responses, you can use care to avoid language that is accusing or attacking. Two "red flag" words to avoid are *why* and *you*. Both of these almost are guaranteed to provoke a defensive response. Instead of saying, "Why did you hurt me!?" you can say, "When you did that, I thought you were trying to hurt me. When I thought that, I was angry." Remember, the event itself doesn't produce emotions. How you perceive or interpret the event based on your beliefs and thoughts produces emotions. You are responsible for your feelings; others cannot make you feel a certain way. But your hurt feelings (which are normal and acceptable) warn you that something is wrong and needs to be resolved.

A Suggested Outline for Confrontations

1. Observation: What I *heard/saw* you say/do was . . .
2. Explanation: What I *thought* when you said/did that was . . .
3. Revelation: What I *felt* when I thought that was . . .
4. Invitation: What I *would like* now is . . .
5. Presentation: What I *will do* to help is . . .

 From your forgiveness list in Step 8 on page 165 select one of the amends you need to make. From the suggested outline find the statements you will use and write them below.

    1. Observation: What I *heard/saw* you say/do was _____

    _____

2. Explanation: What I *thought* when you said/did that was _____

_____

3. Revelation: What I *felt* when I thought that was _____

_____

4. Invitation: What I *would like* now is _____

_____

5. Presentation: What I *will do* to help is _____

_____

Avoid accusation

The first statement merely is an observation of the facts as you see them—stated in order to avoid making an accusation. The second statement is an explanation of your thoughts about the matter: you state your conclusions in order to investigate them further. In the third statement you reveal your feelings or emotional response. (Be very careful to use "feeling words" like happy, sad, glad, mad, afraid, etc.) In the fourth statement, you invite or propose the change(s) you hope to see in the other's behavior, words, or attitude. And finally, in the fifth statement you present yourself as an ally (rather than master) who is willing to support positive change while recognizing that another person's behavior, words, and attitudes are his or hers alone and are not yours to dictate or control.

Restitution

Being honest, open, and direct may take some practice after years of deception and manipulation, but no substitute exists. When we were engaged in eating-disordered behavior, we wronged others by pride, control, secrecy, lying, and avoidance through passive-aggressive behavior (like giving others the "silent treatment," gossiping, hurting ourselves in order to cause others pain). To make things right, we may need to do more than go to the people we've offended and confess our wrongs. We may need to make restitution. For example, we go to the grocery store from which we stole, and we pay for the stolen merchandise.

To help us clear our consciences and correct or repair as much of the past as possible (realizing not everything is repairable), we begin by taking the list of those we wronged, which we developed in Step 8, and look for the best ways and opportunities to make restitution to them. This may involve paying back or returning money or goods, or openly admitting to the people we harmed that we were wrong, that we sinned against them, and that we want to ask their forgiveness.

Barbara's story continues

Barbara's knees knocked together as she walked into the manager's office. In a voice that trembled slightly, she said, "My name is Barbara. I have stolen items from your store. I've come to do whatever is necessary to make up for my actions." She fully expected him to reach for the phone and call the police.

Instead, a look of amazement appeared on the manager's face. Since he said nothing, Barbara went on to confess her past actions. She explained that she now was in recovery for her bulimia and that she wanted to be honest with both God and others.

With tears in his eyes, he accepted Barbara's amend.

The store manager said he recognized Barbara as a regular customer. Then he said an amazing thing. He explained that his son was battling alcoholism. He knew that making amends was a part of the recovery process. With tears in his eyes he accepted Barbara's payment for the goods she took. He thanked her for her honesty and assured her that she always would be welcome as a customer there. Barbara wept with relief as she felt the weight of the world removed from her shoulders.

Our pride certainly will be hurt if we go to those whom we have wronged, admit our wrongdoing, apologize and seek to make amends to them. But again, pride is part of the condition from which we are recovering. One of the best things we can do to support our recovery is to let pride die. If we let Him, God will change our ways of thinking, feeling, and acting.

✎ **As you complete each amend you listed in Step 8, fill in that portion of the list. May God grant you grace and courage to make your amends and clear your conscience. The growth is worth the hard work. God will give you the courage as you rely upon Him.**

> ## Key Concept for Lesson 3
> Life change comes when I take action and make my amends.

✎ **Review this lesson. Name at least one thing God wants you to do in response to this study.**

_____

✎ **Write a prayer asking Him for the grace to help you do it.**

_____

_____

_____

_____

Defeating unhealthy thoughts

When you pursue healthy ways of viewing yourself and relating to others, you defeat the thought patterns which led to your eating-disordered behavior. Step 9 helps you to continue the process of learning how to turn outward rather than inward. It reinforces the knowledge that you don't have to be anxious about whether or not others believe you are OK. You are completely accepted by God! This, in turn, helps you to continue relating to others with the knowledge that you are acceptable, even without their approval. Finally, by seeking to repair and heal damaged relationships through healthy confrontation, you continue learning how to contribute both to your own life and to the lives of others.

Step Review

✎ **Please review this Step. Pray and ask God to identify the Scriptures or principles that are particularly important for your life. Underline them. Then respond to the following:**

Restate Step 9 in your own words: _____

_____

_____

_____

What do you have to gain by practicing this Step?

_____

_____

_____

_____

Reword your summary into a prayer of response to God. Thank Him for this Step, and affirm your commitment to Him.

_____

_____

_____

_____

_____

_____

_____

_____

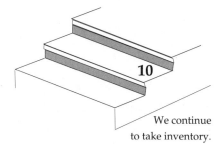

STEP

10

We continue
to take inventory.

Pressing On

MAKING PROGRESS

"How appropriate for it to be called a 12-Step approach," thought Barbara, as she added an entry to her journal. She put her pen down and reflected further on that thought. She had taken many important, new steps in her life. She thumbed through the well-worn journal pages detailing the history of many of these steps. Some had taken her back to work on old painful memories and heal wounded relationships of the past, and some carried her forward toward new choices, new places and new relationships. Steps backward, steps forward . . . and steps into her future . . . steps she would have been afraid to take before, but now, with the power and presence of Christ she knew she could take them with confidence.

She recalled that she had stumbled badly in the early months of her recovery. She gave up in frustration more than once. Through the prayers of her family and friends, her counselor, her sponsor, her support group, and the presence of Christ, she knew she would succeed.

She had taken another job about eight months ago. She still felt a little uncomfortable and insecure after the bad experience on her last job. At first she felt that everyone was watching her. She never ate in front of others—no need to risk unneeded comments about her eating habits. After a month on the job, she began to relax a little. She noticed that the people around her were kind and happy. She also saw something else about them and wondered why she hadn't noticed it before: they were free from obsessions about food and weight.

As Barbara became better acquainted with her co-workers, she found that some of them were Christians. Before long, she had visited the churches of her new friends to see if it gave a clue as to why they were so different.

Step 10   *We continue to take personal inventory, and when we are wrong, promptly admit it.*

Memory verse   *I have been crucified with Christ; and it is no longer I who live, but Christ lives in me; and the life which I now live in the flesh I live by faith in the Son of God, who loved me, and delivered Himself up for me.*

–Galatians 2:20

Overview for Step 10   **Lesson 1: Continuing the Journey**
Goal: You will develop a plan for continued spiritual growth.
Lesson 2: Monitoring Our Emotions
Goal: You will develop a practical plan for dealing with strong or painful emotions.

182

Continuing the Journey

We continue to take personal inventory, and when we are wrong, promptly admit it.

> *Blessed are the pure in heart, for they shall see God.*
>
> –Matthew 5:8

Key Concept:
I can replace old thoughts and feelings with new, Christ-honoring habits.

 Read the following review of the Steps, and mark your progress. Circle each Step that you practice with reasonable regularity. Underline each Step with which you are struggling.

In Step 1 we admitted that we had a problem which was controlling our lives and admitted that this problem was making our lives an unmanageable mess. In Step 2 we recognized the existence and power of God—a power greater than, and outside of, ourselves—and we acknowledged that He alone could restore us to sanity. In Step 3 we became willing to let Him change us by accepting His control of our lives. In Step 4 we "cleaned house" and uncovered some of the self-defeating patterns that had governed our lives.

In Step 5 we agreed with God about what we had learned about ourselves in Step 4, and we disclosed to another person the things we had kept hidden and secret in the past. In Step 6 we submitted our inventory to God. We asked Him in faith to remove the patterns of sin from our lives. In Step 7 we asked God to replace our false belief systems—which governed our thought patterns and resulting actions—with the truth of His Word. In Step 8 we listed those with whom we needed to make amends, and in Step 9, we carried that further by not only addressing those whom we had offended but forgiving those who had offended us. In that Step we began to learn to change the way we typically relate to others, especially in matters requiring personal confrontation.

Now in Step 10, we as faithful stewards of the lives God has given back to us, continue to take responsibility for our attitudes and actions. We can be aware that the old patterns of dysfunctional thinking and acting can reappear—and will from time to time.

Did you underline some Steps because you are still struggling with them? If so, congratulations for your awareness and honesty. Remember the slogan, "We seek progress, not perfection." Beware of the feelings of failure that occur because of Satan's accusations.

Like swimming upstream

Remember that recovery is like swimming upstream. It is hard work. Old thoughts and feelings do not just go away. We replace them with new, Christ-honoring habits. As a result of this constant challenge we must watch for and avoid danger areas. We use our inventories to identify these areas and to bring them to the Lord in confession and repentance as soon as we discover them. We learn to monitor them on a daily basis as a form of maintenance.

The potential for slipping does not have to rob us of the joy we have in our new life. Our old self was nailed to the cross with Christ. This made it possible for us to say victoriously, "I have been crucified with Christ; and it is no longer I who live, but Christ lives in me; and the life which I now live in the flesh I live by faith in the Son of God, who loved me and delivered Himself up for me" (Galatians 2:20).

affirm–v. validate, confirm; to express dedication to (Webster's)

His life for yours. Quite a lopsided bargain. But God in His love would have it no other way. You can experience His life to the fullest. You can relish it and shout about it. Most of all, you can **affirm** His life in you. Let Him so live His life in you that it becomes a genuine part of your very being—the real you.

 Write Galatians 2:20 in the margin to help you memorize this passage. Think about it as you answer the following question.

What evidence do you have that Christ is living His life in you?

_____

_____

Fact, not feeling

You may not always feel like Christ is living in you. You may be all too frequently reminded of the presence of your old, sinful nature. That nature seems to cover up all evidence that you even are a Christian. But feelings, or lack of them, do not change the fact that you are dead to the old ways and alive to the new in Christ.

Step 10 is a means of daily confirming that your old way of life is dead and affirming the life which Jesus Christ is living in you. Working Step 10 will help you identify: (1) the destructive patterns of behavior which keep creeping up out of the swamps of the past, and (2) new patterns of behavior which are the emerging evidence of Christ's life in you. This is the double victory Christ gives to you—destroying the old, sinful nature and strengthening the new, holy nature. You can rejoice in the good news that you are growing and that new things are happening to and through you as a result of God's work in your life!

One Fruit, Many Parts

But the fruit of the Spirit is love, joy, peace, patience, kindness, goodness, faithfulness, gentleness, self-control; against such things there is no law.
—Galatians 5:22-23

In Galatians 5, the apostle Paul describes one of the unmistakable evidences of new life in Christ: the fruit of the Spirit. Often, the fruit of the Spirit is incorrectly referred to as "fruits" of the Spirit. The Holy Spirit develops different character traits in you—love, joy, peace, patience, kindness, goodness, faithfulness, gentleness, and self-control, but all these together make up the fruit of the Spirit. The one fruit of the Spirit is a Christ-like character. Not all believers have the same spiritual gifts or the same ministry, but God desires to develop all aspects of the fruit of the Spirit in every believer.

Take time to consider the characteristics which the Spirit desires to develop in your life. They reveal the activity of the life of Christ within you.

Love

More than one word for _love_ exists in the language of the Bible. The word _agape_—used in the Greek New Testament for God's love—is the unconditional acceptance and desire for the highest good of another. This results in fair, honest, and open styles of relating.

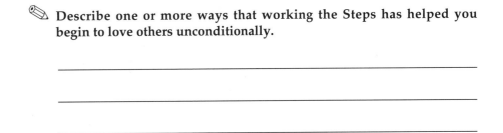 **Describe one or more ways that working the Steps has helped you begin to love others unconditionally.**

_____

_____

_____

Joy

Joy is derived from a word which means gladness and gratitude. You develop an "attitude of gratitude" as you see the positive changes God is making. You see your growing ability to lead a normal, healthy life, and you see healing take place in your once-damaged relationships. You eventually may say with the psalmist, "It was good for me that I was afflicted" (Psalm 119:71).

Peace

The Bible word for *peace* means tranquility, harmony, freedom from anger. Peace results from confronting the source of your anger in an appropriate way rather than lashing out at others or turning your anger on yourself. You also gain peace when you learn to accept and tolerate others, especially in relation to those differences about them that you cannot change.

Patience

Patience means perseverance, endurance, long-suffering. Simply put, patience means to "hang in there!" You may get anxious occasionally when you cannot control what is happening; in the past, anxiety may have meant BINGE TIME! or STARVE TIME! Having patience means that you can endure, by considering your options and making good choices.

Kindness

Practicing *kindness* involves doing things that are the most loving and helpful for others. That does not mean "being nice" to them just so they always will like you. When you have genuine love for others, you consider what is best for them, not whether or not they like you. You can be kind even in confronting people for wrongs they have done to you. Kindness includes being open, honest, and direct. Sometimes kindness hurts, but it never harms.

Goodness

Goodness means having moral integrity. It means having an earnest desire for God to lead you into patterns of thinking and relating which are loving, honest, and open, and for which you need never be ashamed.

Faithfulness

Faithfulness means trustworthiness. As you continue in recovery, you will become increasingly responsible. People will realize that they can count on you for reliability and strength.

Gentleness

Gentleness means meekness, not weakness. To be gentle means to draw back from being impulsive in anger or given to a raging response. Instead we consider our response thoughtfully, not with a goal to get even, but to resolve the problem.

Self-control

How our eating-disordered thinking challenges this one! *Self-control* means possessing the strength to govern yourself. From where does this "strength" come? Remember that your endless efforts to stay in control by self-will helped lead to your eating disorder! It made your life chaotic and unmanageable. On the other hand, God gives power to manage your life in the right way. Self-control will make you faithful, responsible, and a trusted steward of your attitudes and actions.

A Self Test for the Fruit of the Spirit in My Life

The definitions of the character traits on the previous page are a guide for checking the growth of the fruit of the Spirit in our lives. Do not think that we can grow the fruit ourselves; that is God's job. Our job is to abide in Christ. What we can do is daily tend to its growth and cultivation, water it with the Word of God, and feed it with obedience.

Maintenance requires that you be attentive to your emotions.

This list of character traits can be used as a vehicle to maintain your daily spiritual health. Such maintenance requires that you be attentive to your emotions—instead of stuffing and avoiding them—and take care that you do not isolate yourself by withdrawing from others.

✎ **Using the definitions and examples on the previous page, rate how much you think the fruit of the Spirit is growing in your life. Circle the number on the chart that represents your estimate.**

Just a Sprout	1 2 3 4 5 6 7 8 9 10		Strong and Thriving
	love		
Just a Sprout	1 2 3 4 5 6 7 8 9 10		Strong and Thriving
	joy		
Just a Sprout	1 2 3 4 5 6 7 8 9 10		Strong and Thriving
	peace		
Just a Sprout	1 2 3 4 5 6 7 8 9 10		Strong and Thriving
	patience		
Just a Sprout	1 2 3 4 5 6 7 8 9 10		Strong and Thriving
	kindness		
Just a Sprout	1 2 3 4 5 6 7 8 9 10		Strong and Thriving
	goodness		
Just a Sprout	1 2 3 4 5 6 7 8 9 10		Strong and Thriving
	faithfulness		
Just a Sprout	1 2 3 4 5 6 7 8 9 10		Strong and Thriving
	gentleness		
Just a Sprout	1 2 3 4 5 6 7 8 9 10		Strong and Thriving
	self-control		

What Did You Discover?

✎ **Make a list of the items to which you gave the lowest numbers. These are the character traits you most need to develop. Pray for God to help you grow in these areas.**

_____

_____

"I am the vine, you are the branches; he who abides in Me, and I in him, he bears much fruit: for apart from Me you can do nothing.

–John 15:5

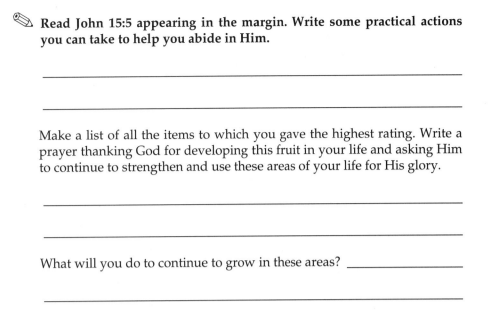

✎ **Read John 15:5 appearing in the margin. Write some practical actions you can take to help you abide in Him.**

_____

_____

Make a list of all the items to which you gave the highest rating. Write a prayer thanking God for developing this fruit in your life and asking Him to continue to strengthen and use these areas of your life for His glory.

_____

_____

What will you do to continue to grow in these areas? _____

_____

If you are anorexic, your only safe food focus is making out a healthy weekly menu with the advice of a nutritionist or dietician. Stick to that menu, without changing it or obsessing over it.

If you are anorexic, you may need to risk by eating your "forbidden" foods. Pray and ask God for courage to conquer your fear.

Keeping a Journal

A journal is another useful means of checking our progress in recovery. Writing and periodically reviewing a record of our feelings and actions may play an important role in our treatment and recovery.

As part of your record you can identify potential triggers for relapse (see Step 2, pages 53-54) as well as develop a strategy to prevent or stop it. If you are bulimic, or a compulsive overeater, your journal may include the following:

- Types/amounts of food you eat in normal meals during the day.
- Types/amounts of food you eat during a binge.
- Time/place a normal meal.
- Time/place you binge or purge.
- Thoughts and feelings before, during, and after you eat a normal meal.
- Thoughts and feelings before, during, and after you have a binge or purge episode.

Do not include a record of body weight or calorie intake, since these areas too easily become abnormal focuses of attention and control. These should be the responsibility of your physician or dietician.

General Tips

- *First-two-bites rule*—Generally, we taste only the first two bites of any food. To help prevent bingeing, eat the first two bites of every food slowly and completely. Learn to describe each taste sensation. This will slow your eating and eventually will result in your thinking of food as *food*, not as a *feeling*.
- *Never skip a meal. Always eat at scheduled mealtimes and in only one particular area.* Don't eat in front of the TV or in a work or other area.
- *Avoid keeping a list of "forbidden foods."* Forbidding certain foods makes them all the more enticing and triggers the urge to binge. You may have a list of restricted foods. Allow yourself small portions of these restricted foods in conjunction with regular meals rather than forbidding them completely.

• *Include representative portions from all basic food groups in your daily food plan.* Consult a registered dietician, if necessary. *First Place* (item number 7227-72) is a complete Christ-centered health program that includes a balanced food exchange plan. For more information on nutrition see *Nutrition for God's Temple*, 2nd Edition, (Nashville: LifeWay Press, 1994).

• *Eat at a table, with proper utensils.* Eat from a plate or bowl, not from serving dishes or packages.

• *Pray before you eat.* Ask God to help you cultivate an "attitude of gratitude" for His provision.

• *Check your weight no more than once a week.*

Additional Items to Include in Your Journal

Reflecting on my day   The following are end-of-day reflections. If you choose to do your journal entry in the morning, reflect on the previous day.

• What have I learned today . . .
    . . . about God
    . . . about myself
    . . . about others
• How have I felt today at different times?
• What do I feel good/bad about having done today?
• How have I been kind/unkind to myself today?
• How have I been honest/dishonest with others today?
• What have I accomplished/failed to accomplish today?
• If any unfinished business remains from today, have I turned it over to God, knowing that I will return to it tomorrow, according to His will?

➔ **Reflect on the life of Christ being lived through you. Affirm His life in yours. Commit yourself to give Him freedom to work even more in your life. Focus on one of the parts of the fruit of the Spirit in your life this week.**

✎ **If you haven't already done so, begin a journal of your recovery. If you already have started one, make an entry in it about something you learned or decided as a result of this lesson.**

> **Key Concept for Lesson 1**
> I can replace old thoughts and feelings with new, Christ-honoring habits.

✎ **Pray and ask God how this concept can apply in your life. Now please review this lesson. What has God shown you that you can use?**

_____

_____

➔ **Memorize this Step's memory verse:**

I have been crucified with Christ; and it is no longer I who live, but Christ lives in me; and the life which I now live in the flesh I live by faith in the Son of God, who loved me, and delivered Himself up for me.

–Galatians 2:20

LESSON 2

Monitoring Our Emotions

We continue to take personal inventory, and when we are wrong, promptly admit it.

> *Trust in the LORD with all your heart, and do not lean on your own understanding. In all your ways acknowledge Him, and He will make your paths straight.*
>
> –Proverbs 3:5-6

Key Concept:
We continue recovery by identifying and appropriately dealing with emotions.

The outline for your journal includes some general questions about feelings. Learning how to deal with your emotions properly is crucial to recovery, so you may want to include a more detailed inventory of emotions in your journal.

In Step 7 you learned that your reactions to events influence your emotions. Your emotions also are products of your family background, past and present experiences, and relationships. You may not like your emotions. You may believe that your feelings led to your eating-disorder. You may have learned to repress painful emotions. If you were abused as a child, you may have become numb and unable to feel either anger or joy, hurt, or love. As a defense mechanism you may have forgotten many painful events.

Many ways exist to block pain in our effort to gain a sense of value and control, but you can begin to reverse this trend. You do so by "tuning in" to your feelings and finding someone who will encourage you to be honest about your emotions. You then can use your feelings as a guide to determine whether your response to a situation is based on the truth or a lie.

Important signals

Feelings are neutral—they are neither right nor wrong. What you do with them determines sin or obedience. Emotions are signals which tell you something about your environment. You must be honest about your feelings if they are to serve the purpose for which God intended them. To help yourself be attentive to your feelings, you can create a list of "feeling words" and practice using them. Below is a partial listing:

- Anger (indignation, irritation, annoyance, rage)
- Anxiety (uneasiness, fear, panic)
- Humiliation (embarrassment, feeling foolish)
- Depression ("the blues," sadness, worthlessness)
- Fear (alarm, timidity, apprehension)
- Happiness (pleasure, contentment, joy, gladness)
- Inadequacy (insufficiency, weakness, "can't" mentality)
- Resentment (unresolved anger, desire to punish)
- Sad (sorrowful, melancholic, mournful)
- Shame (hopelessness, low self-esteem)

Learning to identify and understand your emotions is a skill. Developing the skill takes time. As a start, try using in your journal this six-part plan.

- Recognize the feeling.
- Describe your situation.
- Describe your response to the situation—feelings, thoughts, and actions.

- Reject false beliefs.
- Replace false beliefs with God's truths.
- Respond with the fruit of the Spirit.

Here is an example:
- Recognize—Ask yourself: What am I feeling? How many of the "feeling words" (from the list on the previous page) am I experiencing right now?
- Describe the situation—What is happening that is causing me to feel this way? What are these feelings suggesting I do?
- Describe your response to the situation—How is the situation affecting me? What am I thinking about? What am I trying to avoid? What are my thoughts?
- Reject—Which false belief(s) am I believing?
  –I must meet certain standards to feel good about myself (fear of failure).
  –I must be approved (accepted) by certain others to feel good about myself (fear of rejection).
  –Those who fail (including myself) are unworthy of love and deserve to be punished (fear of punishment/tendency to punish others).
  –I am what I am. I cannot change. I am hopeless (shame).
- Replace—Identify the truth from God's Word that applies to the situation:
  –Justification: God has forgiven me completely; therefore, I am fully pleasing to Him, despite my performance (Romans 3:19-25; 2 Corinthians 5:21).
  –Reconciliation: I am totally accepted by God; therefore, I don't need the approval of others to have a sense of value (Colossians 1:19-22).
  –Propitiation: I am deeply loved by God. Because Jesus bore the punishment for humankind on the cross, I don't need to punish others or myself (1 John 4:9-11).
  –Regeneration: I am absolutely complete in Christ. Because of His renewing work in me, I can change. I need never be ashamed (2 Corinthians 5:17).
- Respond—Choose any characteristic of the fruit of the Spirit which is a healthy response to these circumstances and emotions. Ask God to provide what you need to respond properly.

  –Love: unconditional acceptance and desire for the highest good of another
  –Joy: gladness and gratitude
  –Peace: tranquility resulting from resolved anger, acceptance, tolerance
  –Patience: persevering; exercising endurance, long-suffering
  –Kindness: doing those things that contribute to the highest good of another
  –Goodness: exercising moral integrity in thoughts and behavior
  –Faithfulness: being trustworthy, responsible
  –Gentleness: being in control and acting in love
  –Self-control: submission to God for strength to govern your life properly, in accordance to His Word

✎ **Practice using this six-part method. Think of the last time you experienced strong or painful emotions. Write about the experience below.**

- Recognize the feeling _____

- Describe the situation _____

  _____

- Describe your response to the situation—feelings, thoughts, and actions.

  _____

  _____

- Reject false beliefs _____

  _____

  _____

- Replace false beliefs with God's truths _____

  _____

  _____

- Respond with the fruit of the Spirit _____

  _____

  _____

Therefore let him who thinks he stands take heed lest he fall.
–1 Corinthians 10:12

This looks like a simple plan, but actually it is a complex process which takes time and work! PLEASE DO NOT EXPECT TO MASTER THIS IMMEDIATELY! After having spent a lifetime of avoiding our emotions through compulsive behavior, just learning how to identify and understand painful feelings is a tremendous accomplishment in itself! Our eating-disordered behavior caused us to avoid knowing and dealing with our feelings, circumstances, and behaviors responsibly. Looking at ourselves closely will be new, awkward, and often painful. However, as we get used to the habit of doing this on a regular basis, we gradually will begin to enjoy the growth, maturity, and health it produces.

Relapse Intervention

We are certain to experience strong emotions—rejection, a sense of failure, an unkind word or deed—and before we know it, we're on the way to a binge or purge. What can we do? What would you do if you fell overboard from a boat in the ocean? What would you do if you became separated from your friends while hiking in a forest? In both cases, the first thing you likely would do is CALL FOR HELP!

Call for help!

Calling for help also is the first response when you begin to slip in your process of recovery. Record these names and phone numbers, and keep them where you can get to them when you need them.

Sponsor's Name: _____ Phone: _____

Pastor's Name: _____ Phone: _____

Recovering Friend: _____ Phone: _____

Other Source of Help: _____ Phone: _____

If you cannot get a response from any of these sources of help (remember, other people are not responsible for your behavior), refer to your "Feelings List," get out your journal, and begin writing:

- What am I feeling right now? List the emotions.
- Objectively describe your situation.
- (For women) What day is it in my monthly cycle? What changes might be occurring in my body (medications, monthly cycle, etc.) right now that might affect my feelings?

Other Helpful Activities:

- Look again at your list of feelings. Try to identify the need behind each one. Unpleasant feelings often are an indication of unmet needs or expectations in our lives.
- Now, look to those needs. Is there someone (more than one?) who can help you meet some of those needs? List name(s). Get his/her (their) phone number(s), and contact that person (or persons).
- Repeat the "Serenity Prayer" found in the margin. How does it apply here? What can you change, and what do you need to surrender to God?
- Read your Bible! Read Psalm 91. (Keep a marker there and read it often, especially in times of trial.)
- Read *Search for Significance* LIFE Support Edition.
- Attend your support-group meeting. If your regular meeting is not available when you most need help, check your phone directory for a listing of support-group meetings in your community (such as Overeaters Anonymous); call to find out if one is in progress NOW, and GO!
- Repeat the following affirmation and meditate on its message.

My Identity in Christ

Because of Christ's redemption,
I am a new creation of infinite worth.

I am deeply loved,
I am completely forgiven,
I am fully pleasing,
I am totally accepted by God.
I am absolutely complete in Christ.

When my performance
reflects my new identity in Christ,
that reflection is dynamically unique.

There has never been another person like me
in the history of mankind,
nor will there ever be.
God has made me an original,
one of a kind, really somebody!

God,
Grant me the
serenity to
accept
the things I
cannot change,
the
courage to
change the
things I can,
and the
wisdom to
know the
difference.

- Find someone else who might need help and offer to help him or her.
- Trust God to provide you with a way of escape (1 Corinthians 10:13).
- Remember that you have been crucified with Christ (Galatians 2:20).

Key Concept for Lesson 2
I continue recovery by identifying and appropriately dealing with emotions.

Monitor feelings

Why is all of the above necessary? An old saying in 12-Step groups is, "If you fail to plan, you plan to fail." Your eating disorder was part of your strategy to avoid having to face yourself honestly and confront squarely the problems in your life. Taking a personal inventory still may be new and awkward for you. By keeping up with your feelings and monitoring your life through regular self-examination, you can continue to grow into and enjoy the health God wants you to have.

✎ **Review today's lesson. Name at least one thing God wants you to do in response to this study. Ask Him for the grace to help you do it.**

_____

✎ **Affirm Christ's life in your emotions. Commit to His control any feelings or attitudes you need to change. Make an entry in your journal about something you learned or decided as a result of this lesson.**

Step Review

✎ **Please review this Step. Pray and ask God to identify the Scriptures or principles that are particularly important for your life. Underline them. Then respond to the following:**

Restate Step 10 in your own words: _____

_____

_____

What do you have to gain by practicing this Step in your life?

_____

_____

Reword your summary into a prayer of response to God. Thank Him for this Step, and affirm your commitment to Him.

_____

_____

_____

STEP
11

Abiding in Christ

11

We grow
in relationship with God by prayer,
meditation, and Bible study.

"BIBLE STUDY CHANGED MY LIFE"

As Annie grew in her relationship with Christ, her time for personal devotions began to take on new meaning and importance. No longer was Bible study just something she was "supposed to do" as a believer, but it was something she dearly wanted to do. It brought her closer to the One who was healing and remaking her life.

"I saw the Bible study especially as something absolutely essential for my healing. I poured over the Psalms and saw in them the spiritual ointment for my many wounds from the past. I hung onto the Gospels' accounts and words of Jesus: here was my Savior and Healer in action. I walked with the apostles through the lands and doctrines of the early church and put my modern faith in the setting where it all began.

"But most of all, I literally watched the Bible change my life. It wasn't obvious to me at first what was happening; however, others who knew me pointed out the difference. I was being transformed by the renewing of my mind, as one of my favorite verses says (Romans 12:2). I saw the transition from reading the Word out of obligation to studying because I want to know the Lord. It hasn't always been easy. At first it was enough just to read about the people in the Bible—their problems and their victories—with little commitment on my part to do anything. But that soon began to cause all sorts of problems. People who knew I was a Christian confronted me when I acted contrary to the faith, and I began to feel a healthy guilt when I did something wrong."

Step 11   *We seek to know Christ more intimately through prayer and meditation, praying only for knowledge of His will and the power to carry that out.*

Memory verse   *If you abide in Me, and My words abide in you, ask whatever you wish, and it shall be done for you.*

–John 15:7

Overview for Step 11

Lesson 1: Prayer
        Goal: You will identify four key elements of prayer.
Lesson 2: Meditation
        Goal: You will describe aspects of meditation.
Lesson 3: Bible Study
        Goal: You will review elements of effective Bible study.

194

LESSON 1

Prayer

We seek to know Christ more intimately through prayer and meditation, praying only for knowledge of His will and the power to carry that out.

> *Blessed are those who hunger and thirst for righteousness, for they shall be satisfied.*
>
> –Matthew 5:6

Key Concept:
Prayer is the means by which I can have a love relationship with God.

Jesus Christ's main purpose in becoming human was to reconcile you to God. He wants to have a love relationship with you. By offering His Son as a sacrifice on Calvary, God took the first step in establishing that relationship. When you accepted that sacrifice, the barrier of sin that separated you from Him was removed. God also provides all the resources you need to enjoy fellowship with Him through His Holy Spirit and through His Word, meditation, and prayer.

Communion with God

Prayer provides an opportunity to speak to God. Meditation or contemplation provides opportunities to reflect on the goodness and strength of God. The Scripture is God's Word of instruction and confirmation. Your love relationship with God lays the foundation for your obedience and provides the means by which you abide in Christ.

✎ **According to the paragraphs you just read, what are elements of your communication with God? (Place a check in the appropriate boxes.)**

❍ Praying to God
❍ Teaching others about God
❍ Meditating about God

❍ Studying God's Word
❍ Obeying God

The elements of communication with your Heavenly Father and establishing a close relationship with Him are prayer, meditation, and Bible study. You may have added obedience, which also is an important element in your relationship with God. Generally, however, obedience grows out of the fellowship rather than laying the foundation for it.

God wants us to have a consistent walk as we abide in His Son, and He provides all the resources for us to do so. Abiding in Christ is the joyful alternative to going back to our old eating-disordered behavior patterns.

intercede–v. to intervene between parties with a view to reconciling differences; mediate (Webster's)

And in the same way the Spirit also helps our weakness; for we do not know how to pray as we should, but the Spirit Himself intercedes for us with groanings too deep for words.
–Romans 8:26

One of the activities of the Holy Spirit is to **intercede** for you in prayer. Sometimes you can pray with clear intent. You can ask God for a specific request or tell Him a specific need. As you do so, the Spirit guides your prayer. He places on your heart those people and things about which you need to speak to God.

At other times, you may feel confused. All you can do is go to the Lord in prayer. At those times, too, the Holy Spirit prays for you. Even when you cannot clearly express yourself as you would like to—even if the words don't come out right—God's Spirit lovingly understands, as the verse at left indicates.

Some people don't pray until they have a problem. This approach is what some have called "foxhole religion." A soldier, stuck in a foxhole with bullets flying on a battlefield, makes great promises to God. He vows he'll keep these promises if God will just get him out of the battle safely.

How sad to pray only when you "get in a fix." You miss the fellowship, support, and communion with God that occurs when you are constantly aware of His presence and spend time in conversation with Him. Prayer is not bargaining with a vending-machine God. Prayer is an audience with the King of creation—a conversation with the Almighty. Prayer can move mountains. It is an essential link with God. It helps you abide in Christ.

Prayer is an audience with the King.

Elements of Effective Prayer

Have you wondered, "So how do I pray?" Here is a simple summary of the elements in an effective prayer life. If you practice these kinds of prayer on a regular basis, you will be working Step 11.

Praise
The 12 Steps are a program of humility. A warped sense of self-esteem accompanies our addictions. When we are prideful, we act as if we are God. When we are down, we believe we are pond scum. Either way the addiction wins. It remains in control. Humility involves recognizing that we are people of infinite worth because God loves us, but we are not God. Growing in humility includes recognizing the greatness of God. We praise God in prayer, not because He needs our praise (see Psalm 50:7-15), but because we need the humility which accompanies acknowledging God as God. In praise we direct thoughts and words of worship to God for who He is: His character, His lovingkindness, His power, His handiwork.

✎ **Write a prayer of praise to God. Express to Him your love and adoration for who He is. You may want to use additional paper.**

_____

_____

_____

Petition
You present your petitions, or requests, to Him in prayer as well. He wants—you need to give Him—your concerns and the burdens of your heart. Philippians 4:6 expresses the attitude of trust you can have. You can trust Him to do what is best for you and for those for whom you pray.

Be anxious for nothing, but in everything by prayer and supplication with thanksgiving let your requests be made known to God.
                    –Philippians 4:6

✎ **How do you suppose God feels when His children approach Him with their requests?**

  ○ *Go away kid. You bother me!*   ○ *My child, I am so glad to see you!*

In Step 2 we learned that many of us have a concept of God that the first response you just read represents. We expect God to say, "Can't you see I'm busy?" That God is just a product of our imaginations. Our Father longs for us to spend time with Him.

But an hour is coming, and now is, when the true worshippers shall worship the Father in spirit and truth; for such people the Father seeks to be His worshippers.

–John 4:23

✎ **Read John 4:23, printed in the margin, and the story of the father which appears below. Then describe what the father in the story and the Heavenly Father in the Scripture have in common.**

Don is grieving. His only son has gone away to college. Some call it empty-nest syndrome. Don says he's just missing someone he loves very much. He says, "I look forward to his calls and visits. I just love to hear his voice."

✎ **What do the father in the story and the Heavenly Father of whom Jesus spoke have in common?**

_____

Did you note the word *seeks* in John 4:23? The Scripture says God actually seeks—goes in search of—worshippers. Both God and Don share the deep desire to spend time with their children.

Thanksgiving

Another element of prayer is thanksgiving—showing gratitude for what God does for you and others for whom you pray. Thanking God is a way of acknowledging that He is God. It also is a part of your "attitude of gratitude," which results from the new things He is making possible in your life. Gratitude is a wonderful replacement for bitterness and pride.

Gratitude is a wonderful replacement for bitterness and pride.

✎ **Practice thanksgiving by writing in the margin at least five things for which you are grateful to God. Write them in the form of a prayer of thanksgiving.**

Confession

Confessing our sin—so that we can experience forgiveness and a renewed fellowship with God—is another key purpose and benefit of prayer. You already have explored 1 John 1:8-9 which promises that when we confess our sin, God always forgives us and cleanses us from *all* unrighteousness. Confession is not a duty where we pay for our sin by beating ourselves. Confession is taking God up on His loving invitation. Confession frees us from the guilt that drives us to repeat the offense.

Sample Prayers

Most 12-Step groups use the Lord's Prayer—sometimes called the Model Prayer.

Our Father who art in heaven, Hallowed be Thy Name. Thy kingdom come. Thy will be done, On earth as it is in heaven. Give us this day our daily bread. And forgive us our debts, as we also have forgiven our debtors. And do not lead us into temptation, but deliver us from evil. [For Thine is the kingdom, and the power, and the glory, forever. Amen.]

–Matthew 6:9-13

✎ **Read the Lord's Prayer, which appears in the margin. Below write the words from the prayer that express the following elements:**

praise _____

petition _____

thanksgiving _____

confession _____

Prayer is not a formula. The elements of praise, petition, thanksgiving, and confession are not always a part of every prayer. Our compulsive, addictive thinking wants a nice neat formula to "get it right." After all, we feel the things we do must be perfect. When we pray, whether our prayer is from a prayer book or from our thoughts, we need to let it be from the heart. Openness, honesty, and directness are the necessary vehicles for a meaningful relationship with God, just as they are necessary for meaningful relationships with others.

The "Serenity Prayer" summarizes the very heart of the recovery process. Only the first part of the Serenity Prayer commonly is used in 12-Step groups. In the margin you will find the entire prayer as Reinhold Neibuhr originally wrote it.

✎ **The complete version of the Serenity Prayer appears in the margin. Explain why the Serenity Prayer is so valuable for those of us recovering from addictions or compulsions such as eating disorders.**

_____

_____

The prayer asks God's aid with issues related to boundaries. So much of our recovery deals with knowing and taking responsibility for things which are our business while we allow others to be responsible for their own behavior.

The AA statement of Step 11 says ". . . praying only for knowledge of His will for us and for the power to carry that out." Jesus taught us to pray, "Thy will be done." One expansion of the Steps says, "seeking His wisdom and power to live according to His will as He reveals it to us."

✎ **Why is praying for God's will so important for our continuing recovery?**

_____

_____

You may have answered the question in any of a number of ways because God's will is such a central issue of recovery. Since addiction grows out of self-will, we daily place our will under God's authority.

✎ **Compose a simple prayer of your own. Think about the typical elements of prayer (praise, petition, thanksgiving, confession) and use the example of the Lord's Prayer and the Serenity Prayer.**

_____

_____

_____

_____

_____

God, grant me the Serenity to accept the things I cannot change, the courage to change the things I can, and the wisdom to know the difference; Living one day at a time, enjoying one moment at a time, accepting hardship as a pathway to Peace; taking as Jesus did, this sinful world as it is, not as I would have it. Trusting that You will make all things right if I surrender to Your will, so that I may be reasonably happy in this life and supremely happy with You forever in the next. Amen.[1]

If you abide in Me, and My words abide in you, ask whatever you wish, and it shall be done for you.

–John 15:7

➜ **The Step memory verse appears in the margin. Repeat John 15:7 three times. What does God promise if we abide in Christ and His words abide in us?**

_____

✎ **Name at least one thing God wants you to do in response to this study. Ask Him for the grace to help you do it.**

_____

_____

LESSON 2

Key Concept:
Meditation is spending time thinking about, contemplating, or pondering the things of God.

Meditation

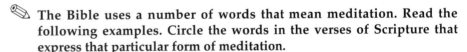

We seek to know Christ more intimately through prayer and meditation, praying only for knowledge of His will and the power to carry that out.

> *Now we have received, not the spirit of the world, but the Spirit who is from God, that we might know the things freely given to us by God, which things we also speak, not in words taught by human wisdom, but those taught by the Spirit, combining spiritual thoughts with spiritual words.*
> –1 Corinthians 2:12-13

Many Christians, concerned about current New Age practices, become suspicious at the mere mention of the word meditation. Modern Western minds may have images of a guru-like person sitting in a cross-legged lotus position and chanting in a monotone. They fail to realize that meditation is a biblical word and concept. Throughout history meditation has been important for great church leaders.

✎ **The Bible uses a number of words that mean meditation. Read the following examples. Circle the words in the verses of Scripture that express that particular form of meditation.**

Consider. *And the peace of God, which surpasses all comprehension, shall guard your hearts and your minds in Christ Jesus. Finally, brethren, whatever is true, whatever is honorable, whatever is right, whatever is pure, whatever is lovely, whatever is of good repute, if there is any excellence and if anything worthy of praise, let your mind dwell on these things.*

–Philippians 4:7-8

Practice. *The things you have learned and received and heard and seen in me, practice these things; and the God of peace shall be with you.*

–Philippians 4:9

Study and Apply. *Take pains with these things; be absorbed in them, so that your progress may be evident to all.*

–1 Timothy 4:15

You may have circled the words *let your mind dwell*, *practice*, and *be absorbed in*. All of these terms are biblical expressions for meditation.

Here is an extended definition for Christian meditation. Meditation is *both a mental and spiritual process of thinking, conversing, planning, anticipating and reflecting. Meditation is for the purpose of developing and enriching one's spiritual devotion.*

A major difference

A major difference exists between Christian meditation and the meditation of the Eastern religions. Eastern religions originate from a non-personal concept of God. They rely on emptying the mind of conscious thought, because they have no personal God to get to know. In some instances, they entrust their minds to evil spirit-guide counterfeits.

Christian meditation is the opposite of its Eastern counterfeit. In meditation we seek to develop a deeper understanding and personal relationship with the true God who really exists. Don't be surprised that Satan would crudely copy and misuse God's useful, peaceful, and holy gift of meditation. Don't be discouraged from reclaiming your spiritual heritage of meditation.

Elements of Effective Meditation

Commit to apply or use what you learn.

Meditation will allow you to develop a clearer understanding of and deeper relationship with God. Pray before beginning any contemplative activity. Pray for guidance, wisdom, and peace as you meditate. You will find the greatest value in meditating on Scripture. If possible, memorize the Scripture passage so you can recall it and reflect on it at any time. Focus your thoughts on certain parts of the passage as you create a mental picture. Reflect using all of your senses—seeing, hearing, tasting, smelling, and touching as you do the activity. Ask questions about the passage, formulate answers to related problems or needs, and commit to apply or use what you have learned.

Using Psalm 1, try the following exercise. Use the resources of your mind and spirit in thinking, feeling, imagining, talking to others and to yourself. Complain to God if you need to as you meditate—with worship, spiritual insight, or solving problems as your goal.

To meditate on Psalm 1, find a place quiet to sit and relax. Begin with the following prayer.

Lord Jesus, I want to grow in my relationship with You by meditating on Your Word in these moments. As I meet with You in this way, I pray that I may receive wisdom and power to carry out Your will and plan as You reveal them to me. Help me to be nourished and refreshed by Your Spirit during this meditation. Draw me closer to Yourself and Your healing power. In Your Name, Lord Jesus, I pray. Amen.

Begin by slowly reading the passage aloud. Highlight or circle words which, for whatever reason, may stand out to you.

The blessed person

¹Blessed is the man who does not walk in the counsel of the wicked or stand in the way of sinners or sit in the seat of mockers. ²But his delight is in the law of the Lord, and on his law he meditates day and night. ³He is like a tree planted by streams of water, which yields its fruit in season and whose leaf does not wither. Whatever he does prospers. ⁴Not so the wicked! They are like chaff that the wind blows away.⁵Therefore the wicked will not stand in the judgment, nor sinners in the assembly of the righteous.⁶For the Lord watches over the way of the righteous, but the way of the wicked will perish.

–Psalm 1, NIV

Think about the phrase *counsel of the wicked*. Counsel means to teach by asking questions and allowing others to draw the conclusions that the counselor wants the counselee to draw.

What are you doing when you *walk in the counsel of the wicked, stand in the way of sinners,* **or** *sit in the seat of mockers?*

_____

_____

What are some of your feelings as you think about these things?

_____

_____

Apply the Word when you meditate. When have you found yourself *walking in the counsel of the wicked, standing in the way of sinners* or *sitting in the seat of mockers?* How did the Word affect you?

_____

_____

Delight in the Lord

Read verse 2. What would your life be like if you really delighted in the law of the Lord—if your greatest desire was to please and honor God out of a sense of love and delight?

_____

_____

Imagine yourself as a *tree planted by streams of water*. In what way will you be like that tree when your delight is in the law of the Lord?

_____

_____

In verse 4 chaff refers to unusable husks of grain, such as wheat, which are separated from usable grain during threshing and winnowing (beating the grain out of the husk, and then blowing off and scattering the unusable hulls by letting the wind carry it away). Imagine as best you can the threshing and winnowing process. Write down why you think the psalmist uses this as an illustration of what happens to the wicked.

Paraphrase verses 5 and 6. _____

_____

_____

Therefore the wicked will not stand in the judgment, nor sinners in the assembly of the righteous. For the Lord watches over the way of the righteous, but the way of the wicked will perish.

–Psalm 1:5-6

What good counsel as a strategy for your life can you glean from this passage?

_____

_____

More about Cathy

Cathy wanted to spend time listening to God. She tried several times to meditate regularly. Her morning schedule started early as she prepared breakfast for the family and took her daughter to school. Although she took time in the morning to pray for daily direction, things usually were so hectic that she couldn't slow down her mind enough to meditate. She tried to meditate after her evening Bible study and had some success, but she often fell asleep while she was in the middle of her thoughts. She finally found a means to meditate that worked for her. She said, "I tried to meditate with the times and methods the others in my support group were using, but nothing seemed to work for me. Still, I wouldn't give up because I wanted that experience with God. 'Why not meditate during my walks?' I asked myself. Each evening I walk over to a friend's house about five minutes away, and we walk for a half hour. During the walk to my friend's house and back I began thinking about God and His Word, and I focused on verses I had memorized earlier. I've been doing this for more than a year now, and I count that time with God as very dear to me. Because my friend is a believer, we sometimes discuss the verses I meditate on."

Key Concept for Lesson 2
Meditation is spending time thinking about, contemplating, or pondering the things of God.

✎ **Review today's lesson. Name at least one thing God wants you to do in response to this study. Ask Him for the grace to help you do it.**

_____

_____

➥ **Practice John 15:7—your memory verse for this Step. Use the verse as the basis of a prayer to the Father. For example, you may want to thank Him for His promise in the verse, to ask Him to help you to abide in Him, or to praise Him for His faithfulness to answer prayer.**

Select two or three verses upon which to meditate this week. Commit to spend a minimum of five minutes a day in contemplation with God. Do this either after your prayer time or at some other time during the day. Keep a journal of thoughts you have as you meditate.

Bibe Study

LESSON 3

Key Concept:
God speaks to me through the Bible.

Many biblical principles guide us in recovery.

Do you not know that you are a temple of God, and that the Holy Spirit dwells in you?
–1 Corinthians 3:16

We seek to know Christ more intimately through prayer and meditation, praying only for knowledge of His will and the power to carry that out.

> *But know this first of all, that no prophecy of Scripture is a matter of one's own interpretation, for no prophecy was ever made by an act of human will, but men moved by the Holy Spirit spoke from God.*
> –2 Peter 1:20-21

As you live and learn, you will hear many things which may or may not be correct or good. God's Word is designed to help you sort out these things. You will hear things from religious leaders and feel things as a result of time spent with God in prayer and meditation. Test all of these against the Scriptures. The Bible is the final authority on matters relating to faith and practice. We should accept nothing that contradicts God's Word.

Though it does not use the language of modern psychology, the Scripture teaches principles for dealing with all of life's important issues. For example, the Bible doesn't deal by name with anorexia, bulimia, or compulsive overeating but many biblical principles guide us in recovery.

✎ **Read the following portion of Doug's story. Look for ways the Bible made an impact on a specific area of his life.**

Doug tells about an experience that showed him clearly the Scriptures' role of confirming truth. "I used to smoke cigarettes," he said, "I believed it was up to the individual believer as to whether or not to smoke. Oh, I'd heard all the health problems cigarettes could cause, but I was young and didn't think anything would happen to me. Besides, I was going to quit in a few years, anyway. I really thought I could quit anytime I wanted to. I reasoned that my decision to smoke was a matter of my freedom to make my own decisions. When fellow church members suggested I shouldn't smoke, I asked them to show me where the Bible said anything about my smoking. I knew they couldn't, so I kept right on smoking . . . and coughing . . . and panting for breath when I walked anywhere.

"One Bible passage that caused me to examine my smoking was 1 Corinthians 3:16. That verse talked about my body being a temple of God. My defenses began to unravel even more when I heard on the news the results of a recent research study: smoking cuts short a person's life, on average, by seven minutes per cigarette. Seven minutes a cigarette . . . about one minute for each minute I smoked. I didn't have to do the arithmetic to tell my little habit was costing a lot more than what I was paying for tobacco. I quit about two weeks later. I did this right after I stumbled across Ecclesiastes 7:17 in my daily Bible reading.

Do not be excessively wicked, and do not be a fool. Why should you die before your time?
—Ecclesiastes 7:17

It works if you work it!

Consistent, not compulsive

Describe a time when the Bible has convicted you of a specific needed change in your life. Did the conviction lead to positive change or simply to more guilt?

_____

_____

You may have thought of an occasion when, just as Doug described, the Scripture brought conviction and healthy change in your life. Do not be discouraged if you thought about another type of experience. Many times we have felt the need for change, but we have been unable to accomplish that change. Remember the slogan (appearing in the margin) about the 12-Step process. A more complete and accurate statement might be: "Jesus Christ works to change our lives if we continue to abide in Him by following the Steps!" You don't have to be defeated. Now you can work the Steps and rely on the Lord.

Elements of Effective Bible Study

In order to get the most out your Bible-study time, approach it in a planned, organized fashion. You can find many helpful books and study guides on the subject in bookstores, but the following guidelines may be of help in getting started.

Be consistent. Try to have a regular time and place to meet with God, with as few interruptions as possible. Although a daily time allows you to get daily guidance, don't be afraid to start with only three to four days a week and work up. You also may vary your study on alternate days by reading for shorter times and by studying more deeply for longer times. Whatever you do, be consistent. Don't worry if you have to miss or shorten a session because of travel or illness. Stay close to your schedule whenever possible.

Start with prayer. You are studying God's Word. Who can interpret it better than the author Himself? Ask for guidance in understanding and applying what you read.

Use learning helps. Use a notebook to record insights. Use a concordance to help you cross reference ideas. Other study aides may include: topical reference guide, Bible dictionary, and commentaries.

You may find two Bible study aids particularly helpful. They are called *Step By Step Through the Old Testament* and *Step By Step Through the New Testament*. Both these books are the same size as and are written in the same interactive style you have become accustomed to in *Conquering Eating Disorders*. They will help you to learn how the entire Bible fits together and how the various books add to the message of Scripture. Since they are written in a short-lesson format, they will help you develop the discipline of daily Bible study. Like *Conquering Eating Disorders* they are best studied in a group. Both Step By Step books are available from the bookstore or other source where you purchased *Conquering Eating Disorders*. They may be ordered by calling 1-800-458-2772. Begin with the the New Testament study and then move to the Old Testament.

Ask questions; look for answers. Whatever Bible study method you choose, ask questions about what you read, and seek answers in the text. Three

What should I do about what I learned?

important questions that are appropriate for any passage in the Bible include: What does this tell me about God? What does it tell me about me (or people in general)? What should I do about what I learned?

Commit to obey. The doers of the Word, not just hearers, experience life change. Listen to the words from the Book of James. *Do not merely listen to the word, and so deceive yourselves. Do what it says. Anyone who listens to the word but does not do what it says is like a man who looks at his face in a mirror and, after looking at himself, goes away and immediately forgets what he looks like. But the man who looks intently into the perfect law that gives freedom, and continues to do this, not forgetting what he has heard, but doing it—he will be blessed in what he does* (James 1:22-25, NIV).

More of Annie's story

Annie said, "I still remember how I felt after I lied to Mrs. Greene about why I wasn't going to church on a particular Sunday. I just needed to get some rest after a particularly demanding week, but I told her I had the flu. No big deal, except that I felt awful for not being honest. Funny how that is now, since I used to make a life-style out of lying and covering up when I practiced my anorexia. God is at work inside and outside through His Spirit and His Word, and He'll do the same for anybody else who'll let Him."

Making Time for God

Time is one of the biggest obstacles many believers have in maintaining a close personal relationship with God. You may resist approaching God because you feel you owe Him a large chunk of your time. Of course, you do "owe" everything to God, but not in the same sense that you would "owe" another person. God has paid all your debts! Your response to Him is gratitude—not obligation. Because God loves you, He is delighted with your efforts to spend time with Him, especially if it means having to say no to something else in order to keep the appointment with Him.

Start slowly, but be consistent. You may want to spend 10 to 15 minutes with God each day or even every other day. You can read 10 verses of Scripture and spend the rest of your time in prayer and meditation. The point is, get started and stick with it. Find a quiet place. If necessary take the phone off the hook. Ask your family to keep you from being disturbed. Avoid unnecessary noises and distractions. Choose a time when you're likely to be free of interruptions. If you like the morning hours but know that on one particular day you will be interrupted, change that day's meeting with God to a later time in the day when you do not expect an interruption. Finally, commit yourself to trust, obey, and practice what He tells you in your time together.

If you abide in Me, and My words abide in you, ask whatever you wish, and it shall be done for you.

—John 15:7

Every relationship takes time to develop and maintain. God, more than anyone else, knows this. As you continue to grow in Him, you'll find yourself wanting to spend more time with Him. You'll gain a special blessing in knowing that God cherishes your time together, too. Abiding in Christ (John 15:7) is the result of time spent with Him in prayer, meditation, and Bible study coupled with your commitment to obedience.

Key Concept for Lesson 3
God speaks to me through the Bible.

✎ Review today's lesson. Name at least one thing God wants you to do in response to this study. Ask Him for the grace to help you do it.

_____

_____

Step Review

✎ Please review this Step. Pray and ask God to identify the Scriptures or principles that are particularly important for your life. Underline them. Then respond to the following:

Restate Step 11 in your own words: _____

_____

_____

_____

What do you have to gain by practicing this Step in your life?

_____

_____

_____

_____

Reword your summary into a prayer of response to God. Thank Him for this Step, and affirm your commitment to Him.

_____

_____

_____

_____

_____

_____

_____

_____

Notes
[1]Reinhold Neibuhr, "The Serenity Prayer" (St. Meinrad, IN: Abbey Press).

STEP 12

Assisting Others

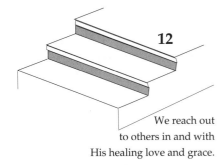

12

We reach out to others in and with His healing love and grace.

NO SECOND-CLASS BELIEVERS

When Barbara first entered recovery, she heard several persons tell how God transformed their lives through a dramatic spiritual experience. As she worked her program, she kept asking, "When will my moment come? When will God transform my life." One night when she heard a speaker at a meeting address that very issue, she felt great relief.

The speaker explained the difference between what she called a spiritual experience and a spiritual awakening. "Some people have a dramatic experience at Step 3," she said. "Bill W., the co-founder of Alcoholics Anonymous, was like that. He had a spiritual experience that freed him from the overpowering compulsion to drink." She continued that most people have a slower spiritual awakening. They work the Steps and learn to trust God one day at a time. Then one day they realize that their lives have been changed. They can't name a time, but somewhere between the decision in Step 3 and the portion of Step 12, which reads "having had a spiritual awakening," God has changed their lives. "Now here is the important part to remember," the speaker said. "One type of experience with God is not better than the other. The person who has the spiritual experience at Step 3 still needs to work the rest of the Steps. God gives to each person the type of experience he or she needs to grow."

Barbara left that meeting walking on air. She always had felt like a second-class Christian, with a second-class recovery as well. Now she realized that what God was doing in her life was as valid and valuable as what He did with anybody, anywhere. (You'll work again with Barbara's story on pages 208 and 210).

Step 12   *Having had a spiritual awakening, we try to carry the message of Christ's grace and restoration power to others with eating disorders and to practice these principles in all our affairs.*

Scripture   *God was in Christ reconciling the world to Himself, not counting their trespasses against them, and He has committed to us the word of reconciliation. Therefore, we are ambassadors for Christ.*

–2 Corinthians 5:19-20

Overview for Step 12

Lesson 1: A Spiritual Awakening
    Goal: You will describe two types of spiritual transformation.
Lesson 2: Sharing the Message
    Goal: You will prepare to share your recovery testimony and your testimony of faith.
Lesson 3: Practicing the Principles
    Goal: You will practice applying the Steps to a life situation.
Lesson 4: Where Do I Go from Here?
    Goal: You will identify resources for continued growth.

A Spiritual Awakening

Having had a spiritual awakening, we try to carry the message of Christ's grace and restoration power to others with eating disorders and to practice these principles in all our affairs.

Go home to your people and report to them what great things the Lord has done for you, and how He had mercy on you.

–Mark 5:19

Key Concept:
Not all spiritual transformations are alike, but a spiritual change is essential to recovery.

All of these are the work of one and the same Spirit, and he gives them to each one, just as he determines.
–1 Corinthians 12:11, NIV

You just read more of Barbara's story on page 207. Her story is typical of what happens in many people's lives.

 Compare the story about Barbara with the message of 1 Corinthians 12:11, which appears in the margin. The Scripture passage speaks of spiritual gifts. It says that the Holy Spirit gives different individuals different gifts as He chooses. Check the best summary of Barbara's story.

○ Everyone must have the same spiritual experience.
○ Those with a dramatic experience or gift are more spiritual.
○ If my experience is gradual, I must be doing something wrong.
○ God works with every person as a unique individual.
○ Even those with a dramatic experience need to mature.
○ Other _____

Your spiritual awakening began when you asked Jesus Christ to be the Savior and Lord of your life (Step 3). Your experience may have been dramatic or very simple. Your experience with God may have begun long before your eating disorder or your recovery began. In that case, you may see your recovery as God's caring for you because you are His child. On the other hand, your experience with God may have begun at recovery. In that case your spiritual awakening included your new birth experience. Certainly the passage from 1 Corinthians teaches us that God works with His children as individuals. In the same way you may have chosen either of the last two summaries of the story in the exercise, or you may have written your own. The key is to reject the first three answers. Don't attempt to have someone else's experience.

Don't attempt to have someone else's experiences.

Two Models: Experience and Awakening

These two models exist for our relationship with God and for our recovery. As you consider whether your recovery has been more of an experience or an awakening, remember that neither model is "best." They are different, and each model has a danger.

 What might be some dangers of having the "dramatic spiritual experience" type of recovery?

_____

_____

What might be the dangers of having the "slow spiritual awakening" type of experience?

_____

_____

_____

Possible dangers

You may have additional insights into the two models. You may have answered that the dramatic experience might result in pride. It might lead you to try to force others into the same mold and to have little patience with those whose experience was different than yours. It also might lead you to think that you have arrived after Step 3 and that you have no need for the other Steps. The slow awakening model might lead you to put yourself down, to feel that you are less worthy than others, or to give up too quickly.

 Has your relationship with God been more of a dramatic spiritual experience or the gradual spiritual awakening?

_____

Sharing Recovery

God created you in His own image. God is loving and giving and reaches out in love to you without trying to control or manipulate you. It follows, then, that you will be healthiest and happiest when you are involved in reaching out in ministry to others, without trying to manipulate or control them to meet your own needs. The goal of that new beginning is to accept the **commission** of God and to become willing to care for others and reach out to them as God cares for you. Your commission is from God Himself, who gave you the ministry of reconciliation, committed to you the message of reconciliation, and appointed you as an **ambassador** of His kingdom (2 Corinthians 5:18-20).

commission–n. authority to act for, in behalf of, or in place of another (Webster's)

ambassador–n. an authorized representative or messenger (Webster's)

We are not perfect, so we cannot expect to live perfectly or give infinitely to others. By now we are all too aware of our limitations and failures. Even our best efforts will save no one. We can help some people because of—and possibly in spite of—our weaknesses. Learning the delicate balance between healthy service and compulsive attempts to change others is difficult if our lives have been governed by the never-ending performing and people-pleasing tendencies common with eating-disordered behavior.

Living in humility

Living in balance means learning humility by recognizing our limitations and trusting God to meet our needs. We no longer have to search for purpose, worth, meaning, and security through dependent relationships, career, performance, compulsions, addictions, or causes.

Proclaiming His Excellencies

Your past and your personality are uniquely yours and can be used for God's glory. God has called you to share Him with others. His Spirit enables you to influence those around you. Your influence can last for all eternity. You have the ability to see the world's spiritual poverty through God's eyes and to offer God's magnificent solution.

But you are a chosen race, a royal priesthood, a holy nation, a people for God's own possession, that you may proclaim the excellencies of Him who has called you out of darkness into His marvelous light.

–1 Peter 2:9

Go therefore and make disciples of all the nations, baptizing them in the name of the Father and the Son and the Holy Spirit, teaching them to observe all that I commanded you.

–Matthew 28:19-20

✎ **According to 1 Peter 2:9 printed in the margin, what is the goal of being specially chosen by God?**

_____

Peter said that God's purpose was that we proclaim the excellencies of Him who has called us.

✎ **Read Matthew 28:19-20. As you yield your life to Him and to the truth of His Word, what does Christ want you to do?**

_____

_____

How does your understanding about the lost condition of those who do not have Christ affect your desire to share your faith?

_____

_____

How does your perception of the painful slavery felt by those with eating disorders affect your desire to share your hope?

_____

_____

Key Concept for Lesson 1
Not all spiritual transformations are alike, but a spiritual change is essential to recovery.

✎ **Pray and ask God how this concept can apply in your life. Now review this lesson. What has God shown you that you can use?**

_____

_____

_____

Specially commissioned

By the authority of Christ Himself, you have been commissioned to carry the message of His peace to all who struggle with life's complexities. This includes those with eating disorders. You are one of His ambassadors.

➤ **In prayer, accept your personal commission to represent Christ among the people you know. Do not worry about how you'll do it, or even if you can do it. Leave those details to God. Tell Him you are willing. Rest in faith that He will give you the confidence you need. Thank Him for trusting you with such an awesome and wonderful responsibility.**

<table>
<tr><td>

LESSON

2

</td></tr>
</table>

Sharing the Message

Key Concept:
I have the privilege and the
responsibility to share both my
recovery and my faith.

*Having had a spiritual awakening, we try to carry the message of Christ's
grace and restoration power to others with eating disorders and to practice
these principles in all our affairs.*

> *But sanctify Christ as Lord in your hearts, always being ready to make a
> defense to every one who asks you to give an account for the hope that is
> in you, yet with gentleness and reverence.*
>
> —1 Peter 3:15

An ambassador represents his or her country. In the same way, you represent
the kingdom of God and the One who called you into the freedom you now
experience. You have the privilege of sharing with others how they can
become free. Helping others is, in part, the telling of a story. The story tells of
your progress toward health through the power of Christ.

In Step 3 we described the decision to turn our lives over to Jesus Christ as our
Lord and Savior. That Step also applies to our repeated decision to turn over
to Christ the details of our lives—especially our addictions. In this lesson we
will examine how to share the message. Many people need the message that
Jesus Christ is the answer to their food addiction, everyone needs the message
that Jesus Christ is the answer to our sin problem. We who are in a Christ-
centered recovery process have a unique opportunity to share both messages.

A unique opportunity

Your Recovery Testimony

In the space below, you'll find an outline to help you organize your testimony
to transmit effectively the message to others. Fill in each space with the
appropriate details, and use this outline as a guide to help you tell your story.

✎ **What was your life like before you began recovery? Describe how you
thought, felt, and acted. You may want to use additional paper.**

_____

_____

_____

_____

_____

How did you begin to realize that you had an eating disorder?

_____

_____

_____

_____

Describe what made you reach out for help.

_____

_____

_____

Describe how God changed your life through the recovery process.

_____

_____

_____

How is your life different now than it was before you began working the Steps?

_____

_____

_____

_____

By writing down some of the many changes that have occurred in your life since you entered recovery, you are gathering some good material to share with those who are new to the program. The Scriptures give many helpful hints for successful sharing. Here are two; see if you can find others.

Brethren, even if a man is caught in any trespass, you who are spiritual, restore such a one in a spirit of gentleness; looking to yourself, lest you too be tempted. Bear one another's burdens, and thus fulfill the law of Christ.
–Galatians 6:1-2

✎ **Read Galatians 6:1-2. How would you try to restore in a "spirit of gentleness" another person with an eating disorder? List several different possibilities.**

_____

_____

For you yourselves know how you ought to follow our example; because we did not act in an undisciplined manner among you, nor did we eat anyone's bread without paying for it, but with labor and hardship we kept working night and day so that we might not be a burden to any of you; not because we do not have the right to this, but in order to offer ourselves as a model for you, that you might follow our example.
–2 Thessalonians 3:7-9

✎ **Read 2 Thessalonians 3:7-9. Is your example to others as important as what you say to them? Below explain your thoughts.**

_____

_____

Barbara had been in recovery for five months when she was asked to visit the local high school and to speak to a support group of young women who had eating disorders. Still unsure of her own confidence, yet wanting to be of help, she reluctantly agreed. As she shared her story, she felt many emotions return even though she hadn't had them for months. At first it was just annoying. Then as some of the high school students shared their recent experiences, Barbara began to feel very uncomfortable. She began to put herself into many of the experiences they shared. She secretly wished she could be the one

Dangers of helping

practicing the eating-disordered behaviors, while at the same time she hated the thoughts she had. She thought about the time her mother had caught her purging; she remembered the day she stole the cupcakes from the corner market; she remembered the weekend she was home alone and how much food she had eaten. By the time the support group session ended, Barbara was visibly shaken. Yes, she'd be willing to do this again, but next time she'd arrive a little more prepared about what to expect.

✎ **What can you do to help ensure that helping another person won't cause a downfall in your recovery? List several possible safeguards.**

_____

_____

Helping others without damaging our recovery is a challenge for all of us. We have to learn to care without taking away other people's responsibilities. We can ask ourselves if we are allowing others to make their own choices.
- Am I feeling their feelings for them?
- Am I continuing to work my own program?
- Am I becoming exhausted or resentful about time spent "helping" others?

Your Christian Testimony

You have the opportunity to share your faith.

You not only have opportunity to share what God has done for you in the area of food addiction, you have opportunity to share your faith. Use an outline similar to the one you used to describe your recovery to prepare to share your faith. The easy-to-remember outline is: 1) what my life was like before I met Christ, 2) how I began to realize that I needed Christ, 3) how I received Christ, and 4) what my life is like now. Don't use religious or "churchy" language. Write your testimony. Then share it with your sponsor and possibly with your pastor. Enlist their aid to help you make it as clear and easy to communicate as possible.

✎ **What my life was like before I met Christ— (Hint: think of what motivated you to trust Christ. You may write something such as "I was fearful, lonely, or lacked purpose.) You may need to use additional paper.**

_____

_____

_____

_____

How I began to realize that I needed Christ—

_____

_____

_____

How I received Christ— (Hint: People don't automatically understand what receiving Christ means. Explain how you prayed to ask Christ to forgive your sins and to come into your life.)

_____

_____

_____

_____

Specific changes

What my life has been like since receiving Christ— (Hint: Don't paint a false picture of living "happily ever after." What are some specific changes Christ has made in your motivations, relationships, and behavior? How does He strengthen you in your troubles and encourage you in your times of depression?)

_____

_____

_____

_____

If you were of the world, the world would love its own; but because you are not of the world, but I chose you out of the world, therefore the world hates you. Remember the word that I said to you, `A slave is not greater than his master.' If they persecuted Me, they will also persecute you; if they kept My word, they will keep yours also.
–John 15:19-20

As you experience the joys of encouraging others who have eating disorders, and as you mature in your relationship with God, you will begin to feel like sharing His transforming love and power with those who are outside the program. The urge to share that you feel is the work of the Holy Spirit. Out of fear of rejection, you may shy away from this responsibility. Christ warned that not all would accept the message you bring in the same way that not all accepted the message He brought. If you take a stand for Him, you can be assured that at least some people will reject you and Christ.

What a comfort to know that the Father accepts you in spite of others' rejection! Jesus said that the reason you are rejected is because you are His and because He has chosen you. Almighty God has chosen you! He has made you new, set you apart, and reconciled you to Himself. You are special to Him, even though the world may not be too thrilled with your commitment to Christ.

Sadly, we often forget that we are special and chosen. At times, we wish we belonged to the world. When we are faced with the choice of being rejected for taking a stand for Christ or going along with the world, we may feel that it is easier to choose the world. The fear of rejection is great, but God has provided a solution to the fear of rejection! We no longer have to accept the opinions of others as the basis of our significance. Instead, the love and acceptance of the infinite, Almighty God frees us to live for Him. We can step out in faith and lovingly tell people about Christ's offer of forgiveness and healing.

✎ **Read Acts 1:8 and answer the following questions.**

But you shall receive power when the Holy Spirit has come upon you; and you shall be My witnesses.

–Acts 1:8

What is your personal role in evangelism? _____

_____

What is the Holy Spirit's role in evangelism? _____

_____

Your role is not to change other people but to share what God has done.

God always provides the resources for the tasks He calls you to do. His Spirit will give you the power to share your testimony effectively and to overcome the fear of sharing. Your job is simply to tell the story—what you've seen, heard and experienced through His healing touch. Do not worry if others reject the message; your role is not to change other people but to share what God has done in your life. As in a courtroom, the witnesses give the testimony and the lawyers argue the case. Never confuse the two—you are His witness.

The following list provides some practical ways you can give the message of Christ's saving and healing power to those with eating disorders. Add your own ways to it. Look for opportunities to use them.

Ways to Give the Message of Hope to Those with Eating Disorders

- Become a sponsor of someone in recovery.
- Volunteer to assist in an existing support group.
- Volunteer to start a support group at your church.
- Volunteer to help in Overeaters Anonymous.
- Volunteer to help in an outpatient clinic for eating disorders.
- Share your story with groups or individuals when they ask.
- Give your testimony in a church service.
- Provide materials on eating disorders to your church staff.
- Encourage the distribution of information on eating disorders through your employee benefits program at work.
- Write a book or a collection of your own experiences.
- Pray—encourage others to pray—for those in recovery or who need recovery.
- _____

- _____

> ### Key Concept for Lesson 2
> I have the privilege and the responsibility to share both my recovery and my faith.

✎ **Pray and ask God how this concept can apply in your life. Now review this lesson. What has God shown you that you can use?**

_____

_____

➜ **In prayer, thank God that all the struggles and pain of your past were not wasted. They can be used to instruct and encourage others. Ask Him for opportunities to share your experiences and your faith. Watch for His divine appointments to share His comfort and peace, and plant the seeds to reproduce your victory in the lives of others.**

LESSON 3

Key Concept:
God continues to transform my life as I walk in His principles.

Practicing the Principles

Having had a spiritual awakening, we try to carry the message of Christ's grace and restoration power to others with eating disorders and to practice these principles in all our affairs.

> *So that you may walk in a manner worthy of the God who calls you into His own kingdom and glory.*
>
> –1 Thessalonians 2:12

The final Step begins with the words, "Having had a spiritual awakening." Because we have followed these biblical principles, God has changed our lives. Some see a dramatic change, while others struggle with what seems only slight progress. Our experience encourages us to promise you that these Steps lead to change. The challenge is to continue in this change by practicing the Steps in all areas of our lives.

Practicing the Principles

Many times when we encounter problems, stressful situations or painful, traumatic events, God not only helps us get through them but moves us into much better circumstances and surroundings than before. Unfortunately, even when the results are positive, we may remain bitter or continue to harbor resentment because the "bad guy" didn't get punished. We may continue to be angry about how the negative circumstances came about, or we may find any number of other ways to remain "peevish." Sometimes we feel like we're getting hit by more than we can stand and certainly by more than we deserve.

Sometimes we feel like we're getting hit by more than we can stand.

Practicing the 12 Step principles means incorporating those principles into our thoughts and behaviors every day. It means admitting our powerlessness in difficult situations. It means believing and trusting God to take care of the things we cannot. It means turning our situations and ourselves over to Him, and it means continuing to take our inventories, make our amends, and deepen our relationship with God.

 As you read the following story, think about how you could use the Steps to deal with—or lessen the impact of—the events described.

You are at work, trying to complete a project which is due that day. You have invested a tremendous amount of time and effort on this project, and you are looking forward to its completion.

A bad day

As you access your computer file, you discover that a fellow employee accidentally downloaded and lost all of your work. When you do your best to confront him by using the guidelines in Step 9, he seems unconcerned and refuses to take any responsibility for the loss. Your boss is very unhappy and does not care that the error is not your fault. She lets you know that the project still is due and that your job may be hanging by a thread. Your other co-workers seem equally unconcerned about your problem. None offer to help, and all have excuses why they are unable to come to your rescue when you ask them.

A very bad day   You stay very late at the office. A longtime friend who happened to be in town wanted to come by your house to see you, but you didn't have time. When you finally leave for home, you find that one of your tires is flat and you do not have a spare. You glance across the street and see the flashing neon sign outside "The 24-Hour Doughnut and Pastry Emporium." You run in panic to the public pay phone next to the doughnut shop to call your sponsor, only to look inside the window and see your sponsor seated at the counter—eating doughnuts. How would you feel if this happened to you?

✎ **Think of the formula for the first three Steps—I can't, God can, I think I'll let Him. How would you apply Step 1 to the situation?**

_____

_____

How would you apply Step 2? _____

_____

How would you apply Step 3? _____

_____

✎ **Apply the "Serenity Prayer" to the above situation (see page 198). What are the "things you cannot change" in this story?**

_____

_____

Beyond your control   You probably identified a number of things in the situation that were beyond your control—your co-workers, attitudes and actions, your boss' behavior, even whether you will continue to have a job. You now know that you have the option of believing God and turning those items over to Him.

What things can you change? _____

_____

You may have identified only one thing you could change in the story. You could change your attitude toward all the horrible things that were going on.

✎ **List principles from other Steps which also apply to the above situation, and describe how they might apply.**

_____

_____

_____

_____

_____

Work the Steps

You could—cautiously here, without beating up on yourself—inventory your own behavior to see if you contributed to the problem or to your co-workers' indifference. You could definitely use some prayer and meditation to cope with the situation. You might even remind yourself, "At some time in the future this is going to be a great illustration for leading a meeting on the topic of coping with stress."

Obedience as the Way of Joy

When we travel from state to state on the highway, we find different traffic laws for different types of terrain, conditions and types of roads, various sizes of towns, and many other circumstances. We follow these laws, not because we want to appease someone's need to control us, but because our safety and well-being, as well as that of all others on the road, are at stake.

His commands are given for our good.

This illustrates the authority of Jesus. We do not earn His favor by our obedience (we already have His favor!). Rather, we submit to His authority and obey Him because His commands are given for our safety and sanity, and for the safety of others.

The 12 Steps provide a framework—a guide—for life and health in Jesus Christ. He is the source of health. The 12 Steps point toward Him. We can help others in their spiritual awakening, but He alone is the One who saves. In our helping, we both draw the attention of others to Him and experience the strength and health God gives as we reach out in His love to others.

➥ **Pray for at least one person today who is struggling with an eating disorder or who is in recovery. If you haven't already done so, make yourself available to that person.**

Look at the course map again and see where God has taken you in your road to recovery. Take a moment to reflect on each of the 12 Steps you took, and thank God for His being there with you—each step of the way.

Step 1: Admit powerlessness.
Step 2: Come to believe in Him.
Step 3: Turn our lives over to His management.
Step 4: Courageously make an inventory of our lives.
Step 5: Confess our sins to Him and to another person.
Step 6: Allow Him free rein in changing the patterns of our lives.
Step 7: Seek Him to renew our minds and transform us.
Step 8: Face the wrongs we have committed against others, and become willing to make amends.
Step 9: Make amends.
Step 10: Continue to take inventory.
Step 11: Grow in relationship with God by prayer, meditation, and Bible study.
Step 12: Reach out to others in and with His healing love and grace.

Key Concept for Lesson 3
God continues to transform my life as I walk in His principles.

Pray and ask God how this concept can apply in your life. Now review this lesson. What has God shown you that you can use?

_____

_____

<table>
</table>

LESSON 4

Where Do I Go from Here?

Having had a spiritual awakening, we try to carry the message of Christ's grace and restoration power to others with eating disorders and to practice these principles in all our affairs.

> *I have no greater joy than this, to hear of my children walking in the truth.*
> 3 John 4

Key Concept:
Discipleship is a life-style.

By the time Cathy completed the written work on Step 12, she understood that the Steps are a lifelong process. She learned some principles and developed disciplines that she will be practicing for the rest of her life.

Cathy, the sponsor

Cathy knew the process was not over, but she felt let down and a little bewildered. For months she had practiced the daily discipline of writing in her 12-Step workbook. For months she had met regularly with her sponsor. Now she felt a sense of accomplishment for her efforts, but she wondered to herself, "Where do I go from here?"

Cathy's feeling is common to those who complete their initial Step-work. Now when Cathy sponsors another person through the 12 Steps, she is sensitive to the question, "What's next?" She has begun to provide some suggestions. This final lesson in *Conquering Eating Disorders* will share some of these resources.

 Think about areas for continued growth in your life. On the list below check your top three priorities.

___ Understanding the Bible,
___ Memorizing Scripture,
___ Developing my prayer life,
___ Building witnessing skills,
___ Changing unhealthy relationships,
___ Knowing God's will,
___ Becoming a discipler,
___ Caring for the physical needs of your body,
___ Other _____

Remember that character development and spiritual growth are not instant. Things that are worthwhile take time.

And do not get drunk with wine, for that is dissipation, but be filled with the Spirit.
Ephesians 5:18

Ephesians 5:18 reflects a helpful comparison. Getting drunk, using food to medicate our emotions, or any other addictive behavior does something for us. The immediate payoff is relief. The problem is that the benefit is temporary and destructive. Spiritual growth gives the benefits but without the destructive side effects. Spiritual growth does for us in a healthy and Christ-honoring way what our addictive behaviors did for us in an unhealthy way.

Spiritual growth

Cathy has learned that she does not complete the 12 Steps. What she does is continue her spiritual growth. She continues to work the Steps, especially Steps 10, 11, and 12. She simply expands those Steps to include additional actions to improve her understanding of God's will, her prayer life, her discipleship. She may choose to go through the 12 Steps again, or she may want to pursue other concepts in her growth.

The following resources all are written in the interactive format you have used as you studied *Conquering Eating Disorders.* All of these books are intended for group study. They can help you to continue working Steps 11 and 12. You can determine the particular area in which you need to grow. Then you can use one or more of these resources to help you with that process. They will enable you to continue your spiritual growth.

To build your self-worth on the forgiveness and love of Jesus Christ:
• *Search for Significance* LIFE Support Edition, by Robert S. McGee, Johnny Jones, and Sallie Jones. Continues the work of replacing the four false beliefs with the principles from God's Word. *Search for Significance* LIFE Support Edition expands upon some of the work you have done in *Conquering Eating Disorders.* (Houston: Rapha Publishing), product number 7264-62; Leader's Guide, product number 7269.62.

To identify and replace codependent behaviors:
• *Conquering Codependency: A Christ-Centered 12-Step Process,* by Pat Springle and Dale W. McCleskey. The learned perceptions and behaviors called codependency—a compulsion to rescue, help, and fix others—often add to our addictive behaviors. *Conquering Codependency* applies the 12 Steps to these habits. (Houston: Rapha Publishing), product number 7200-33; Leader's Guide, product number 7201-33.

To deal with painful experiences from your past:
• *Making Peace with Your Past: Help for Adult Children of Dysfunctional Families,* by Tim Sledge. This study offers practical, biblically based guidance to lead you and other adults to identify, understand, and come to terms with the feelings and problems of growing up in a dysfunctional family.

To understand God's will for your life:
• *Experiencing God: Knowing and Doing the Will of God,* by Henry Blackaby and Claude V. King. Find answers to the often-asked question, "How can I know and do the will of God?" This study helps Christians discover God's will and obediently follow it. (Nashville: LifeWay Press), product number 7203-00; Leader's Guide, product number 7225-00.

How can I know and do the will of God?

To help you grow in your prayer life:
• *Disciple's Prayer Life: Walking in Fellowship with God,* by T.W. Hunt and Catherine Walker. This course helps adults learn to pray through experiences based on prayers of the Bible. Its sessions offer practical experiences that strengthen and deepen prayer lives and help churches develop an intercessory prayer ministry. (Nashville: Convention Press), product number 7232-18.

More about the Bible

To help you know more about the Bible:
- *Step by Step Through the Old Testament*, by Waylon Bailey and Tom Hudson. This self-instructional workbook surveys the Old Testament, provides a framework for understanding and interpreting it, and teaches Bible background. (Nashville: LifeWay Press), product number 7602-71; Leader's Guide, product number 7606-71.

- *Step by Step Through the New Testament*, by Thomas D. Lea and Tom Hudson. This 13-unit self-instructional workbook surveys the New Testament, provides a framework for understanding and interpreting the New Testament, and teaches Bible background. (Nashville: LifeWay Press, product number 7609-12; Leader's Guide, product number 7610-12.

To help you learn how to disciple others:
- *MasterLife: Discipleship Training*, by Avery T. Willis, Jr. This six-month in-depth discipleship process for developing spiritual disciples and leaders trains persons to help carry out Christ's vision to make disciples of all nations. For more information write Adult Discipleship and Family Development, MSN 151, 127 Ninth Avenue, North; Nashville, Tn 37234.

Give Jesus first place in your life.

To help you grow in developing a healthy life-style:
- *First Place: A Christ-Centered Health Program*. This program applies biblical insights and the latest nutritional information in a support-group process. In *First Place* groups people learn and practice healthy eating, exercise, and spiritual growth habits. (Nashville: LifeWay Press), product number 7227-72; Leader's Guide, product number 7228-72.

Step Review

✎ **Please review this Step. Pray and ask God to identify the Scriptures or principles that are particularly important for your life. Underline them. Then respond to the following:**

Restate Step 12 in your own words: _____

_____

What do you have to gain by practicing this Step in your life?

_____

_____

Reword your summary into a prayer of response to God. Thank Him for this Step, and affirm your commitment to Him.

_____

_____

_____

_____

_____

You may desire to learn more about nutrition and living a healthy, balanced life-style. *First Place: A Christ-Centered Health Program* can provide the help you are seeking.

First Place is a total health program, focusing on weight management. Some persons join *First Place* because they want to lose weight. Others join to maintain a weight loss. Still others join to learn to live a healthy, balanced life.

Not only does *First Place* give nutritional guidance, but it also gives balance in all areas of life: spiritual, mental, emotional, and physical. The nine commitments a *First Place* member makes are:

1. Attendance
2. Prayer
3. Scripture Reading
4. Memory Verse
5. Bible Study
6. "Live-It"
7. Fact Sheets
8. Phone Calls
9. Exercise

First Place is best used in a weekly group format. You have discovered the value of encouragement from others who are facing similar issues. *First Place* can provide this same encouragement.

First Place does not come with pre-packaged food. The food program is based on the one recommended by the American Diabetic Association.

You will need the following materials:

First Place Member's Notebook (#7227-72)
One of four Bible study packs:
  Giving Christ First Place (#7243-72)
  Life Under Control (#7260-72)
  Life That Wins (#7257-72)
  Everyday Victory for Everyday People (#7256-72)

A leader will need the above materials plus *First Place Leader's Guide* (#7228-72).

To order the above materials or to obtain more information about *First Place* call Customer Service at 1-800-458-2772.

The Twelve Steps of Alcoholics Anonymous*

1. We admitted we were powerless over alcohol—that our lives had become unmanageable.

2. Came to believe that a Power greater than ourselves could restore us to sanity.

3. Made a decision to turn our will and our lives over to the care of God *as we understood Him.*

4. Made a searching and fearless moral inventory of ourselves.

5. Admitted to God, to ourselves, and to another human being the exact nature of our wrongs.

6. Were entirely ready to have God remove all these defects of character.

7. Humbly asked Him to remove our shortcomings.

8. Made a list of all persons we had harmed, and became willing to make amends to them all.

9. Made direct amends to such people wherever possible, except when to do so would injure them or others.

10. Continued to take personal inventory and when we were wrong promptly admitted it.

11. Sought through prayer and meditation to improve our conscious contact with God *as we understood Him,* praying only for knowledge of His will for us and the power to carry that out.

12. Having had a spiritual awakening as the result of these steps, we tried to carry this message to alcoholics, and to practice these principles in all our affairs.

*From *Alcoholics Anonymous,* 3d ed. (New York: World Services, 1976), 59-60. The Twelve Steps are reprinted here and adapted on the following pages with permission of Alcoholics Anonymous World Services, Inc. Permission to adapt the Twelve Steps does not mean that AA has revised or approved the content of this workbook, nor that AA agrees with the views expressed herein. AA is a program of recovery from alcoholism. Use of the Twelve Steps in connection with programs and activities which are patterned after AA but which address other problems does not imply otherwise.

The Christ-Centered 12 Steps for Codependency

Step 1

We admit that we were powerless over other people; our needs to be needed and our compulsions to rescue others have made our lives unmanageable.

Step 2

We increasingly believe that God can restore us to health and sanity through His Son Jesus Christ.

Step 3

We made a decision to turn our will and our lives over to God through Jesus Christ.

Step 4

We make a searching and fearless moral inventory of ourselves.

Step 5

We admit to God, to ourselves, and to another person the exact nature of our wrongs.

Step 6

We commit ourselves to obey God and desire that He remove patterns of sin from our lives.

Step 7

We humbly ask God to renew our minds so that our codependent patterns can be transformed into patterns of righteousness.

Step 8

We make a list of all persons who have hurt us and choose to forgive them. We also make a list of all persons we have harmed, and we become willing to make amends to them all.

Step 9

We make direct amends to people where possible, except when doing so will injure them or others.

Step 10

We continue to take personal inventory, and when we are wrong, promptly admit it.

Step 11

We seek to know Christ more intimately through prayer and meditation, praying only for knowledge of His will and the power to carry that out.

Step 12

Having had a spiritual awakening, we try to carry the message of Christ's grace and power to others who struggle with codependency and to practice these principles in every aspect of our lives.